Creative Tension

Kenneth Boulding, March, 1970
(*photo by Eldon Hamm*)

Creative Tension

*The Life and Thought
of Kenneth Boulding*

Cynthia Earl Kerman

Ann Arbor
THE UNIVERSITY OF MICHIGAN PRESS

Grateful acknowledgment is made to Prentice-Hall,
Inc. for permission to include material from Kenneth E. Boulding, *Principles of Economic Policy,* ©
1958. Reprinted by permission of Prentice-Hall, Inc.,
Englewood Cliffs, N.J.

Foreword

I have to confess to a slight embarrassment in writing a foreword to my own biography. It is hard to maintain that scholarly objectivity which one hopes would mark a foreword to somebody else's biography, for I cannot disguise the fact that this biography is about me. This makes it impossible for me to judge whether anybody else would find it interesting. I have not, after all, played much of a role on the great stage of the world. The highest political office I have achieved was that of disqualified alternate at a county political convention. I have never wandered very much in the corridors of power, and outside a brief stint with the old League of Nations I have never even worked for any public body. I have taught a lot of students, but none of them, I hope, regard me as a guru, and I have written a lot of books and papers, none of which, however, ever became a best seller. I have founded no school, though I have been active in some interesting intellectual movements. I can only think of two justifications, therefore, for publishing my biography. One is that I have had a good life, and I have enjoyed it a great deal; some parts of it, naturally, more than others. In an age of alienation and general malaise, perhaps having enjoyed life is worthy of record. The other reason is that Cynthia Kerman is an unusually talented writer and I imagine she could make anybody's life sound interesting. What she has written about me is only a tiny sample of human experience, but she has done it so well that I am sure it will interest many, even in that large majority of the human race who have never heard of the subject.

Cynthia Kerman indeed is unusually well qualified to write this volume. My wife and I and Cynthia and her husband, Ralph Kerman, were all members of the Ann Arbor Meeting of the Religious Society of Friends, and we have been friends, as we say, with a small "f", as well as with a capital "F", for many years. The religious aspects of my life, therefore, Cynthia Kerman knows from inside, and as perhaps this is the least accessible of any person's life, she has a great advantage here over anyone who would look at it from the outside. For about two years in the 1960s, Cynthia was my secretary and handled the ever-increasing volume of correspondence, books, and papers, which are the main visible evidence of my professional life. She has, therefore, an inside view of my professional life, as well as of my religious life. In the parts of my life where she does not have personal experience, she has done a remarkable job of research. She went to England and interviewed most of the people now living who had known me as a child, in school, or as a college student. She interviewed many of my colleagues and friends. She even probed my psyche with psychological tests. One thing I have learned from this experience is never to trust autobiographies. If I tried to write an autobiography myself it would not be half as accurate, as well researched, or as perceptive as this volume, for the memory is notoriously fallible and self-evaluation is notoriously biased. For the subject, indeed, a volume of this kind is even better, because truer, than a psychoanalysis, which after all never rises much above the level of autobiography.

No biography, of course, tells all. A library would not suffice to describe the complexity of the simplest and humblest human being, and I cannot honestly pretend to be either very simple or very humble. Mrs. Kerman has caught in a remarkable way the complexities and tensions of a life: the tension between the religious and the secular, the family and the profession, the pacifist and the naturalized American, the economist and the philosopher, and the stutterer and the public speaker. That I have enjoyed my life as much as I have — and I have enjoyed it a great deal — may be due to the good luck of having these tensions at just the right level, an Aristotelian or Toynbean mean, large enough to avoid dullness, small enough to avoid disaster.

In another very fundamental sense, this biography cannot tell all. It is, I hope, an interim report. I find myself at sixty-two in good health, with a lot of things I still want to do. What's past, indeed, is prologue. There are few people as fortunate as I in having a prologue written by an able, trusted, and objective friend.

KENNETH E. BOULDING

Preface

To try to describe a multifaceted personality, condensing an incredibly complex whole into two, four, or six dimensions, seems almost as much an act of violence, and as little related to truth, as to dissect a living plant in order to find the secret of life. Many times in the course of this project I have been appalled at the audacity, impossibility, and hazards of the job I had set for myself. Nevertheless, keeping firmly in mind two of Kenneth Boulding's cardinal principles, "Anything worth doing is worth doing badly," and "Don't get it right, get it written," I have plunged boldly ahead in gathering material, and in putting down on paper what seems to me (as far as my observation and judgment have carried me) to be relevant and reasonable. It must be remembered that this *is* only an interim report — the book is far from closed. Each tomorrow brings more fruits of this life and more surprises. The goal has been to begin to know and understand some of the background, some of the thinking, and some of the motivation of a man who is even more multiple and unpredictable than most samples of the genus Homo sapiens.

In the pursuit of this end I have had incalculable

Preface

assistance from Kenneth Boulding himself and his wife Elise Boulding, who have both freely given me quantities of their most precious commodity, time, a friendly accommodation to anything I have asked of them, and access to a lifetime's collection of personal and professional papers. In addition I have been blessed with the full cooperation of their children, Russell, Mark, Christie, Philip, and William. The help of Kenneth's cousin Edwin Wells and his wife Muriel, and his friends Fred Watts, Muriel Parkinson, and Ernest Dundas, has been unstinting and generous. The warm welcome and willing interviews I was given by his many other friends and relatives made my research most enjoyable. These include his aunt Florence Dowell, his cousin Robert Hendrie, and his friends Ronald Shaw, Bernard Ash, William Baxter, Harold Loukes, Sir Robert Shone, Lilian Shaw James, Leslie Stone, Maeve Marwick, Dora Wilson Craghill, Harold Walton, Martin Hoffman, James Sculthorpe, Rex Kissack, Thomas Ellis, Roberta Martin, Arthur and Esther Dunham, Carlene Blanchard, Carolyn Hamm, Mabel and Eldon Hamm. My thanks for interviews and insights go, also, to colleagues and observers William Palmer, Daniel Fusfeld, William G. Shepherd, Daniel Suits, Herbert Kelman, Robert Angell, David Singer, Robert Hefner, William Barth, Clinton Fink, Elizabeth Converse, William Gamson, Harold Jacobson, John Platt, Peter Steiner, and Arthur Booth.

Special assistance in reading and commenting on individual chapters is acknowledged to Dr. John Copps, Dr. Robert Hefner, Dr. David Singer, Dr. John Platt, and Dr. Frederick Wyatt. I am also very grateful to the Horace H. Rackham School of Graduate Studies of the University of Michigan for a grant which enabled me to travel to England for many of these interviews, and to the Danforth Foundation for the fellowship which facilitated my years of graduate study, some of which went into this manuscript. My mother, Barbara T. Earl, devoted many hours to unearthing turn-of-the-century material about Liverpool and typing copies of sheaves of old letters of that time and place. The speedy and accurate work of my typist, Mary Kirschner, was a lifesaving factor when the pressure was greatest. And the information could never have been compiled without the research facilities and competent, helpful staff of the Michigan Historical Collections, nor the writing completed without the practical help and daily encouragement of my husband and children, who have rearranged many days and given up many shared pleasures for the sake of the work in progress.

Thanks are due Kenneth Boulding for permission to quote from his documents and papers, and Prentice-Hall for permission to use the verses and excerpts from *Principles of Economic Policy.*

I owe particular thanks to Dr. Martin Gold for his wording of the title and for continuing critical evaluation and constructive proposals for improvement; to him and Dr. Elizabeth Douvan for lending their warmth to incubating this egg from its earliest beginnings; to Dr. Joe Lee Davis for presiding over the hatching; and to Dr. Robert Sklar for pushing it out of the nest.

Contents

Part I. Patterns of Thought

Ideas and Writings

Ideologies and Attitudes

Part II. Patterns of Life

Family and Culture

xiii

Contents

Illustrations

Part I
Patterns of Thought

1

From Economist to Philosopher

Man is a highly improbable being.

— KEB, *The Meaning of the Twentieth Century*

PROLOGUE

In a large auditorium on an afternoon in March, 1970, a tall, solid, hawk-nosed man was engaging in sharp debate with the student-dominated audience. His eyes were shadowed by formidable brows, and his graying hair swooped back from a high forehead to hang low behind his ears. He was known as a campus radical, supporter of far-out causes, yet his thesis was antirevolutionary:

> What you revolutionists are saying is, "The brain operation has to be done now, if we have to use a meat axe." But the means determine the ends — we have to use the instruments of change which are appropriate. A revolution changes role occupants, but it hardly ever changes the system.

He was invited there through his reputation as a popular speaker, yet those who heard him for the first time (if they were not caught up in his rhetoric) might have wondered how a man with such a pronounced stutter could gain renown in public speaking. He had made his name as an economist, a measurer and predictor of social forces, yet he hinted at the most important societal changes coming in unexpected, unmeasurable ways: "After sixty years I have come to believe that the creative things happen in the cracks, within the system." His intellectual incisiveness was well recognized, yet his tone was warmly emotional, not coldly rational. "You won't like this," he spit out, "but revolution is sentimental semantic pollution: it lands you precisely where you were before. What do you do in the streets? The thing to do is to get off the streets and on your fanny and *think* about some things!" He was a man appreciated by many for his wit, his light touch on any topic, his way of spoofing sacred cows, yet he was tragically in earnest in his pleading for a rejection of violence and the need to live by love. "What is means and what are ends? The end is nonviolence, benevolence, the love relationship. I don't have any ends, only means which *are* ends — if you violate these, you violate my ends."

In terms of his time and culture, what *is* Boulding's special point of leverage? Is he a radical or a conservative, preserver of traditional values or attacker of the system? Is he an economist or a social philosopher, a flippant entertainer or a practical man? Men who have read his books, worked and talked with him differ on these questions. Is he a mystic or a scientist, a poet or an intellectual? Flashes of both emerge in every contact. Those who pick up traces of British accent or know he was born in Liverpool may ask, is he really American or is he a misplaced Englishman? And the psychologically inclined may wonder, is such an ambiguous figure whole or fragmented, torn by conflicts or highly integrated? And how did he get that way?

I

In December of 1949, three weeks before his fortieth birthday, Kenneth Boulding stood on another stage. A brilliant young economist, he was to be awarded one of the highest honors of the American Economic Association, the John Bates Clark medal, given once every two years. The minutes of the meeting report it as follows:

> After a diligent screening of a large number of meritorious candidates by the Committee on Honors and Awards and after careful consideration by the Executive Committee, the John Bates Clark medal was awarded to Kenneth Boulding. President Ellis read the citation — "To that American economist under the age of forty who is adjudged to have made a significant contribution to economic thought and knowledge" — and, with a few felicitous remarks on the achievements of Professor Boulding and his contributions to economics, presented him with the medal.[1]

Solidly established by the publication eight years earlier of a widely used textbook which had recently come out in a revised edition, he stood now in the mainstream of pure economics. In his revision of *Economic Analysis,* he had incorporated the newly accepted Keynesian revolution into his text, retaining the freshness of arrangement and the clarity and spice in presentation that had made the first edition so powerful; about one hundred fifty colleges, as the publishers were happy to announce, had adopted it. In addition, at the end of the war he had published a work on the economics of reconstruction and development, and he had, currently in press, a major piece of original thinking in economic theory. Many articles in economic journals had helped establish his reputation, and already more than half of this flow of published articles were being solicited from him by journal editors.

In the teaching profession, too, he stood at a kind of peak. He had just been hired, almost setting his own terms, by the University of Michigan. (He learned later that the chairman of the department who hired him already knew Boulding was to receive the Clark Medal, though it was a well-kept secret from the recipient himself: "The joke was Sharfman, the old fox — he was on the selection committee — he knew!") It was a major appointment for the Economics Department at Michigan and a major advance (chosen from about a dozen offers that year) for Boulding.

But pure economist though he may have appeared in 1949, other seeds were already sprouting within. An economic man, according to Boulding, is one who is always counting the cost, weighing the benefits, making only the rational choices in terms of a carefully drawn graph of indifference curves. He cares not for fine frenzies, self-sacrifice, love, religious devotion, or loyalty to friends or country. He is, of course, an abstraction, a fiction; Boulding knows very well there never was such a man, and that even economists are not economic men. He himself had always been a double man, carrying on a second life of speaking, writing, and publishing in the circles of the Religious Society of Friends where he was well known for his devotional articles and poetry; but he did not list these in his bibliography.

He was not yet ready, however, for the synthesis of these two halves of his life. The years just past had seen the broadening of his experience from pure theory to agricultural economics to labor economics to a fruitful intellectual exchange between economists, sociologists, and anthropologists in a small academic community. Immediate exposure to sociology through his wife Elise's work for her master's degree in this field had strengthened his sense of the world of social science outside economics and of the interrelatedness of separated areas of knowledge. And as he was to say later, "The pursuit of any problem in economics always draws me into some other science before I can catch it." [2] He had mined by the bright light of his keen intellect some of the important problems in economic theory; but he had a suspicion of diminishing returns, an image of his fellow miners grubbing in narrow dead-end passageways while a network of judiciously laid tunnels could open up a world of variegated wealth.

In short, he was looking for connections between fields of knowledge, for the threads of theory that would tie together economic man, biological man, sociological man, psychological man, perhaps even religious man, and bring the fragmented back together again. His price for going to Michigan had been just this: a portion of his time free to organize interdisciplinary faculty seminars for adventurous minds to explore ideas together, from the points of view of many different specialties. From the firm ground of solid recognition in his field, he was about to set foot on the swampy borderlines between disciplines.

For such an exploration he was eminently fitted. His is the kind of mind that always sees the other side of a question or problem, sometimes in an actual three-dimensional sense. (To illustrate his theory in *A Reconstruction of Economics,* he indulged in some three-dimensional diagrams which his fellow-economist Daniel Suits described as "horrors" — although he went on to admire the spatial perception that conceived them, and to recall how he had once seen Boulding expertly stack the pieces of a tetrahedron puzzle in his hand, with immediate grasp of how the pieces had to fit together. "He sees things in ways that other people don't," Suits commented.) Whichever side of a problem Boulding examines, the opposite seems to be visible to him too, and to require consideration and exposition. For him there are no limits to the juxtaposition of the unlike; all boundaries are permeable. Nothing and no one can remain isolated; there is always another point of view that can shed light on the subject at hand.

And while he sometimes decries the "rage for order" that leads man to see order where there is none, it could not be denied by anyone who has read much of his work that one of Boulding's most persistent traits is the seeking of order, the building of specifics to generalities. In 1936, he wrote in the introduction to an ambitious but unpublished work, "I have a secret and insidious passion for generality and for system." In some of his early articles, he

7

took a familiar segment of economic theory and demonstrated that it could be viewed as a special case of a larger, more general theory which he then outlined. For instance, he regards Keynes's liquidity preference theory of interest as in a way a special case of his own "liquidity preference theory of prices." [3] The sliding scale of size, from the world to be discovered in the atom to our universe seen as an atom, had fascinated him from his youth. This theme occurred in a poem he wrote at sixteen, and is represented again in this sonnet written at thirty-one:

> I speak a mystery: that there is no end
> To greatness or to smallness. Did we shrink
> To atom's size we would not reach the brink
> Of manifoldness, but would see extend
> A new great universe, whose atoms rend
> Themselves in turn to universes: think
> Ourselves but great enough, and all stars link
> In one small molecule, whose tremors send
> Some speck of vaster light to worlds outside
> Our mote of galaxies. This greater world
> Is but an atom in a greater, furled
> Each one in each, endlessly multiplied.
> Thou, love, hast taught me this, for now I know,
> As Truth is Love, that Love is fashioned so.[4]

To find a principle, like growth, or communication, or conflict, that can be applied to many kinds of organisms or organizations is an extremely exciting exercise for him.

And what does such a mind in such an exercise bring forth that other people can use? What difference does it make to a community or a culture or a world that such a person is there? Good ideas, that reflect reality seen more clearly or in a new shape, can strike sparks and spin off more ideas, create more useful images, lead to a better understanding of self, society and where we all are going. The function of the farseeing generalist, the clear perceiver and purveyor of ideas, the integrator of knowledge and combiner of opposing points of view, can be a reflection, a confluence, and a bridging of the polarizing forces present in a culture. These elements are brought together in Boulding not as a muddy mixture but as a pattern, a mosaic. To see in one mind an intense commitment to the scientific method and a deep religious faith, a welcoming of change and a cherishing of stability, rigorous mathematical analysis and the soft warmth and cold depths of poetic exploration, a tender response to beauty and suffering and a bursting, infectious, extravagant humor, is to know that all this is possible, these modes can coexist. It is, after all, Boulding's first law: "Whatever exists is possible."

II

One of Boulding's most recent books shows in more detail what he has to say to society. *Beyond Economics,* published in 1968, is actually a collection of articles written between 1948 and 1967, the period, in his words, of his "transition from being a fairly pure economist to being a rather impure social philosopher." [5] It can serve as an almost visual sequence of the building of his thought from its sound, simple, and somewhat mundane (though always aesthetically pleasing!) foundations to its shaping into a complex castle with a number of wings, and perhaps a few airy turrets.

The book is divided into four sections, each shown developing in a series through time. These are Economics, General Systems and Society, Religion and Ethics, and Politics. We may consider economics as the foundation and core, the others as the wings of the castle; even so, a closer look will show that a strong respect for man as an end in himself penetrates the essays on economics, and that the economic man's collection of data, rational decision-making, and wise use of the elements in the environment can have application to ethics and politics as well as

9

Fig. 1. A Castle of Boulding's Thought (a monastery model built between 1937 and 1940)

to general social systems. In fact, Boulding's own description of the theme of this book is that "economics is too good to be left to economists and it enjoys a kit of intellectual tools which can be used in some quite surprising places."

Several basic Boulding ideas to be met in this book might be considered building blocks of much of his thinking. They are carved from the shared quarry of human knowledge. Because he leans so little on footnotes and academic paraphernalia, he often gives the impression of an ingenuous observer of the world. We almost have to remind ourselves that, of course, he is widely read and well acquainted with a spectrum of theories across many disciplines. It is his selecting, ordering, and sometimes visualizing new shapes in the stone, which is his gift to the reader.

One such Boulding idea is his concept of the three kinds of social organizers: the threat system, the exchange system, and the integrative system. In the threat system a relationship is maintained by coercion, with one or both parties holding the power and the will to do harm to the other if certain requirements are not met — it is based, in other words, on the production of "bads." The exchange system, in contrast, is based on the production of goods, and the shifting of the ownership of these in such a way that both parties benefit. The integrative system is the kind of relationship that is based on identification, love, or loyalty, in such a way that benefit to the other is conceived of as benefit to the self. It is characterized by giving (either material goods or nonmaterial service or devotion) without tangible returns. No social systems are purely one or another of these, but the military and international systems relate more closely to the threat system, the economic world to the exchange system, and the institutions of church, family, and nation to the integrative system. It is the integrative system that gives legitimacy to the exercise of authority and provides the kind of glue that holds society together and keeps renewing the potential of community.

Perhaps it would increase the clarity of this triple concept if we laid out the three systems in a kind of "social map" (fig. 2). It is evident they are all different ways of learning, as well as relating (this is why Boulding sometimes calls them "social genes"); so we divide the process of learning into three sections. Then there are overlapping areas where a social process shares elements of two of the systems. In addition, Boulding's two kinds of ethical systems, the "heroic" and the "economic," are related to these social organizers. It is easy to see that the economic ethic, which is based on rational calculation of values against costs, belongs to the exchange system. The heroic ethic, which is essentially sacrificial devotion to a cause,

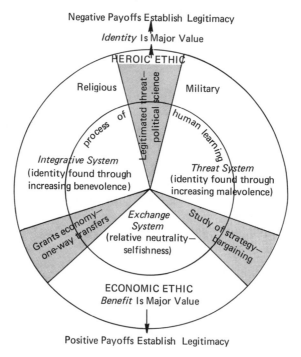

Fig. 2. Boulding's Social Map

has several varieties. In its religious form, it is closer to the integrative system; in its military form it belongs to the threat system. These competing ethics will be discussed more fully in chapter 7.

It is possible to trace in *Beyond Economics* the time-sequence of the growth of Boulding's concept of "social genes." The moment of its birth seems to have been between December, 1961, when he presented the paper "The Relations of Economic, Political, and Social Systems," (*B.E.,* p. 98) and March, 1962, when he gave the lecture "Ethics and Business: An Economist's View" (*B.E.,* p. 227). In the first of these he identifies population, exchange, threat, and learning systems as four subsystems of the social system, and then, rather as an afterthought, adds a fifth that he describes but does not name except tentatively as a "love system." But by the second moment in time represented here, his concept of "social organizers" has been pared from five to three, leaving population as an aspect of almost any system, and the learning process as a major force in evolution. In this lecture he describes the three social organizers in essentially the same terms he has used in his writings ever since: the threat system a negative-sum game, the exchange system a positive-sum game, and the integrative system a game without counters or scores.

Another major concept frequently appearing in Boulding's thinking is that of the application of ecological analysis to social systems. Here again we can trace a time-sequence of this thought. The image of "society as a pond" occurs in the very first essay in *Beyond Economics,* written in 1948. Here populations in equilibrium are described as:

> Baptist churches, post offices, gas stations, families, counties, states, wheat farmers, chickens, and so on, which . . . exhibit complex cooperative and competitive relations one with another. (*B.E.,* p. 8)

The same image occurs from time to time (e.g., in 1961, *B.E.*, p. 242), but comes to a much fuller development in the 1966 essay, "The Economics of the Coming Spaceship Earth" (*B.E.*, p. 275), in which this "systems" thinking becomes more than a tool of analysis for the social world and is applied to the total earth ecology. Here the social is combined with the biological and physical-chemical as interacting systems, pressing to the now-familiar conclusion that the only way man can survive is by recycling earth's resources after use instead of continuing to exhaust its mines and pollute its reservoirs.

The world of knowledge as a "Republic of the Mind" is a metaphor he likes to develop. He worries about frontiers and trade barriers between disciplines:

> Specialization has outrun Trade [in the market of the intellect] . . . and the Republic of Learning is breaking up into isolated subcultures. . . . One wonders sometimes if science will not grind to a stop in an assemblage of walled-in hermits, each mumbling to himself words in a private language that only he can understand. (*B.E.*, p.85)

Thus he has been led to explore and integrate foreign intellectual provinces.

The idea of evolution versus entropy is another building block used again and again, in a pattern similar to that of Norbert Wiener's description of the islands of more highly organized matter in a sea of increasing entropy.[6] He was certainly aware of Wiener's formulation; he reviewed *The Human Use of Human Beings* in 1952. "Evolution," says Boulding, "builds increasingly complex castles." It keeps adding useful, improbable, sometimes beautiful things to our world, while entropy keeps tearing down this improbable organization to its eventual end as a "thin brown soup." Production and organization are similar building-up processes while consumption and death are a tearing down. But knowledge is a kind of magic which does not obey the laws of entropy but keeps increasing irrepressibly. When it is spent it is not diminished, the sharer of knowledge still keeps what he had, and, in fact, knowledge often grows in the sharing. "There is no way of uneating the Apple"; only by nuclear destruction could the accumulation of knowledge be stopped. Knowledge can even be thought of as the basis of evolution, as more complicated organisms develop more complex information systems and feedback mechanisms, to the point where (Boulding argues) social systems now have to become self-conscious and develop a learning process (information gathering and feedback mechanisms) in order to survive in this present era of very rapid system change.

The continuing struggle between evolution and entropy is only one of the tensions recurring in Boulding's thinking. The static and the dynamic seem to be the most generally repeated opposing poles in *Beyond Economics*. They appear in many forms. In economic theory, the relative importance of the stock and flow concepts are weighed. Stock is a static or snapshot valuation, while flow is dynamic; but the snapshots at successive moments, of course, can serve as frames of a movie. Between the ideas of homeostasis and ecological succession, he recognizes the value of homeostasis for analysis, but considers it incomplete without adding the dynamic concept of cumulative change. Control, which seems more a balanced, static state, he sees as necessary for the establishment of justice, which, in turn, gives greater opportunity for freedom, a dynamic state. The open, dynamic system of the "cowboy economy," romantic, excessive, and violent, has to be replaced now, in his view, by the "spaceman economy" and its static closed system. But then again, the economic man and the exchange system (with their staid and static overtones) both stand in opposition to and yet require the heroic or prophetic man and the integrative system (the dynamic, unpredictable) in order to persist in useful form. The claims of these two kinds of forces are clearly strong and interwoven in his thinking.

Creative Tension

Kenneth Boulding has never shied away from questions of value, and, in fact, introduces them boldly where the hard-nosed fear to tread. He insists that we can hardly study anything fairly without consciously examining our assumptions and values about it, and laying them out in some kind of order. In the total impact of his book, *Beyond Economics,* not only do the threads of many ideas become clear, but a sense of the interrelation of these ideas on a value scale is also developed.

Three major elements of basic importance to Boulding begin to emerge as one essay in this series leads to another. These are knowledge, organization, and the value of humanity. In a way they have an equivalence for him: high-level organization is a value; knowledge has a high value; knowledge is a kind of high-level organization; and developing humanity to its highest potential (using knowledge) is essential. Each has a parallel concept. He describes them in his preface as the basic dimensions of his political philosophy: Freedom (toward which, for Boulding, knowledge is the means), Progress (for which organization is the direction), and Justice (which arises from placing a high value on man). And each includes a number of other concepts which also interplay across the element-boundaries. It is a fairly complex picture, and may be more easily seen if it is drawn as a three-dimensional pyramid, each side of which has interfaces with each of the other sides, the base of which is the political philosophy, and the apex of which is the learning of community (fig. 3). We might call this the "mountain of Zion," the path that society should follow to become ideal.

We begin with knowledge, in many ways, I am convinced, Boulding's first love. It was knowledge, after all, gained in long hard hours of study, that took him up the scholarship-built rungs of the educational status-ladder; it is knowledge, plus wit, that takes him now from lecture to

Fig. 3. Boulding's Pyramid of Value in Society

lecture and book to book. But knowledge is not only his bread and butter, it is his play. He carries everywhere a lasting deep curiosity about the world, symbolized by the magnifying glass always in his pocket, used for looking at things more closely. For him, knowledge is the key to breaking out of the chain of necessity, to having an accurate enough image of the world and of possible futures so that man can make a viable choice among those alternatives. This applies both to individuals and to society: "Freedom, if I may be pardoned for parodying Holy Writ, is power, law, and understanding, and the greatest of these is understanding." (*B.E.*, p. 273) Knowledge and capital are in many ways equivalent: capital is described as frozen knowledge, and knowledge is the capital structure of information. Knowledge, like capital, is a source of power: "It is not the noisy revolutions of politics but the silent revolutions of skill that change the course of man's destiny." (*B.E.*, p. 28) Nevertheless, Boulding emphasizes the need for the constant infusion of knowledge by the proper valuing of humanity, and fully recognizes the Orwellian dangers of knowledge without such value-criticisms. This is the interface between knowledge and humanity.

There is an interesting parallelism (or interface of the pyramid) between economic development or progress and the evolutionary development of more highly organized structures, or knowledge. Evolutionary development, the formation of more and more complex structures, is the reverse of entropy, which is the breaking down of complexity and the dissipation of energy. Boulding equates production with the organization of matter into more improbable structures (that is, more complex, less likely to occur by chance) and consumption with entropy: the breaking down of these structures into something less organized and more probable. (Anyone who has seen an elaborately decorated three-layer cake, a totally improbable organization, dissolving into crumbs on the onslaught of a group of guests, will tend to agree.) Economic progress, in Boulding's analysis, depends on an excess of production over consumption, which makes possible the accumulation of capital. Since production rests on knowledge, and capital represents "frozen knowledge" — that is, knowledge in tangible, material form — the educational process becomes crucial in economic development.

Economic development or progress also depends on human values. Forming the opposite edge of this "Organization" concept, where it joins the "Humanity" side, is Boulding's theory that progress cannot occur without the innovations provided by the eccentric, the heretic, the prophet. Thus the examiner and proclaimer of man's values has an essential place in the economic development of a society.

Knowledge is crucial to organization, the value of humanity is crucial to knowledge — and organization, in its progress-form, is crucial to humanity. Boulding holds that we have to have riches to have economic justice. It is his conclusion that only when there is something left over to reinvest in the economic process can it operate at a level to benefit all; we cannot solve the problem of poverty by redistributing from the rich to the poor, but only by making everyone richer and the poor productive. The modestly expanding economy, with opportunities and flexibility (based on the margin of accumulation), presents the alternatives that make freedom and justice possible.

Economic justice is not, of course, the only kind of justice, nor is justice the only concept on the "humanity" side of the pyramid. Boulding's foundational conviction that people must be treated as ends, not means, is most forcefully presented in "An Economist's View of the Manpower Concept." (*B.E.*, p. 14) To learn community with all mankind, "the great moral arrow that gives meaning and direction to human history," is at the heart of Boulding's goals. He would operationalize man's ancient dream of peace by means of an "information system feeding into adaptive conflict control." Threats and coercion are, he believes, "a half-way house which may hopefully be left behind," and his political philosophy "looks forward shamelessly to a world in which war has been abolished, in which a realistic sense of community covers all mankind, and in which the learning process that leads to the good life is open to all." (*B.E.*, pp. *vii–viii*)

Again and again there occurs a reference to something more, something surprising, something perhaps divine, operating through and beyond all. Boulding's concept of humanity includes an element of potential divinity. "The love of God escapes both the test tube and the formula." Prophets are seen as the great innovators, in economic life as well as in social inventions and religious insights, who shake a static society into the next step of a dynamic evolution. The existence of "slack" — resources left over, time left over, something extra — is a basic change factor. The future is never predictable (evolution is the growth, after all, of improbable structures); knowledge will keep growing in ways we cannot guess; randomness is an important element in the universe. And the world, no matter how much we pin it down, refuses to be enclosed: "The bulging and slatternly corpus of knowledge obstinately refuses to fit the neat corsets of the system builders." Reality is always a "great multidimensional splodge."

Economics, says Boulding, introduces value and humility into the sciences. Through its study of the ranking of choices, "Economics, grubbing around at the roots of the tree of knowledge, brings up insights within the framework of its narrow world which are of the same stuff as the brave questions which make the fine flowers of ethics, philosophy, and religion." (*B.E.*, p. 219) For him, grubbing around at the roots or looking up at the crown of the tree of knowledge, the value of man as knower, but never knower of all, is the beginning and ending of the search. The section on Religion and Ethics (*B.E.*, pp. 177–238) clearly acknowledges his religious heritage: he is at last able to integrate his religious life with his social-scientific proclivities. The touch of the sophisticated mystic is not segregated to one wing of the castle.

A word should be said about style, as we examine this sampler of Boulding. A thorough education in British schools with their classical emphasis (he went from the worst to the best of these), parents and grandparents who were grounded and founded in the Bible, a lifelong love of books, and a phenomenal memory that keeps Alice and Gulliver, John Bunyan and Balaam's Ass always at his fingertips, have made him a storehouse of allusions. (Occasionally he gets a citation wrong, as he rarely bothers to look it up, and fellow-economist Herbert Stein once caught him out misquoting a passage from Wordsworth that Samuelson had quoted correctly.[7] He laughs shamefacedly as he tells this story on himself.) But the twist of his humor, and his gift of seeing unlikely likenesses, generally put his allusions in unexpected places, and bring to his writing a birthday-present quality of happy surprise. For example, the "Pinocchio principle" explains what happens when an organization sets up a puppet organization, which then gets up and walks away. Then there is the macroeconomic world described as "a Wonderland full of widow's cruses and Danaïd jars, where nothing is what it seems, where things do not add up, where the collective result of individual decisions is something totally different from the sum of these decisions." We find a "square person in a round role," and rival philosophies of history, "an egg theory of hens or a hen theory of eggs."

Metaphor is his natural mode; it seems to come as easily as breathing. "There is no recipe for unscrambling . . . the magnificent omelette of social experience"; "a necessary implement in the inquirer's tool chest"; "strait jacket of a niggardly natural environment"; "hot abstraction to be handled with long tongs"; Hitler and Stalin as "pimples on the changing countenance of time"; "bulldozer economics" and "scalpel economics"; "wallpaper systems" that repeat themselves in a constant pattern — all these are to be found in the first few pages of *Beyond Economics.*

Shifting images from physical, biological, and social systems give one a start sometimes. They may appear in his picture of death as a "system break" or a "semipermeable boundary," or in his comparisons of a flame, a river, and a university as similar "open systems" where the role occupants change but the system goes on, ingesting and excreting molecules, water drops, or students. Social machinery is applied at different levels of magnitude in the passage, "The political organization of the world is bankrupt. It is as obsolete as the sword. Unfortunately, we have no social institutions for bankrupting it decently and quietly . . ." (*B.E.,* p. 129) But perhaps one of the wildest stretches of imagination occurs in his description of the gravimeter. If, he suggests, the physical world were as difficult to predict as social systems are, with the gravitational constant changing as rapidly as do such vital quantities as the price level or the range of the deadly missile,

21

. . . we would literally never know how to get out of bed. On Monday we fly through the window and Tuesday we would crack our head on the floor . . . we would have to have a gravimeter by the bedside to tell us before we even got up whether to make a desperate leap or a gentle movement. . . . We desperately need a social systems equivalent of the gravimeter by the bedside. (*B.E.,* pp. 107–8)

IV

After twenty years of wandering in the swamps between the academic disciplines, Kenneth Boulding does have dirty feet. Not everyone in his department at the University of Michigan was sorry to see him leave for Colorado in 1968. Some economists feel he has left the fold, a kind of traitor to his early promise, and is no longer one of them. Some of his Michigan colleagues felt he was not "pulling his load" in the teaching program since he took so much time for what they regarded as peripheral activities, writing and speaking in areas other than economics. At times up to half of his teaching load was a course in general systems, only nominally listed as economics. One economist said, "He is much admired as an economist — by noneconomists."

He was billed by *Business Week* in 1969 [8] as a "heretic among economists" who was chosen for the high post of president of the American Economic Association "more in recognition of his achievements as the fairly orthodox Keynesian he was rather than as the social philosopher he has become." When I asked him if he thought of himself as an economist, he answered, "Oh, yes, I'm an economist — I *must* be — I'm President of the American Economic Association!" Later, more soberly, he described economic problems he was currently working on, but they were "the sort of problems which arise out of general social science. On the whole I have no interest at all in the type of problems which are bothering the average economist."

There are other economists, more sympathetic to what he is doing, who still regard him as one of them. It seems to be rather a matter of definition of the field of economics, whether one considers him in it or not. (He is fond of quoting a phrase from Jacob Viner, one of his graduate school professors at Chicago: "Economics is what economists do." With this definition, he could slip under any fence!) But in any case, both those who criticize him and those who admire him note with awe and real enjoyment his power with words. Even one who feels he has betrayed his profession adds, "But the world is lots more fun to live in because he's here!" Reviewers of *Beyond Economics* ranked him with Milton Friedman, John Kenneth Galbraith, and Robert Theobald; *Business Week*'s article calls him "the legitimate heir of Adam Smith," and unequivocally adds, "on paper and in person, Boulding is one of the most articulate — and one of the wittiest — men in the economics profession." Recent reviewers have also called him "an exceedingly bright practitioner of the 'dismal science,'" "an economist-turned-humanist," and "chief ambassador from economics to the other social sciences and to the fields of religion and ethics." [9]

However, his credentials as a social scientist are still somewhat questionable. Boulding's definition of "research" — which he has not, I think, spelled out, but which can be deduced behaviorally — may be his alone. It carves out a niche for his own special mode of operation. His statements on "proposed research" submitted from time to time to the department he was working for, and his recurrent memoranda on "proposals for a program of research in such and such" suggest clearly that its meaning to him is speculation or theoretical inquiry. Here is an example, a proposal for a "research program in general economics" written about 1946 at Iowa State University. It deals with the development of basic principles: a restatement of the theory of distribution, the relations between prices and wages, and the impact of monopoly. He envisions this in terms of a group effort, with "constant, though not excessive" interaction between these theorists and others working in applied fields. The nature of his image of research is most clearly indicated in the words: "Research of this kind is not a mechanical process, but one which depends to some extent on the unreliable processes of 'inspiration.'" The results of this research, published in his book *A Reconstruction of Economics* several years later, drew this comment from economist M. Bronfenbrenner: "The volume is a succession of exercises in pure economics. There are no empirical verifications, statistical or otherwise, and likewise no predictions regarding the actual world." Funding for research seems to mean to Boulding, paying him for time to let him think.

A scientist today is supposed to be more data-based than in Adam Smith's day, when science and philosophy were equivalent terms. It is the extremest of understatements to say, as *Business Week* did, "Whatever he says about the need of more information, Boulding himself could hardly be called a data-gatherer." Boulding is reported to have declared once that he had never done any empirical research. (His early history seems to belie this, but even so, it was many years ago.) Can he really make a contribution to social science without data-gathering? He would certainly be regarded as a more solid scientist if he had some controlled studies to his credit, if he stated his theories in terms that could be operationalized and tested, or even if he were more careful about sources and prior research or less eager to jump to theories from minimal clues. But those who have worked with him, read his writing, and listened to him speak suggest that this is not his role. His mode is rather that of spinning off ideas.

For example, Herbert Kelman reported the spinoff effect of one "Bouldingism" on him:

> Kenneth said, "You know there are these ads about 'Take your family to the church of your choice' — well, there ought to be an ad saying 'Join the army of your choice: Fight for the country of your choice.'" So after awhile I

wrote an article about that, "The Internationalization of the Military." [10] I am more stimulated by his throwaways — the gems he drops by the wayside — than by his official work.

Other colleagues at the University of Michigan have made these comments: "Kenneth has more ideas per day than most people have per month" (economist William Palmer); "He is an entrepreneur who begins things, begins them intelligently, and begins things that don't occur to many people to begin. He's got guts and doesn't hesitate to get out in front" (economist Daniel Suits). Psychologist Robert Hefner's summation was, "He makes the conceptual leap, in Thomas Kuhn's sense. By moving out of the narrow area in which he was trained he was able to view a large number of areas from different perspectives." (As Kuhn points out, the major advances in science are made by men who are relatively untrained in, or just moving into, the specialty where they make the new and original contribution.) [11] Boulding is a producer of ideas, and he may be at the root of one or two creative revolutions.

But he is also a salesman, a middleman, a merchant of ideas. He has called himself this, from time to time, seeing the need for the translation of the world-view of Keynesian economics into terms the layman and the politician can understand, the need for the introduction of social science data into the images of the international system on whose basis statesmen make decisions, the need for all of society to see more clearly the alternative futures which are thundering down on us. He is a missionary of reality-images. The salvation he wants for man will come (if it comes) through an ethical system built on a view of the world as a community, applied to accurate images of the natural and human environment, and tempered by humility. He wants all of us to see life steadily and see it whole, and his considerable powers are bent toward that end. Not only, according to Boulding, is the unexamined life not worth living; the unexamined society is not worth living in.

2

Economics: The Rock
of Respectability

Economists are understood
To study goods, if not the Good
Although their goods, we often find
Are pale abstractions of the mind

—KEB, *The Skills of the Economist*

I

From this overview of the development of Boulding's
thought in the fruitful period from 1948 to 1967, and the
point to which his escapades have brought him in the academic world, let us turn more intensively to some of the
details of his intellectual history.

His first article was submitted to the [British] *Economic Journal* in 1931, while he was an undergraduate at
Oxford. He still has among his papers the letter of acceptance from Lord Keynes, who was then its editor. Three
articles followed in 1934 and 1935, growing out of his
graduate study in Chicago, developing and expanding
some ideas on which he was in sharp disagreement with
Frank Knight, then one of his professors. In these papers
he developed a population theory and applied it to the
theory of capital.

26

As he reported in a conversation in 1969, the controversy centered

> around the concept of the period of production, as to whether it means anything really. I now think it probably doesn't, but I was very much on the side of the period of production at that time and Knight was very much against it. It's a controversy which crops up in economics every generation, it has thirty-year cycle . . . it never comes to anything.

The "period of production" is the length of time between the input of raw materials and the output of the finished product. The controversy arose over the relative valuation of certain factors of production which serve as inputs at different times, and the role which capital or investment plays in the process. For Knight, capital was a relatively homogeneous fund or a fixed amount of durable goods; Boulding could see it only as a heterogeneous stock of items acquired and replaced at various times, each with a different life expectancy, and a value varying with its age — hence the usefulness of the population theory.

He maintains it was this argument which made his name, because Knight published an article called "Mr. Boulding and the Austrians" attacking his position; then, of course, he had to reply; and he was fairly launched. Another controversial article was published in 1936, while he was teaching in Edinburgh. He was introduced to Paul Samuelson, a rising young rival economist, through an intellectual controversy in the pages of the *Quarterly Journal of Economics* in 1937. In the next few years he was asked to do book reviews by a British and a Canadian economic journal, and a lecture he gave in Toronto was published. The lecture material grew out of studies he had done on British milk and meat problems, and was his entry into the subject of economic development.

All through these early years he was, of course, trying to break into the field of his career choice, and constantly measuring himself against his inner intuitions of dunder-headedness or brilliance and the outer measures of competence. Those who know him only by reputation tend to assume that he followed the normal academic route to the Ph.D. degree; or, aware of his M.A. from Oxford, they judge this required an equivalent effort; or they are deceived by his protestations of scorn at such meaningless formality, and assume that he never cared about higher degrees. None of these is correct.

Thoroughly grounded in all the great economists and freshly excited by the appearance of Keynes's theory, he achieved a "first" in the School of Politics, Philosophy, and Economics when he graduated from Oxford in 1931. In his year of postgraduate study there, 1931–32, he hoped for the degree of B.Litt. Though his topic was accepted and he wrote his thesis, it was judged not ready to submit and he did not receive the degree. On arrival at the University of Chicago with a graduate fellowship, he actively pursued the possibility of a Ph.D. for a time, but he gave it up and received no degree in his two years there. He then began teaching, first in Edinburgh and then in upstate New York. Although he wrote to a friend in 1938, "How thankful I am that the special privilege I enjoy as a distinguished (?) foreigner makes me immune from the Ph.D. plague," he was still pursuing a higher degree. He applied for the M.A. from Oxford and it was granted in April, 1939. (This requires, surprisingly enough, no submission of a thesis or other work, but only elapsed time after graduation and the payment of a fee.) [1]

At the same time he inquired about the D.Litt. at Oxford, and was told that to receive this he must submit published work: "There is no definition of the standard; it is simply a question of what the judges decide, but they must decide that it is an 'original contribution' to learning in science; and at least a year must elapse between its publication and its submission for the Degree." [2] In May, 1943, two years after his first book was published, Boulding duly sent it with his £10 fee in "application for permission to supplicate for the degree of Doctor of Letters." In January, 1944, he received a letter informing him his application was not granted. It looked as if he had to depend on his writings if he were to gain prestige; and these proved, though not immediately, to be enough.

II

He had, in fact, been writing several books along with his articles. The first was the thesis called "Capital Migrations" written in his postgraduate year at Oxford and taken with him to Chicago. It did not suit either him or his advisers well enough to be submitted for the B.Litt. at Oxford or the Ph.D. at Chicago, and while he had some hopes of publication and polished it further, I have found no evidence that it was ever sent to a publisher. He turned instead to a detailed theoretical examination of the business firm as a complex of processes held in a "particular equilibrium" which would form a building block of the larger theory of "general equilibrium," with emphasis on the *process* as the atom of economic behavior. He finished this 300-page manuscript in March, 1936, and, under the title of "Investment and Production: The Theory of a Single Economic Process," sent it to Frank Taussig at Harvard, who turned it over to the Harvard Press. Although both Taussig and a former Oxford mentor, Ogilvie, commented very favorably on the manuscript, Harvard Press rejected it a year later. A London publisher agreed to publish it only if Boulding would subsidize part of the cost; later, an altered version of it seems to have been sent, again unsuccessfully, to two American commercial publishers.

By this time, however, he had his next book underway, which turned out to be *Economic Analysis*. While he was in correspondence with several publishers about it, the manuscript was accepted by Harper's practically on the strength of the outline and preface. It was published in 1941. In it, Boulding put together what he had learned in five years of study and five of teaching. In his youthful enthusiasm, he overturned old categories. His original contribution was his arrangement of the material in terms of tools of analysis: supply and demand first, with applications to the simplest cases, then marginal analysis applied to an expanded range of variables. He also included material from the frontiers of economic thinking, though little of Keynes was yet digested and incorporated by him or other economists at that time.

The book was hailed by many for its freshness of approach, lucid style, and depth of penetration, though some criticized it for too broad a range, and some for "immaturity," or lack of relation to major problems of economic policy, or for certain "fallacies" peculiar to the author. (This may have been an echo of his earlier journal controversies.) Coming onto the market in the year the United States entered World War II, its sales were not fantastic, but it very quickly gained and held a steady place as an economics text, though rivaled and partly displaced a few years later by Samuelson's. By 1944, the publishers were asking Boulding for a revised edition, and eventually third and fourth revisions were added, each incorporating the innovations in theory and technique and the broadening of his own concepts that had occurred in the interim. Role behavior, theory of organizations, and extensive references to "models" were added between the first and fourth editions, as well as material on economic dynamics and linear programming. Students from all over the world have reported that they cut their teeth on *Economic Analysis,* which brought Boulding to remark one day that he felt like "a wet-nurse to this generation of economists."

His second book on economics, *Economics of Peace,* was aimed at a more popular audience. It came as a surprise to his colleagues, appearing amidst an outpouring of books on the economics of war. He was frankly trying to sell Keynesian ideas for controlling cycles of deflation and inflation, focused in a pet project, the "adjustable tax plan," which he borrowed from his friend Albert Hart. However, much of the book was an analysis of the problems of reconstruction and of development in the postwar world. It was written mainly in 1942–43, coming out of his work the previous year with the League of Nations spent in studying such issues; but it was not accepted by a publisher until the spring of 1944 nor actually printed until 1945. "It was never an uproarious success," says Boulding. "Nobody paid a great deal of attention to it."

It received many warm reviews, however, though there were some objections to his analysis or point of view. Perhaps the most sharply critical note (except those of Marxist reviewers) was struck in the sentence, "Every professional reader will doubtless be impressed both by the wisdom of Boulding's discussion in areas outside the reader's competence and by its shortcomings within that area." [3] There was another flaw, in the tone, which several reviewers noticed. The book had a sermonizing, moralizing, soapbox flavor in its exhortations toward a more humanistic economic policy and world view — quite different from the sophisticated presentations of the same moral values in later Boulding works. He had said once in his college days, "I don't much care for preaching, but I would rather preach than listen to sermons." He was to do much preaching, but later learned to make his sermons more palatable to modern ears by couching them in social-scientific terms, or coating his most earnest sentiments with the sugar of humor.

His second venture in a popular work on economic policy began as a revision of *Economics of Peace* but became an entirely different book, *Principles of Economic Policy,* published in 1958. In this work, a clear and objective ordering of goals of economic policy (progress, stability, justice, and freedom) is followed by detailed applications of these goals as yardsticks to the various segments of the economy, and a final chapter analyzing value systems. Opening each chapter is a capsule condensation of its message in serio-comic verse. For the introductory chapter, the verse runs as follows:

Our policy, to be effective,
Must chase a suitable objective,
So, our economy should be
Both Growing, Stable, Just, and Free.
The Dog would surely be a Dunce
Who tried to chase four things at once,
Yet this is just the way we plan
The task of Economic Man!

Boulding had learned to present his views with wit and style — and yet leave the reader room to feel there are alternatives of acceptance or rejection of the ideas open to him. As one reviewer described it, "The book is stimulating, honest (it emphasizes not only what we know but also what we do not know), and tolerant (it avoids black–white statements and eschews dogmatism)." [4] The book had a fair success as a text but did not seem to make an enduring place for itself, although it was translated into Spanish and Portuguese in the ensuing ten years.

The pivotal theoretical book in his economics bibliography — as Boulding sees it, his most original contribution to the field — was *A Reconstruction of Economics,* which was in press when he went to Michigan, published in 1950, reissued as a paperback in 1962, but is now out of print. It is a difficult, technical work, in which he tried to correct some of his dissatisfactions with existing theory. The "balance sheet" is a central concept in his analysis, with asset preferences as the main behavioral clue to explain the dynamics of capital theory. He does a great deal of analysis in terms of the identities comprising the exchange system of the whole society. This "macroeconomic" theory of distribution leads to some rather startling discoveries: for instance, the individual decisions of businessmen to save or not to save have, in many cases, very little influence on total business saving. Aggregate changes in the system are instead controlled by the mathematical requirement that certain elements in the system add up to the same total as certain other elements. (That is, gross profits plus wages have to equal the total of business accumulation, household absorption, and a transfer factor of debts and payments.) Boulding proposed the concept of *assets* or *capital* as fundamental to economic theory instead of the income, or flow concept. He also set all of economics squarely in the ecological environment of general social systems.

Unfortunately for the future application of Boulding's brain to economics, this book was a failure. He recognizes there were some flaws in the analysis, but still has a lingering feeling that it somehow failed to get the reception it deserved. The reactions of sympathetic economic colleagues were: "He attempted a tour de force which didn't come off" (William Palmer). "It was his effort to move modern economics into the general systems area, and it didn't take; the profession went off in other directions" (Daniel Fusfeld). It was called a "genuinely bad book" by another economist, and an even less sympathetic colleague called it "a disaster." It received in the journals both serious criticisms and enthusiastic reviews. It was not followed with enthusiastic acceptance, nor enlarged upon, refined, or extended by other professionals. There are those, however, who feel it should have been. Ben Seligman, in a study of recent economic thought, makes the following judgment:

> The *Reconstruction of Economics,* containing Boulding's major technical contributions, unfortunately has not received the attention it merits. And the failure of others to follow up its many fruitful suggestions merely indicates a sad reluctance to pursue new lines of theoretical investigation.[5]

It has been suggested that the failure of this work to excite enthusiasm among economists helped push Boulding in other directions. There is probably some truth in this: had other thinkers picked it up and run with it, he admits he might have been more interested in pursuing economic theory further. But evidence in the book itself and in other aspects of his life, both at the time and several years earlier, indicates that he was already moving in other directions. A paragraph in the preface of *A Reconstruction of Economics* reads:

> I have been gradually coming to the conviction, disturbing for a professional theorist, that there is no such thing as economics — there is only social science applied to economic problems. Indeed, there may not even be such a thing as social science — there may only be general science applied to the problems of society. (p. *vii*)

The first chapter is devoted to a description of society as an ecosystem. The sprouts of general systems were surely breaking through the crust of his thinking even at the moment of his most concentrated attempt to add to the body of pure theory in economics.

III

Seligman, in his analysis of Boulding's economic writings, describes him as making his main contributions in the theory of the firm and the economics of organization. He mentions the usefulness of Boulding's way of looking at flows of goods as alterations in stocks, and of looking at capital as a population, which he calls "one of the more realistic and genuinely satisfactory capital theories in recent literature." The maximizing of "utility" instead of the maximizing of profit as a focus of preference theories, his unique concept of consumption, and his pointing out the "balance sheet" data that provide the information link in an organization, are cited as areas where Boulding is at

odds with standard theory, but making fruitful sugges-
tions. While Seligman recognizes Boulding's connection
with Keynes, he also traces a relationship with the "under-
ground theory" of the American institutionalists, chiefly
John R. Commons, and remarks, "This concern with dis-
senting streams of theory was interesting, for in many
ways Boulding himself has become an important dissenter
from received economic theory."

Boulding himself does not lay any claim to having
founded a "school" or created a new system in economics.
But he does feel he brought some clarity to concepts that
had been muddy. *Economic Analysis,* for instance,
"cleaned up a lot of loose ends in value theory." He considers his most important economics article "A Liquidity
Preference Theory of Market Prices," written in 1944,[6] in
which the fundamental notion is that in the pure market
the function of the price structure is to persuade people
to hold the assets that are there. The method of analysis
in the article, the factor of liquidity preference, throws a
clearer light on the separate determiners of price and
quantity.

Many of his distinctive or original contributions take
us into the misty borderlands between economics and
other fields. His continued insistence that the goals of economics be examined moves us into ethics, as does his work
on the "grants economy" [7] as a measure of the integrative
system. His connection of economics with the national
state and its international policies moves us into political
science and the international system. His emphasis on the
tools of economics in their application to other areas
brings us to general systems. But some of his ideas strictly
within economics are distinctive to Boulding and may
well bear description.

One of these is the notion of consumption, about
which he claims a "conceptual revolution." Traditionally,
consumption has been considered a measure of wealth:
the more one consumes, the happier one is. Boulding,

however, insists that consumption, as the using up of resources (the eating of a loaf of bread, the wearing out of a pair of shoes, the final collapse of a one-hoss shay) is a bad thing; instead, the *enjoyment* of resources is the good thing, and this is not equivalent to using them up. We would be better off, he feels, if clothes, shoes, and houses did not wear out, though he has a little trouble when he applies this idea to food. He developed the idea particularly in two articles in 1945 and 1950,[8] and sums it up briefly in the preface to *A Reconstruction of Economics:*

> Once the emphasis is laid on assets rather than on income it becomes clear that there is a vital distinction between the enjoyment of assets and their consumption — that is, destruction. Consumption, and therefore production and income, are then seen as quantities to be minimized rather than to be maximized in the interests of maximum enjoyment. (p. *ix*)

More recently (in 1966) the idea was cogently related to the pressing requirements of diminishing resources:

> In the spaceman economy, what we are primarily concerned with is stock maintenance, and any technological change which results in the maintenance of a given total stock with a lessened throughput (that is, less production and consumption) is clearly a gain. This idea that both production and consumption are bad things rather than good things is very strange to economists, who have been obsessed with the income-flow concepts to the exclusion, almost, of capital-stock concepts.[9]

Stocks and flows, which are clearly an essential part of the consumption concept, are also represented in a theorem which appears again and again. It is based on a fundamental identity of Keynes, that the accumulation of capital in a system at any time is equal to the production minus the consumption. From this simple identity Boulding develops a great deal of theory in demand and supply and in consumption and production — all perhaps not so surprising — but who else would have thought of calling it the "bathtub theorem"? Though in the first edition of *Economic Analysis* and in earlier articles he had described capital as a lake and income and expenditure as the flow of the stream into and out of the lake, and in the first edition he had developed an elaborate diagram of water in a tank (stocks) with valves (controlled by price) regulating its flow in and out, it was not until the *Economics of Peace* that he came up with this unforgettable tag. If the bathtub is overflowing, he suggests, we can turn off the faucet (stop production with deflation, depression, and unemployment), pull out the plug (expand consumption), or hack a hole in the side (waste the stockpile with war). The bathtub theorem stayed with him, and appears in the index of each of his succeeding books on economics.

Whether it is more useful to descibe and analyze economic processes in terms of the stock (capital or accumulation) or of the flow (income and expenditure) apparently has not been settled. This long argument on stocks and flows, which began in his graduate school days and made his name known in early journal articles (in the shape of the period of production), seems to be very central to Boulding's thinking. Frank Knight and the Austrians (the "Austrian" theory of capital) received several pages of discussion in *A Reconstruction of Economics* (pp. 193 ff.) and a page in the fourth edition of *Economic Analysis* (Vol. II, p. 199). The centrality of stocks and flows to the consumption issue has been mentioned above (p. 36). The argument encompasses an interplay of questions on homogeneity–heterogeneity, population theory, and the philosophy of value. One of its aspects is the question of whether income, or capital, is a homogeneous fund like a liquid, a "quantity of value," or a series of discrete heterogeneous entities. Boulding views value not as a quality inhering in objects or a static "thing" produced in measurable quantity but as a *process* in which valuation is always occurring in time and is changeable over time, even with regard to the same article. Like a population, heterogeneous articles changing in value over time have to be viewed with regard to their age-specificity and must be considered in their aspect of discreteness. If every flow of income or expenditure is a series of discrete payments, as he contends, and if a stock does not maintain a constant value but must be re-evaluated at different moments, then the payment or the heterogeneous valuation becomes the primary concept, and the stock (the counting of an aggregate) takes precedence over the flow (the homogeneous "fund" of value).

Boulding still feels, in spite of meager response from other economists, that to view the stock as the basic concept, and flow as additions or subtractions, is a clearer method of conceiving the process. The whole argument bears considerable resemblance, even to the lumps-or-liquid aspect, to wave and particle theories of light in physics. Perhaps it can only be settled as that controversy was, by believing both: some phenomena can be explained better with one theory, some with the other.

Boulding has been one of the consistent supporters and refiners of Keynesian economics, which has gained wide acceptance in the United States over the past few decades, and he is recognized as one of the ablest and most lucid current exponents of this economic theory. The central element of the Keynesian view, as Boulding explains it, is that it is "Copernican" rather than "Ptolemaic": it views the system as a whole rather than from the point of view of an individual or firm within the system. This, of course, fits extremely well with Boulding's whole systems-oriented approach and is no doubt one of the reasons why he has said that economics was his "launching pad."

3

General Systems and Society: The Fruitful Tree

Knowledge grows by accretion, but we gain truth by pruning the tree of knowledge.

— KEB, Class lecture, 1965

I

After Kenneth Boulding began teaching at the University of Michigan in the fall of 1949, the growth of his thinking on general systems was rapid. It had sprouted in the clefts and crevices of the economic rock, but in a few years its leafy branches were overshadowing its foundations. The sun and soil were good in Michigan: congenial faculty members with interesting ideas in a relaxed environment gave the chance for creative interchange that Boulding finds important to the development of knowledge. For the first few years, he spent each fall semester going around and talking to people, feeling out their interests in a selected topic related to the integration of the social sciences; the spring semester would be devoted to a faculty seminar, with each participant presenting a paper on the topic from the viewpoint of his discipline. These seminars included "Cooperation and Competition," "The Theory of the Individual," "Growth," "Information and Communication," and "Conflict."

Since the "general systems" point of view is so central
an element of Boulding's major contribution to current
thought, a definition in some detail will be helpful. He
spelled this out himself in a 1956 article, "General Systems Theory, the Skeleton of Science":

> Somewhere . . . between the specific that has no meaning
> and the general that has no content there must be, for
> each purpose and at each level of abstraction, an opti-
> mum degree of generality. . . . At a low level of ambi-
> tion but with a high degree of confidence [General Sys-
> tems theory] aims to point out similarities in the
> theoretical constructions of different disciplines . . . and
> to develop theoretical models having applicability to at
> least two different fields of study. At a higher level of am-
> bition, but with perhaps a lower degree of confidence it
> hopes to develop something like a "spectrum" of theories
> — a system of systems which may perform the function of
> a "gestalt" in theoretical construction. . . . [This] might
> be of value in directing the attention of theorists towards
> gaps in theoretical models, and might even be of value in
> pointing towards methods of filling them.[1]

And in more vivid imagery, taken from a 1954 memo:

> Knowledge is a many-storied hotel, with poor elevator
> service. Each floor or "discipline" has many alcoves and
> balconies peculiar to itself. Nevertheless there is some
> sort of common ground plan, which is worth investigat-
> ing. Furthermore the plans of one floor may give leads as
> to the dark corners of others.

Some clues to the early roots of Boulding's systems-
thinking may be found in some of his earliest published
journal articles in which he developed population theory
to apply to "populations" of capital goods (a viewpoint
which was refined to a high degree in a 1955 study of the
automobile population of the United States).[2] This idea
was mentioned in the first edition of *Economic Analysis*
and considerably expanded by the fourth. The related
concept of death as a system break, a passing of defini-

tional boundaries, was actually stated incidentally in a 1936 article [3] in the description of molecules "born" into a lake when they pass the boundary at which the stream, by definition, becomes a lake, and "dying" when they pass the similar boundary at the lake outlet. (This was developed in a 1961 article, "A Pure Theory of Death," included in *Beyond Economics*.) It is also illustrative of the inclusiveness of his definition of economics, or its gradual shading into the more general approach, that he used the figure, the "skeleton of science," to describe economics in the 1940s. "Economics," he wrote in chapter 14 of *Economics of Peace*, "is the skeleton of social science, a rational element in an irrational world."

The implication of systems-thinking — that the interaction of a system with its environment cannot escape consideration — is foreshadowed in a letter he wrote to a friend in 1935, referring to economic theory. In this he objected to thinking of one problem at a time "without considering the effects of these actions outside the particular branch of activity which they directly represent."

But these are loose applications, which only illustrate a fundamental characteristic of Boulding. "He is one of the ten men in the world," remarked John Platt, "who really *thinks* general system theory." Platt himself is one of the developers of this theory.

A helpful clarification of current thinking about general systems was made recently by Anatol Rapoport, one of its founding fathers.[4] He divides the field into "hard" system theory, that portion which can be defined by unambiguous mathematical models, and "soft" system theory, which perceives units of experience in the world maintaining their identities in spite of environmental changes, and draws analogies between many types of such units. The "hard" theory includes system engineering, cybernetics, and such physical studies as meteorology. Its models are characterized by the relationships of certain variable, measurable quantities to the momentary "state" of the portion of the world being described. It is a question how rigorously such a theory can be applied to non-physical units such as ecological or social systems, because identifying the variables and the laws that govern them is a far more complex and less testable task than is the case with physical systems; nevertheless, the systems approach has begun to be helpful even in these areas.

The "soft" system theory can lead to even more interesting questions. Its definition of a system is close to the biological definition of an organism, with a structure, function, and history; it thus creates parallels between systems at many levels, reintegrates the biological and social sciences, and raises important ethical questions about "organisms" at the societal level. Seeking the structural uniformities between physical, biological, psychological, and social systems has been one of the continuing goals of general systems from the time of its earliest public statements.[5]

Boulding, as we have suggested, was thinking general systems before general systems was invented. It may be imprecise to equate the broadening movement of his thought beyond economics with its movement into general systems, but I feel this is supportable, at least within Rapoport's "soft theory" definition. Boulding had always been inclined to look for the "isomorphs" — those relationships and constancies which hold equally well for disparate objects. And it was this tendency of his own mind which drew him so quickly to other minds thinking in similar patterns, as soon as he discovered them.

Some time before he began his seminars at Michigan, he was trying to feel his way to some such cross-fertilization. In the fall of 1946, he actively negotiated for the establishment of a research program in economics which would use the "case history" method of sociological investigation and would involve specialists in economic history, political science, social problems, and statistics. In February, 1948, a letter to a potential university employer included these sentences:

My long range research interests lie mainly in the field of developing a coordinated and empirically tested theory of the "social organism": I am particularly interested in applying the techniques of sociology and anthropology to economic phenomena; I am interested also in applying the methods and insights of economics to other social sciences, particularly political science. Indeed, I find that I can no longer be content with being an economist, and would much rather be a professor of "Social Science" than of economics narrowly conceived.

I have noted already that the released time Michigan offered him to develop his interdisciplinary interests was one of the major factors in his decision to go there; the Survey Research Center also appealed to him, and he wrote in a letter of January, 1949, just after he had decided, "Ann Arbor looks like a good place to integrate the social sciences, if they are integrable."

I I

From the trunk of Boulding's growing integrative interests, thus nourished in a new soil, sprang a number of branches. One of the first of these was his book *The Organizational Revolution,* written in the summer of 1952 and published in 1953. The book asks the question, "Why did organizations of all kinds suddenly begin to enlarge after about the 1870s?" (this is the period which intellectual historian John Higham calls the "Age of Consolidation") — and answers it with a combination of biology, economics, sociology, and psychology. Biology specifically supplies the powerful idea of the limitation of the size of an organism by the functions of its members, especially the need for absorption of nutrients from the outside and for communication among its parts.[6] Boulding applied this idea in the hypothesis that organizations broke through the "size barrier" largely by making structural changes that became possible with development of mechanical aids for communication and social inventions for

43

diversification of function, leading in turn to the possibility of more complex, and therefore larger, combinations of people. This entailed an increase of conscious coordination rather than the less-planned "family" type of cooperation in small organizations, and necessitated attention to power networks, feedback, and effector systems.

The purpose of this study, funded by the then Federal Council of Churches under a grant from the Rockefeller Foundation, was the examination of the ethical implications of burgeoning organization. Boulding, analyzing the paradoxical case of the organization that defeats its own goals, examines particularly the communication structure. Correct information passed from the receptors to the executive is essential, as are realistic images of the systems involved, for effective action. The dictator, on the other hand, Boulding writes, "sits in a dark room looking at the world on what he thinks is a television screen, but is actually an old movie, made out of his preconceptions and previous conclusions" (*The Organizational Revolution*, p. 65). Boulding reasons that the best defense against the perversions of large organizations is the provision of many centers of power (democratic rather than hierarchical decision-making). One-way power and one-way communication lines, from the top down, represent coercion, a major evil in Boulding's view and the main means of preserving bad organizations. He recommends a mechanism for the easy death of organizations that are not functioning in the service of mankind, to make room for the birth of those that may. His preference for pluralism is expressed in a clear opting for the market system of keeping a measure of freedom in society, and for a society in general "polylithic" rather than monolithic, composed of "many quasi-independent organizations, with a considerable turnover among these organizations to permit constant experimentation with mutations" (*The Organizational Revolution*, p. 81).

In the original version (though not included in the

paperback edition) there is a discussion of Boulding's thesis by a collection of economists, sociologists (including David Riesman), and theologians (most notably Reinhold Niebuhr). Niebuhr's comments center around a replacement of coercion as the major evil by the selfishness of man. Boulding, in his reply, gently begs to disagree, suggesting that the two men's differing life experiences have led them to different theological positions: viewing man as essentially sinful vs. viewing him as essentially good but warped by outside constraints.

Reviews were variously appreciative, thoughtful, and critical; almost every organized group he discussed found grounds for objection to what he said, but most reviewers praised his tackling of a major problem in a productive way. The book was certainly a springboard for discussion, and its reprinting in paperback fifteen years after publication shows that it has worn well. But Boulding's most important general systems book grew out of a year in Palo Alto.

The year 1954–55 could hardly have been designed, in Boulding's most expansive moments, to suit better his conception of the ideal state of existence. Imagine a selected group of eminent and creative scholars in various branches of social science, set together on the sun-washed hills above San Francisco Bay, with no teaching duties and an academic year to explore ideas separately and collectively! It was Boulding's faculty seminar writ so large as almost to become explosive. It was, in fact, the inaugural year of the Center for Advanced Study in the Behavioral Sciences (CASBS), and the group of social scientists invited included anthropologist Clyde Kluckhohn, political scientist Harold Lasswell, mathematical biologist Anatol Rapoport, and many other notables.

Kenneth Boulding, though not the most famous, was described as "clearly one of the stars" by an erstwhile junior scholar who was there. The intention had been to invite several established senior people, and gather around

each a coterie of junior scholars, but, in the end, the interaction pattern was much more general than this. I am informed that at the formal opening of the center, when the
directors and advisors came and talked about their hopes
for group products, group activities, and continual *mesh-*
ing and inter*mesh*ing of Center participants, Boulding
broke up the meeting with his interjection, "I think we
are being too *mesh*ianic about all of this!" He followed
this with the repeated comment, "I'm planning to *read* a
book this year instead of writing one, for a change," and
spent most of the first half of the year going around asking
people what book he should read. It was reported that his
colleagues testified, somewhat uncomfortably, that he succeeded in his goal of inquiring and learning: he became
"the most inveterate and embarrassing question-asker of
the year." [7] In the end, the choice was A. A. Vasiliev's *History of the Byzantine Empire,* which served, by his own
testimony, to overturn Boulding's image of a thousand
years of history.

The meshing of that year produced at least three
identifiable concretions through Boulding (without at-
tempting to mention its impact through many other
lives). First was the Society for General Systems.

Through his "Growth" seminar in the spring of 1953,
a correspondence had begun between Boulding and biologist Ludwig von Bertalanffy, who was pursuing many of
the same ideas, applying the concepts of one discipline in
the study of another. Now they found themselves together
at CASBS.

Bertalanffy had, in fact, contributed to the inspiration of a group of scientists who gathered at the University of Chicago in 1949 to consider "whether a sufficient
body of facts exists to justify developing an empirically
testable general theory of behavior." [8] To try to build
such a general behavior theory, and formulate a common
language, a "theory group" began meeting regularly in
1952, with representatives from history, anthropology, eco-

nomics, political science, sociology, psychology, medicine, physiology, and mathematical biology. Ralph Gerard, Richard Meier, and Anatol Rapoport were among the members of this group, with James G. Miller as their catalyst, who were to move to the University of Michigan in 1955 and continue their work there under the aegis of the Mental Health Research Institute.

There had thus been several years of concentrated attention among a body of scholars to the point of view which became known as general systems. When so many of them turned up at CASBS in the fall of 1954, their shared excitement about the possibilities in general systems led to the formation of the Society for General Systems Research, created by calling a kind of caucus at the American Association for Advancement of Science meeting in December, 1954. Other Center Fellows involved were Gerard, Rapoport, and historian Raoul Naroll. Kenneth Boulding became the society's first president, and Bertalanffy its "high priest." Bertalanffy and Rapoport were the first coeditors of the General Systems Yearbook. The first yearbook was published in 1956. By the end of 1969, the society had grown to a membership just under a thousand. The *Yearbook* for 1970 notes in its preface that there is now a London chapter of the society and that a general systems yearbook is appearing in the U.S.S.R., with which an exchange subscription has been arranged. It remarks also that the proliferation of novel speculations in its pages is becoming more disciplined: "Connections between rigorously defined structural and process concepts and their analogical spin-offs are somewhat more firm than in the early years of general systems theory."

The second group for which the year at CASBS was the catalyst was the peace research movement. The "junior scholar" who is the source of my anecdotes is social psychologist Herbert Kelman, who describes himself at that time as one of a group of Young Turks who had started a newsletter — largely an avocational effort growing out of social concern — which they called the *Bulletin of Research Exchange on Prevention of War*. They were mostly psychologists, and felt the need of a wider professional spread to their work. Also at the Center that year was Stephen Richardson, the son of Lewis Richardson, who had done pioneering studies in the 1920s, quantifying historical information about arms races and wars. Stephen had his father's works with him in microfilm, the only form in which they then were available.[9] Boulding, Rapoport, and others became immensely excited by this work; Boulding now refers to those who read Richardson in microfilm as the "Early Church" of the peace research movement. Kelman, Rapoport, and Boulding eventually carried their enthusiasm for research on international systems and quantification of political science into the formation of the Center for Research on Conflict Resolution at the University of Michigan. (Its history is spelled out in more detail in chapter 4.)

The third fruit of the year, in spite of Boulding's resolution, was his writing of a book, *The Image*. Somehow the liquid interaction of the year's ideas trickled through the intricate store his mind already held, and, in nine days at the end of the year, while his wife was packing and gathering up children and goods for the trip back to Ann Arbor, he poured out in dictation, in unbroken sequence, the eleven chapters of this book. He asks in his preface forgiveness for "a certain atmosphere of intellectual exaltation which inevitably pervades it and which no sober editing can quite remove."

General systems gave form to the fountain of ideas. *The Image* develops a theory of knowledge and behavior which relates systems at every level from the mechanical to the societal. Through the mental filter of each person's image of the world, made up out of all his past experience, must pass the perception of any new signals. Groups such as subcultures and nations have shared images, and there is something comparable to an image at even simpler levels of organization. The ramifications of this concept for the theory of organization and the sociology of knowledge and social change are traced in past, present, and future. Then Boulding turns to what the notion can teach us in terms of gaps in theory and what needs to be done to increase knowledge. Here is a real plea for a thorough interdisciplinary movement: All subcultures when cut off from others tend to develop warped images; these need correction by interpenetration. He suggests for this movement what he calls the new science of eiconics, the study of the message-image relationship, cutting across all disciplines to gather threads and weave them together. It is not so much the unification of knowledge as its restructuring, a search for the minimum knowledge, not the maximum, which must be transmitted.[10]

The book was listed under "Philosophy" in the *Book Review Digest,* a new heading for Boulding but one which probably fits his current interests better than any other. Journals of philosophy, anthropology, political science, economics, and sociology gave it attention. Comments ranged from "fiery tract," "crosses the narrow line between sense and nonsense," and "readable but somewhat superficial" to "One wonders whether there is anyone but Kenneth Boulding who could propose a new science . . . in a fashion at once so persuasive and so disarmingly modest and tentative" (*Journal of Political Economy*); to "a brilliant book . . . goes far toward providing a conceptual scheme which has tremendous possibilities for the unification of many different disciplines" (*Yearbook of World Affairs,* 1959). I cannot resist quoting part of Boulding's own description of the book in an unpublished comment on the manuscript; he says, after listing most of what it is *not:*

> Perhaps the best description is that it is an intellectual fox hunt. The author starts up an Idea, and chases it, hallooing loudly, through biology, through psychology, through sociology, through economics, through history,

49

ending up perhaps in philosophy. Whether the author
ever caught the Idea, or whether it finally got away,
those who read the book must judge for themselves. . . .
The Idea is a very simple one, and has been around, living quietly in the underbrush of many minds, for a long
time. . . .

The chase at least served to scout it out from the underbrush, and his hallooing has evidently echoed back
from several directions. A book was produced three years
later by three psychologists and sociologists in residence at
the Center for Advanced Study in the Behavioral Sciences.
They happened to pick up *The Image* from a shelf in the
Center's library, liked the idea, and built their year's
study on expanding it.[11] Boulding notes three quite different kinds of groups who are interested in *The Image:*
people who teach liberal arts in engineering schools; executive, Madison Avenue types; and a group of decision
theory, management science, general systems people. In
addition, I have encountered a dedicated Episcopalian
group which has adopted Boulding's concept of the Image
as a conscious determining factor in historical change and
religious commitment; and this concept has been found
useful in the cross-disciplinary analyses carried out in programs of American studies. What a mixed bag of cus-
tomers! But what better testimony to the inter-subcultural
usefulness of a powerful idea?

A book in many ways closely related to *The Image*
followed eight years later. *The Meaning of the Twentieth
Century* was developed as a series of orientation lectures
which Boulding gave on a student ship sailing for Europe
in the summer of 1963. It is an application of the theory
of the dynamic processes involved in history which is outlined in chapter 8 of *The Image.* In it, Boulding builds
the concept of the great transition from civilization, the
"deplorable interlude" where we have been, to "postcivilization," where we are going if we are lucky. To get there,
or perhaps even to survive, we have to make a leap in eco-

nomic and technological development which is subject to a number of traps: the war trap, the population trap, and the entropy trap — which refers to the possibility of our using up the earth's stockpile of energy resources before we learn how to extract enough energy from continuing sources of supply. The promised land beyond the abyss is envisioned as follows:

> The techniques of postcivilization . . . offer us the possibility of a society in which the major sources of human misery have been eliminated, a society in which there will be no war, poverty, or disease, and in which a large majority of human beings will be able to live out their lives in relative freedom from most of the ills which now oppress a major part of mankind. This is a prize worth driving for even at the risk of tyranny and corruption. There is no real virtue in impotence, and the virtue to strive for is surely the combination of power with goodness.
>
> In any case there is probably no way back. . . . Eden has been lost to us forever and an angel with a flaming sword stands guard at its gates. Therefore either we must wander hopelessly in the world or we must press forward to Zion. We must learn to master ourselves as we are learning to master nature. (*The Meaning of the Twentieth Century*, pp. 23–24)

This thinking did not grow all at once. The two major changes preceding the great transition — the invention of agriculture and the appearance of science — were indicated in *The Skills of the Economist* in 1958; in the same year a chapter in *Principles of Economic Policy* was devoted to describing that Utopian future, summed up in this verse (p. 415):

> We travel — faster than it seems —
> Towards the substance of our dreams.
> A world is almost at our door
> Devoid of poverty and war.
> But won't Utopia be dull?

51

Won't human nature soon annul
The tenuous gains of Social Science?
To that dim thought I shout defiance,
For at the end of every rope
There lies a little loop of hope.

Many of the problems involved were jotted down in an ambitious study proposal which Boulding drew up in the spring of 1960. But the term "postcivilization" and the dramatic image of our society standing at the nodal point in human history were the new contributions of *The Meaning of the Twentieth Century.* The title, quite incidentally, as he reported in a letter to his editor, "came to me one morning, quite unannounced, in the shower."

This book, like his others, received mixed reviews. He was called antihumanistic, impeccable in analysis but too theoretical to be useful, and one of the few who perceive distinctly what kind of an age we are living in. But the buying public, readers and nonreaders of reviews, evidently liked it. It has sold consistently about twenty to twenty-five thousand copies a year.

A third book, also growing out of the same period of 1963–64, but not published until 1970, deals further with dynamic processes in history. Called *A Primer on Social Dynamics,* its impetus arose in the discussions Boulding had during that year while he was teaching in Japan. Many of his students were Marxists, and their dialectical approach to history came into creative conflict with Boulding's bent toward a nondialectical or evolutionary approach, in which progress is not inevitable but certain major culture changes, once accomplished, are irreversible. The ideas fermented then were allowed to age and were only later drawn off and bottled in this analysis of what is dialectical and what is nondialectical in history.

Three more books can be grouped together, as they deal in different ways with the uses of social science in society. These also had their origins in lecture series.

The Skills of the Economist was born in Rio de Janeiro in the summer of 1953, expanded and published in 1958. In a format like his *Principles of Economic Policy,* of the same year, each chapter is headed with a piece of definitive doggerel. (Incidentally, the first of these is quoted without credit by Marshall McLuhan — perhaps he has a memory like Boulding's, which retains choice phrases longer than their sources — in *Understanding Media:*

> In modern thought, (if not in fact)
> Nothing is that doesn't act,
> So that is reckoned wisdom which
> Describes the scratch but not the itch.[12]

It is described as an "annoyed and anonymous stanza" which illustrates the increasing awareness in our current culture of the action of media apart from their content.) *The Skills of the Economist* traces the applicability, and some of the applications, of the tools of the economist for analyzing other sections of the social system.

Puget Sound in the spring of 1966 was the setting for *The Impact of the Social Sciences.* In this work, he tells us in the preface, it is hares, not a fox, he is chasing — or rather rousting out of the thickets for someone else to chase. He again takes up his role as the middleman of ideas, allocating his resources to narrowing the gap which fellow-economist M. Bronfenbrenner bemoaned in a review — the gap "between what the experts think they know and what the intelligent layman can at least criticize rationally." Boulding, on one side, describes the positive effects of the work of social scientists (greatest in economics, very small in politics, and almost nonexistent in the field of ethics and values), and, on the other, prescribes what contributions they might make given a redirection of their talents and a reallocation of misdirected resources.

The last of this trio is the one Boulding called during its composition "the patio book." Its womb was the brick patio of his house in Boulder, Colorado, where he held a seminar in the summer of 1968 for high school teachers of economics. Titled *Economics as a Science,* its chapter headings show best what he is about. "Economics as a Social Science" should surprise no one; "Economics as an Ecological Science" has been anticipated in works from about 1950 on. "Economics as a Behavioral Science" (studying inputs and outputs) describes the classical abstraction of the movement of commodities ("the study of the no-person group"); but "Economics as a Political Science" begins to sound heretical. "Economics as a Mathematical Science" traces the contributions and pitfalls of mathematical analysis; "Economics as a Moral Science" brings us into strange territory indeed (except that we might have guessed Boulding would take us there). This chapter, as a matter of fact, was not drawn up for the peaceful patio but for the Chicago battleground of the American Economic Association in 1968. "Economics and the Future of Man" rounds off the work on the note of a man who feels as if he is standing on a fortified border: "If the formal study of economics boxes itself in so much that real economic problems will have to be studied outside it, this will be worse for economics than it is for mankind."

III

We have now briefly described Boulding's books in the area of general systems and society. Of the splendid array of multicolored ideas spread out in this feast of the mind, how to choose the three or four to put on our plate? The most original, the most elegant, the most persistent (that is, the most "Boulding") — the ones that catch the eye, entice the taste, or stick to the ribs — should be selected.

The pièce de resistance on the general systems table of Boulding's thought is without doubt the Image and the series of systems-levels at which it operates. This idea is summed up in his own words (again from his "fox hunt" description of the book, *The Image*):

Fig. 4. Boulding at his desk in Boulder, Colorado, April, 1969

Behavior, whether of the amoeba, the rat, the man, the group, the state, the firm, or the Federal Reserve Board is determined not by any immediate stimulus, but by the Image — the view of the universe which the organism or organization possesses at the moment. Every Image is endowed with a value structure, and behavior always consists in moving into the most highly valued part of the Image. Thus the Image is a kind of capital-structure of information: it is built up out of Messages, but these messages are themselves filtered through the value system of the image.

This image is built up by all past experiences (that is, all those messages that have been allowed through the filter) and is the individual's perception of his placement in space, time, personal relations, causal relations, a set of emotional intimations, a social system, a historical sequence, and so forth. It includes, besides these images of fact, images of value, which consist of a rating of the factual images on one or more scales of "betterness or worseness."

It must be made clear that while the image may be viewed as a personal stock of knowledge, the concept does not imply anything about the *validity* of that knowledge, or its correspondence with whatever the "real world" may be, except that it is open to question. The image of any person or group, being shaped by previous experience, will be as unique as that experience. Shared images grow out of shared experiences — for instance, a number of people seeing the same news event on television — which are the means of production of "public" as against "private" knowledge. Experiences of the physical world, of large organizations and the broad thrust of events, as well as of the stored knowledge available in museums and libraries, are widely shared and become public images of many people. However, there is a caution even here. The individual filter is always operating, selecting some perceptions and eliminating others in terms of partly recognized and partly unrecognized value ratings. Therefore, for the growth of a shared image, a group must have approximately equivalent value systems.

This is, then, an organic theory of knowledge. Knowledge grows by accretion, the addition of message to message, but these additions are made in terms of an active internal organizing principle which fits them into an architectural arrangement. Some stones are chosen and others rejected; they are not simply tossed into a heap.

This mechanism of choice, which is an essential part of the learning process, brings us to a widely recurring Boulding idea, the importance of disappointment for learning. His mottos, "Nothing fails like success" and its converse "Nothing succeeds like failure," are so pervasive that almost any exposure to his writing or speaking will bring one up against these twin paradoxes. The dynamics of this are as follows. When a message hits the image, several things may happen. The message may not be perceived or noted, either because it is too expected, like an ever-present background noise; or it carries too little saliency in the value-system of the image, like much school-teaching; or it is too threatening, like a message that contradicts our basic assumptions. In this case the message has no meaning, for meaning arises in the *change* of the image. The message, on the other hand, may change the image in some regular way by clarifying or adding to a piece of knowledge already there, or may change it in a radical way, in which case it would probably have to be repeated enough, or somehow be compelling enough, to overcome the considerable resistance to such change that the image offers. It is Boulding's thesis that most fundamental learning comes about when what we expect does not happen, when we get unrejectable messages that are contrary to our pattern, and we are required to revise our image.

We may be reminded here of Festinger's theory of "cognitive dissonance," which holds that the perception of inconsistency between two salient related beliefs sets in motion forces which result in our taking whatever actions are necessary — usually the easiest behavioral path — to make the beliefs consistent.[13]

In ordinary life, messages contrary to our expectations can be handled in several ways. We can reject the message; we can reject the inference on which we based the expectation; or we can reorganize our image of the world. For example, there is a certain walk on the University of Michigan campus where several times I have had a sensation of fine rain falling on a clear sunny day. From long experience I know rain comes from clouds; therefore this perceptual combination is impossible. My first reaction is to reject the message: the sensation of rain must be my imagination. But then the same thing happens again on another day in the same place. My inference, that "the presence of rain means the presence of clouds," now has to be revised to: "the presence of rain means the presence of some visible external agent which could produce moisture." I look around for something above me; there is a tree, of a species I do not recognize, which may by some process unfamiliar to me be exuding a fine mist. I file this away as a hypothesis, temporarily resolving my dilemma. But if there were nothing above me or near me to which I could attribute the sense of wetness, and yet it was still unmistakable — that is, if I could reject neither the message nor the inference — I would be forced to make a drastic reorganization of my notion of the physical world. The point is, the most fundamental learning takes place when something jolts our expectations and forces us to reexamine our image.

The knowledge that we pick up in personal experience and everyday life Boulding calls folk knowledge; that from the distilled and recorded experience of many people, literary knowledge (by which we can do more complicated operations, such as using a map to find our way across the country); and that gained by controlled theorizing and testing, scientific knowledge. The success of the scientific method in advancing learning is due to its built-in protections against the first two kinds of rejection, forcing learning to go to the third step. It is protected against rejection of inferences by extended use of mathematics and the logic of theories, and against rejection of messages by the development of constantly more sensitive instruments to serve as extensions of man's senses and by the practice of retesting and replicating experiments.

The Image's importance in determining behavior, by directing the individual into the most highly valued sector of the possibility-image, is a concept that can be applied at many levels.

Another dimension of the image idea involves a series of system levels and how the image can be an integrating thread among them. As has been mentioned earlier, Boulding conceives the universe in terms of the increase of entropy vs. the rise of organization, that is, pockets of more and more highly organized matter surrounded by a kind of sea of entropy. The levels of this organization can be read as a kind of hierarchy. Simplest is the static structure, the individual object which exhibits some form: a graph, a puzzle, a statue, a picture. Second is the predetermined dynamic structure which operates because it was set that way: the clock that is wound up, or the universe of the eighteenth-century Deists. The third level is the cybernetic one of homeostatic control mechanisms, such as the thermostat, which receive messages and operate controls to keep a set of conditions at a predetermined state. This is the simplest level at which an "image" could be said to exist in a rudimentary form, complete with messages and value system. From this level on, the image becomes more complex and more important in determining behavior. Beyond it is the fourth level, the biological cell, an "open system" maintaining its structure with continuous "throughput"; the fifth, a plant, or society of cells, showing orderly development into different forms, seed to plant to seed; and the sixth, the animal, a cell society with awareness and mobility. The seventh is the level of man, with the capacity for symbolizing, patterning large quantities of information, and interposing the image of a range of potentialities between the stimulus and the act. The eighth, a somewhat nebulous level, is that of social organization, which has its own macrodynamics though it cannot be said to have a conscious image unless man can attain more widely shared images of its processes and laws, and therefore make realistic choices among its alternative directions.

Each level depends on and includes within it the organization of the lower levels, but no level can be completely explained by the systems of the levels below it.

Man, then, with his symbolic culture, may be partly but not wholly explained by studying rats in mazes.

> To psychologists who like alternatives to nickel-in-the-slot, stimulus-response conceptions of man, an Image has considerable appeal. (It is so reasonable to insert between the stimulus and the response a little wisdom. And there is no particular need to apologize for putting it there, because it was already there before psychology arrived.) [14]

Quite clearly, the image involves choice on the basis of values, and it goes far beyond the stimulus-response level. But just as the human organization comprises the static, mechanical, cybernetic, and other levels, the image includes some of the elements of behaviorism: we get our *values* also from experience; here we are shaped, and here what is put in can determine what comes out. Just how this is determined, how we learn our values, is a black box whose lid Boulding would like to pry off. His is a system which integrates the mechanical world-view into a larger framework, accepting it as a part, but not all, of reality.

Among philosophers, the Image has its friends and counterparts. The emphasis on testing by failure of prediction is in a direct line from pragmatists Peirce and James. The concept of the image as interposed between stimulus and response reflects Ernst Cassirer's view of the symbolic system between the receptor and the effector system. This is a kind of spelling out of the function that makes man uniquely human. But at the same time, by the extension of the image in a less complex form (leaving in the receptor and the valuing functions but without the quality of the symbolic pause) to lower levels of organization, we are brought into touch with Teilhard de Chardin's concept of the noösphere and its implications of shared near-consciousness at many levels of the evolutionary tree.

Boulding's philosophy of history, second fundamental idea, is a kind of side dish to the Image, related but distinct. Evolution is central, although, like phyla, civilizations can go into dead ends. Nevertheless, the idea of long-term change on the ecological, organic model appears again and again. Boulding identifies several latent processes, mechanical as well as dynamic, in man's history. Among these are the effects of technological discoveries, which can be very surprising. They cause what he sometimes calls the "ratchet effect," since once a major discovery is made and put into use the civilization never goes back to its former level. He cites as such monumental discoveries the horsecollar (which reduced slavery by enabling man to use animal-power instead of manpower for heavy work) and the rudder (after which men were no longer tied to the coastlines in their navigating). Changes in agricultural methods have done the same kind of thing. In fact, he posits the growing of root crops as one of the major causes of the development of the past three centuries. Root crops eliminated the fallow field and fed stock during the winter, preventing the slaughter that had previously occurred at midwinter and making possible selective breeding. The extra food resulted in an amazing fall in infant mortality in the middle of the eighteenth century, which populated the new industrial cities. He discusses this soberly in the first edition of *Economic Analysis* and in *The Image,* but elsewhere has referred to it with tongue in cheek as the "turnip theory of history."

It is clear that thresholds of development and the discontinuities, as well as the long slow cumulative effects in the process of history, are very important in his thinking. The significance of mutations in evolution, and of innovations as social mutations, is highly emphasized. He again parallels William James, who concentrated on the variations rather than the necessities in the Darwinian scheme.

Boulding often illustrates the powerful role of a small and perhaps segregated community, or an eccentric individual, in developing these mutations. Recognizing the importance of Weber's work on the Protestant ethic, Boulding points out particularly the connections between small nonconformist churches or sects and the historical development of innovations. All isolated subcultures tend to warp their group images, but this kind of warping can sometimes be a creative contribution to society.

> The most important innovation in any society is the *idea* of innovation itself . . . this liberates the society from its previous equilibrium and exposes it to all the terrors and delights of dynamics. Once iconoclasm has succeeded in the most traditional and "sacred" area of life, once "free enterprise" has been successful in religion, the spirit of innovation seizes upon all other areas of life. (*B.E.,* p. 202)

The prophet as innovator — in the spiritual sphere, surely, but also in the economic — is a central figure.

When one realizes the importance of discontinuities in past history, one can also sense the difficulties in making any predictions about the future. Cultural persistence, planned change, and trends observed from social indicators may be fitted into a model, but who is to guess which change processes may suddenly reach a threshold point when quantitative change becomes qualitative change, or when some technological breakthrough will carry a society over a threshold into a different world? [15] Such thresholds have been identified in ecological processes when forces which had been in balance are tipped by the slight increase of one over the others so the whole situation is radically changed. Such nodes in time or "watershed" points or "system breaks" (as when water evaporates into a gas, or freezes into a solid) are of particular interest to Boulding.

His references to random elements and system breaks are legion. For example, in 1953, he published an article called "Projection, Prediction, and Precariousness." "Expecting the Unexpected" was a 1966 title. And dealing with the process of economic development in *The Meaning of the Twentieth Century,* he sums up as follows:

> The sheer random shifts in the power structure which take place in all societies must eventually bring into power those who have both the knowledge and the power [to do what is necessary for development]. From that point on, development is inevitable and irreversible. . . . The developmental process in economics as well as in war and peace may be compared to a watershed or mountain pass. A society may push up the hill toward the pass and fall back many times. Eventually, however, it goes over the top, and that is the point of no return. From then on, the society goes on into a different landscape." (pp. 119–20)

There is a consistency in his emphasis on the breaking through of the unseen into the world. At sixteen he wrote a paper on "The Influence of Wireless," whose main theme was that the greatest events of history are usually unnoticed at the time they occur. Forty years later, *The Impact of the Social Sciences* included the following paragraph (p. 100):

> Who could have known . . . that a carpenter at an obscure town in a tiny province of the Roman Empire would have established a movement that was going to build enormous cathedrals in countries and continents the Romans never heard of? Who would have thought that a charismatic camel driver in the middle of Arabia a few hundred years later would have established a movement that led to a great civilization stretching from Spain to the Philippines, on the edge of which Christian Europe in the Middle Ages was a troublesome, barbaric peninsula? Who would have thought that an irascible old man with a beard in the British Museum in the middle of the nineteenth century would have fired the imagination of a third of the human race in the next hundred

years? For all we know, the most important thing that is happening today is happening in an obscure valley in Ethiopia or Afghanistan and we will not even learn about it for fifty years.

The prophet occupies a central role in the change of the system because he helps to shape the images of the future held by the group to which he belongs, and the image of the future, in Boulding's philosophy of history, is a powerful determinant of what the future will be like. It is not that the future is always what is expected — far from it. There are self-justifying and self-defeating processes in which images play an important part; the actual behavior of events is limited by forces not always or often a part of the image. In fact, Boulding enjoys pointing out the frequent frustration of expectations in social systems:

> In politics prohibition leads to drunkenness, the quest for national security leads to national destruction, the more literate we make people the less educated they become, and the conquest of nature by the physical sciences leads to ever-increasing misery, fear, and degradation. (*B.E.*, p. 12)

To create the desired change, an *accurate* image of forces and processes is necessary. But having an image of change is essential to making changes of any kind, and the belief that man has some power to change events is directly related to his world-view and religious beliefs. "The images that men have of themselves and of the society around them — because of their impact on human behavior — are an important, indeed, almost a dominant element in the course of social evolution" (*B.E.*, p. 243).

Fred Polak, who was a Fellow at the Center for Advanced Study in the Behavioral Sciences at the same time as Boulding, had written a book in Dutch, testing the hypothesis that the rise and fall of images of the future (related particularly to images of how much influence man can have on events) precedes or accompanies the rise and fall of cultures. Elise Boulding, Kenneth's wife, learned Dutch in order to translate it for publication in English,[16] so the family lived intimately with it for some time. Polak's thesis as upheld by the empirical evidence set forth in this book was a powerful ingredient in Boulding's conviction about the role of the image in shaping history.

Boulding is recognized as one of the pioneers in developing and espousing the general viewpoint of systems analysis. The stir he created at Michigan with his interdisciplinary seminars in the early 1950s is still remembered. David Singer, in conversation, has called him "one of the patron saints of the general systems movement"; and a recent reviewer of a book of Bertalanffy's (a little carried away, perhaps) drew a parallel between the early fortuitous association of Bertalanffy, Rapoport, Boulding, Gerard, Miller, and W. Ross Ashby, and that of Jefferson, Madison, Franklin, and Adams! [17]

In his usual fashion, Boulding has drawn broad schematic diagrams and shot off ideas like a train of fireworks, leaving the detailed data-gathering and theory-building to others. He is one of a group (though he does not say so in print) which he describes in *The Meaning of the Twentieth Century* (pp. 191–92) as an "Invisible College": people on the edge of new knowledge, who exchange manuscripts in mimeographed form, who spark ideas off each other, who meet when they can, who recognize no boundaries of nation or culture but know each other by the confluence and complementarity of their ideas.[18] "Its living representatives," he adds, "are still a pretty small group of people. I think, however, that it is they who hold the future of the world in their hands or at least in their minds."

4

International Systems and Conflict Resolution: The Loop of Hope

There is a race between knowledge and disaster, but in this race the longer disaster is staved off, the better chance we have of acquiring the knowledge to prevent it altogether.

— KEB, "Social Sciences," in *The Great Ideas Today*

I

As already noted, the beginnings of Kenneth Boulding's involvement in peace research can be traced to his year at the Center for Advanced Study in the Behavioral Sciences (CASBS). But this was not the beginning of his attention to the problems of peace and war. From his small-boy impressions of World War I through his school days and his mature life, one of his most constant convictions is that war is one of the two or three most pressing problems mankind has to solve, and probably the worst aberration of the human spirit.

Although he wrote a number of themes and essays related to this in his days at secondary school and at Oxford, his first international-systems piece to see print was a pamphlet called *Paths of Glory*. It was published by a section

66

of the British Society of Friends, the Northern Friends Peace Board, a committee he served on while he was teaching at Edinburgh. He was asked to write a pamphlet on the nonviolent method in the fall of 1936, and it was printed in April of 1937. It is a cogent and persuasive development of the theory of nonviolent resistance as it could be applied to international, national, and interpersonal problems.

Five years later, after moving to a teaching job in the United States, he reworked this material into another pamphlet, *New Nations for Old,* again published by a Quaker organization, Pendle Hill, near Philadelphia. In this he contended the age is ripe for the abolition of war because war is now both morally intolerable and economically unprofitable. He did not call for an international governing body but for international coordination of information and assistance with practical problems.

Economics of Peace, already discussed, followed in 1945. While this work concentrates largely on reconstruction and development, it does begin with a chapter describing the costs of war beyond the actual destruction: the continuing gaps in population, both the dead and the unborn (illustrated by a graph from German census figures before and after World War I); the diversion of resources from needed goods and services "to produce that most expensive and often most disappointing of all commodities — victory"; and the damage to psychological capital: "War also tends to destroy the subtle moral bonds that are the unseen underpinning of all economic life."

The strong push he felt toward study in the area of peace and war is indicated by a proposal he made in the fall of 1948 that he be given time to study with political scientists for two years to familiarize himself with the field: "The problem towards which I feel particularly drawn is that of the general theory of national defense."

In addition to the two pamphlets mentioned and the focus of *Economics of Peace,* two articles on economics and international conflict were published by Boulding in 1953–54.

His interest was there and an application of his knowledge to the problem had been begun. But solid accomplishments in the peace research field through the mobilization of a larger group around this goal would not come until 1954–55. What occurred that year was very like the phenomenon of a critical mass: when enough keen minds were gathered together who had individually been moved by a concern, the mutual bombardment produced a chain reaction. David Singer calls this think-tank birth of peace research "the convergence of brilliant and decent people."

Out of the interaction at CASBS, the reading and discussion of Lewis Richardson's work, the appreciation of individual contributions, and the powerful impact of shared endeavor, came the nucleation, at the University of Michigan, of a group of minds brought to bear on how intellectual skills could help achieve world peace.

Actually, the *Bulletin of Research Exchange on Prevention of War* on which Herbert Kelman had been working was already being issued from Michigan. Begun by Kelman, with Arthur Gladstone of Swarthmore in 1950, its editing had been transferred to graduate students Robert Hefner and William Barth at Michigan in 1953. They were scrounging supplies and putting it out in a photo-offset format from the psychology office. They had interested a group of faculty, including psychologist Daniel Katz and sociologist Robert Angell, in working with them; Boulding was not really involved at the time. ("Those young guys needled us," as Angell puts it, "until we had to do something about it.")

But when Kelman at CASBS called a group together to consider the *Bulletin* and how it could be improved, it was like a puff of wind on a smoldering fire. The potential they had seen in studies such as Lewis Richardson's blazed into flame with the idea of transforming the *Bulle-*

tin into a more ambitious interdisciplinary journal, and establishing peace research as a professional activity. Dry kindling was all about them; they were in the midst of prestigious experts. The initial list of sponsors included Harold Lasswell, Paul Lazarsfeld, Clyde Kluckhohn, and Ralph Gerard from CASBS personnel, as well as Boulding, Kelman, and Rapoport. With this kind of backing they found they could get others. It seemed natural to center the operation at Michigan, with Boulding already there and Rapoport going there, and to ask Hefner and Barth to begin the legwork for the larger journal. Kelman continued in a consultative role, and several years later came into a closer working arrangement when he also joined the faculty at Michigan.

At a meeting in Ann Arbor, some time in the winter of 1955–56, the title for the new journal was chosen, *Journal of Conflict Resolution*. Neither Angell nor Boulding remembers who invented it, but Robert Angell feels that the title itself, chosen in a long meeting one day in his office, was a significant contribution: "It's a very common word in the literature now, that was never there before!"

By now Boulding was a leading figure in the new movement. He concentrated on the topic of conflict in the spring, 1956, seminar; he gathered articles for the early issues almost singlehandedly; and he and Bill Barth were the primary fund-raisers. Barth and Hefner moved their operations to the anteroom outside his office. But there was still a problem as to which department at Michigan could be persuaded to issue the new journal under its name, although they had succeeded in getting a small grant from the Rackham School of Graduate Studies to get it started. This was the McCarthy era and the effort was viewed with a certain suspicion. The political scientists did not feel any particular calling to open their field to intrusion by outsiders from other specialties, and some officials of the University did not think the venture appropriate. Finally Wesley Maurer, chairman of the Department of Journalism, agreed to give it his department's sponsorship and the *Journal* was born. The first issue came out in March, 1957.

Even then there was grave danger of infant mortality. When they began publishing, they had funds enough for two issues, and took subscriptions for the first year. At the end of that year they had three issues out and paid for, and no funds in sight to pay for the fourth. The editors and managers had just decided to go out of business and were filing down the stairs from Boulding's office, when there came a phone call from a woman to whom Bill Barth had talked earlier. She had a small foundation and had decided to give her last thousand dollars of foundation money to the *Journal*. Boulding ran to the top of the stairs and called the committee back. They were in business again.

And so the *Journal* did not die. It has not yet reached its final goal, stated in Boulding's editorial in the first issue, to "devise an intellectual engine of sufficient power to move the greatest problem of our time — the prevention of war." But it has achieved its immediate purpose of becoming a professional organ where the theories and research of psychologists, sociologists, political scientists, economists and others, focusing around the issue of conflict in many forms, can be shared, and it serves as a general exchange of theories and data in the area of international systems.

For three years Boulding served as chairman of the editorial board. After that, he continued to remain an active member even when he was no longer teaching at the University of Michigan. His seminar on conflict in the spring of 1956 proved to be the source of several papers later published in the *Journal,* and he was the *Journal*'s intellectual leader in the early years, stimulating and rounding up varied and relevant articles for inclusion, and tossing out ideas for others to pick up on a wide range of research possibilities.

The Journal of Conflict Resolution has succeeded in carving out a new field of scholarship — peace research — in which several companions have since joined. A Peace Research Institute was founded in Oslo in 1959 under the leadership of Johan Galtung, and it started publishing the *Journal of Peace Research* in 1964. Walter Isard in Philadelphia set in motion an annual conference on peace research in 1963, and the proceedings of this group, the Peace Research Society (International), have been published regularly since 1964. And since 1967, *Peace Research Reviews,* edited in Ontario by Alan and Hanna Newcombe, has published a series of topical issues, each gathering together relevant research findings on a selected question.

It was the hope of the liberal, anti-Cold War scholars who banded together to start the *Journal,* with Boulding as a pivotal figure, that the University of Michigan could provide a further focus for research and teaching in this new area — conflict and ways of managing it. After the *Journal* got off the ground, they drew up a proposal for establishing an interdepartmental center around which interested faculty and students could share theory and methods from various disciplines to build a new body of knowledge, conflict studies.

In the ins and outs of university politics, proposing is one thing, achieving another. Several administrative officials were highly unsympathetic. In addition, there was active resistance from the faculty of the Department of Political Science, most of whom felt international problems were *their* province, many of whom were ideologically opposed to the purposes of the center, and some of whom had cherished an unfulfilled dream for a center of their own. Boulding did not make them allies when ("Bless him, never very tactful," as a colleague remarked) he was asked to speak to the political scientists shortly after the *Journal* was begun. This speech was well remembered even in 1972: he said, in effect, that the problems of peace and war were much too important to be left to political scientists, that the kind of work they had done was a disaster, and that in the future, work in the international field ought to be taken out of their hands and given to quite other people.

Only by finding full financial support outside the University of Michigan did the faculty sponsors succeed in establishing the center. Intensive fund-raising efforts by Barth and Boulding brought another anonymous gift soon after the *Journal* was rescued from the edge of oblivion, this time $65,000 to be used for peace research. Faced with this offer, the university agreed to establish the Center for Research on Conflict Resolution; but no college funds were to be committed to it for the first three years. After that time the center's activities were to be reviewed and a decision made as to the amount of support it would receive. The university later did allow a full-time salary for the assistant director and half-time for the director, but funding for secretaries, supplies, and research always had to be found elsewhere. Over the years of the center's life, the Ford Foundation and the Carnegie Corporation were the two largest supporters of its work, with the National Science Foundation also funding considerable research.

The regents gave formal approval to the center on June 26, 1959, and it began operating in July, embarking on a program of conferences and seminars, research and training. One of the earliest research grants the center administered was for a study by Robert Angell and David Singer on the values of Soviet and American elites and their effect on foreign policy. In 1960, studies were initiated on the economics of disarmament, political implications of disarmament, trends and patterns of international interaction, the simulation of crisis decision-making, and ways of measuring international attitudes. Many more followed over the years, to a total of some forty-six separate studies in the areas of international conflict, domestic conflict, and the theory of conflict itself. Boulding's own

CRCR research projects fell in the areas of economics of disarmament, dynamics of social and international systems, and the theory of the integrative system. He lent his imagination and analytic powers to the development of many of the other project proposals as well.

The weekly research development seminar gave faculty, graduate students, and visiting scholars a chance to bounce their ideas off each other and observe edge-of-knowledge thinking in process. A graduate program with a major in conflict studies was developed in cooperation with six departments. And the *Journal,* now shifted to the sponsorship of the center, continued to publish the foremost articles in the peace research field.

Most observers agree that the center's accomplishments were very real. Even from the point of view of adding to the measurable assets of the university, it could not be ignored. Up to 1967, by Robert Hefner's rough calculation, it had pulled in a million dollars in grants and produced a hundred journal articles and nineteen books. Over the full twelve years, the research funds it brought to the university totaled $1,910,100. It also attracted several notable faculty members. Yet it received continued criticism, not all of it unfounded.

Some of this centered around its looseness of administration. The administrative function alternated between Angell and Boulding for the first seven years. Barth remained in a supporting administrative role, and Hefner served first in research and later in administration, through the total life of the center. But the allocation of administrative duties was fuzzy; there were years when the directorship was essentially empty, and this problem was never really solved. Boulding's dislike of detail, impatience with red tape, and disregard for established forms made him particularly inept as a director except to create enthusiasm, generate ideas, and lend status. The center seemed to attract people who were more free-wheeling and informal than some academic types, and the enterprise became a little too casual to suit critics who believed

73

in "running a tight ship." In addition, ideological resistance continued. The center's support of the controversial Black Action Movement and other burgeoning student action groups for social change no doubt increased animosity against it.

There were other difficulties. The university's provision of facilities was temporary and minimal, requiring four moves in twelve years, each except the last one to a more inaccessible and inadequate structure. The center's goals were more diffuse and far-reaching than those of other university centers, and harder to sell to funding agencies. Perhaps the heart of the problem was twofold: endorsing an unpopular cause (which made outside funds hard to get and limited the administration's support), and existing outside the locus of university power. Its interdisciplinary makeup kept it dependent on the associated departments, which controlled fellowship funds, hiring, firing, and salary. This left little freedom of movement for either faculty or students at the center.

In any case, foundation grants decreased, partly under the impact of the Vietnam War; several of the key senior faculty supporters (including Boulding, in 1967) left the university; and, while junior members still were producing considerable work, the center as a unit was less visible. Giving as their reason "lack of financial resources," the university regents, in July, 1971, voted to terminate the center. *The Journal of Conflict Resolution,* however, continued to be published. The impact of the center as the first institutional base of the peace research movement, a model copied later in other places, would remain.

11

In addition to helping found and nourish the *Journal* and the Center for Research on Conflict Resolution, Boulding attended and helped to organize several national and international conferences on peace research. He was one of

74

the first social scientists to join the physical scientists in the Pugwash Conferences on Science and World Affairs, in 1962 and again in 1964. Elise Boulding has also been active in this field, editing for a number of years the *International Peace Research Newsletter*.

Boulding's bibliography shows that from 1957 on, though he did not stop writing on economics and social science, there appeared at first one or two and then a number of articles each year in the international relations or conflict resolution field. In 1961, he wrote a pamphlet for the Institute for International Order, called *Perspectives on the Economics of Peace*. It is thoroughly research-oriented, factual, and operational: no histrionics and absolutely no moralizing (unless we include under this rubric the phrase "producing a rather dubious spiritual product known as 'national security' "). It consists of detailed questions and hypotheses, which could be empirically tested, about "war-proneness," the dynamic economic processes related to war, the economic problems of a stable peace, and the problems of transition to a peace system. His perspective was clearly that of looking, not just for ways of stretching out the intervals between wars, but for ways of adjusting to the radical social changes that the total abolition of war would bring.

At the same time, the young Center for Research on Conflict Resolution was preparing a study, jointly led by Boulding and Emile Benoit, to tackle one thorn of this many-branched issue, that of the economic problems of disarmament. Boulding contributed some ideas and an introductory paper; Benoit did most of the hard empirical and editorial work. This thorough and basic book, *Disarmament and the Economy*, was published in 1963.[1]

It succeeded in showing that economic barriers to disarmament could, in fact, be overcome. Its preface states its purpose and its accomplishment:

> We are under no illusions that disarmament is easy or close, or that the economic adjustments are the major

problem involved. The political problems of disarmament are the most difficult and the most important, and
the economic problems will rise in importance only as
the political problems are solved. It is essential, however,
to know that we can solve the economic problems concerned; otherwise, our fears in this regard, even though
they are below the surface, may operate as a serious handicap in our efforts to solve the political problem. (p. *ix*)

In 1962, Boulding published what is certainly his
most important theoretical work outside of economics,
and one of the major contributions to a field not yet overburdened with theory: *Conflict and Defense*. In a pattern
similar to *Economic Analysis* and *Principles of Economic
Policy*, he first develops the model of a general theory of
conflict, then applies it to a number of cases, international
conflict being one of these.

His general theory of conflict begins with the classes
of conflict processes. The first is the reaction process,
which Boulding names the "Richardson process" after
Lewis Richardson. In this process one party's action
changes the situation of the other, forcing the second
party to react, which again changes the situation of the
first. The phenomenon of the arms race can clearly be described in these terms. The direction of mutual interaction can be predicted depending on the starting point of
each, the initial reaction coefficients or touchiness to a
hostile act, and the rate of change of the two reaction coefficients. There are many elegant graphs to illustrate various combinations of these factors.

Game theory provides another way of analyzing these
reaction processes, but one which assumes rational calcula-
tions about the other's behavior, instead of mere
mechanical reaction. Boulding then explores the theory of
viability: that is, the conditions existing when one party
has the power to destroy or absorb the other. This analysis, again largely graphical, relies heavily on the economic theory of oligopoly, or the competition of two

firms. Conflict within the individual — approach vs. avoidance, the roots of hostility and its various outlets, and the function of symbols in relation to attitudes — is next discussed, then the ecological view, with groups in competition for living space or resources. The epidemiological model examines conflicts between group loyalties or ideologies in the same terms that have been used for the spread of disease. Finally, conflicts between individuals and organizations, questions of autonomy and socialization, are treated before the special cases are examined.

What is surely Boulding's most diverting example is given in the epidemiological analysis of the contagion of hostility and friendliness. Some complicated mathematics with an input of certain assumptions results in this conclusion:

> The end position of the population depends solely on the subtle balance between saints, devils, and publicans. If there are not enough saints, the rest of the population will become entirely hostile; just a few more may make the difference between highly hostile or highly friendly end positions of the dynamic process. (*Conflict and Defense*, p. 139)

These characters appear in an illustration of reaction processes also: the curious will even find a Richardson process graph of the interactions of saint, publican, and devil on page 32.

There is also an appendix to chapter 14 which consists of a chart of ideologies compared in their views of elements such as interpretation of history, nature of ultimate reality, nature of man, theory of value, and nature of evil. All this may sound like a standard analysis of ideologies, illustrating, as Boulding suggests, their similarities of structure — but we can get a glimpse at the fun he had playing with the idea when we catch slots for "Marxism, orthodox," "Nationalism, liberal," or "Worldliness" under the heading "Form of Worship" or "Sacramental

Dogma." As a single example, he lists the sacramental dogma of orthodox Marxism as follows: "Surplus value (substance) not reflected in price (accident). Acts in themselves evil transmuted into good if committed in the service of the revolution."

A pamphlet published in 1967 is the latest of Boulding's books and pamphlets in the conflict resolution area.[2] A slight piece, but something of a position paper, it is an edited transcription of a two-day debate between Kenneth Boulding and free-lance writer Milton Mayer on whether peace research is the way to get peace. Both men are Quakers; both have tongues that are extremely sharp swords; both are devoted to peace; and they agree about almost nothing. Boulding, in defending peace research against Mayer, is almost forced into the corner of defending knowledge against love.

But in this pamphlet we get a description of Boulding's idea of how we might get stable peace, using the figure of a phase system. A fairly extensive quotation gives a sense of his thinking as well as his oral style:

> The diagram of the phases of ice and water has striking parallels to that for peace and war. This is actually very much like the international system; there is a pressure aspect of it, the world war industry, the extent of the threat system. What corresponds to the temperature is what I call the warmth of the system, the level of community, identity, cultural exchange, commonality of interests, and all this sort of thing.
>
> Now if you look at the phase analogy, the water corresponds to stable peace. This is the liquid society, a society in which there's freedom of movement, in which you aren't frozen. There is a thaw even now in the Catholic Church and in the socialist camp; but our State Department just remains a chip off the old block of ice. You see, if you're close to the boundary, a small increase in temperature can melt the ice. This is the reason for cautious optimism. We are in the ice part of the diagram, all right, but there is a great deal of evidence that we're

close to the boundary. Neither peace nor war is stable, neither peace nor war is legitimate.

Then you also ask, how do you get over? What is the most fruitful line of action? There are two lines of action; one is reducing the pressure — this is disarmament — and the other is increasing the temperature. This is cultural exchange. . . . (*The Mayer/Boulding Dialogue on Peace Research*, p. 22)

But we return to a little fuller examination of his ideas. As has been mentioned, in 1942 the basis of his argument for the early end of war was twofold: its increasing horror and its increasing unprofitability — the moral cost and the financial cost. He did not expect men to become perfect and did not feel this was necessary. The key to his hope was the proposition "that war, as a specific human institution, is the result not of conflicts, nor of human wickedness, but of the political organization of the world into a number of separate, sovereign and irresponsible countries." As he pointed out, there are other ways to handle conflicts and wickedness without war (as is done, for example, within a country). "The trouble with the world has not been so much a lack of good will, as a lack of knowledge as to how to make good will effective." Consequently, he recommended an international organization not with a military function but rather as a center of research and information, a clearing house for statistics, and a place for administration of practical problems. The major obstacle he saw was the sense of responsibility for the welfare of others within a country, and the lack of this sense for those outside its borders. The concept of the sacredness of the nation got in the way of the needed extension of the sense of community.

Here, in 1942, were two themes which have run through all his succeeding writings on the subject: the view that the national state is obsolete; and the reliance on research, statistics, and information as a way out of reliance on military force. A third constant present in 1942,

79

and strikingly brought out in the 1967 pamphlet, is the principle of taking man as he is — believing he wants pretty much the right things — and concentrating the effort on making the system work for, not against him. Elsewhere he says:

> It is the moral, patriotic, and self-sacrificing individuals who are most likely to be the active participants in the international system. It is the organization, not the individuals, which is pathological, by reason of the corruption of both the information and the values that have produced it. (*B.E.*, p. 297)

Boulding pointed out the obsolescence of the national state as early as 1931, in a prize essay at New College, Oxford:

> Sovereign national governments are as obsolete as the city-state, and unless that is brought fully before the eyes of the capitalist world, then it cannot be too strongly urged that the world is doomed, and we shall be faced with a partial breakdown of civilization and a slow and painful reconstruction.

Articles and books to the present time have echoed this theme; and in *Conflict and Defense* he refines and extends it.

Nations, like firms, have costs of transport of both goods and "bads" (modes of attack or destruction), which result in a "loss-of-strength gradient": the farther from its center of power, the weaker a country is, and at some point (in the past at least) the loss-of-strength gradients intersect and a second country is stronger from there on. In such a case both countries are unconditionally viable in their own territories, with an overlapping area where they are in competition. The most stable situation occurs when countries are a long way apart, with a high cost of transporting violence, and a rapidly diminishing efficiency of operation as its scale increases. "It is because of a failure of all three of these conditions that we face an acute breakdown of the system of national defense in the world of today" (*Conflict and Defense,* p. 242).

The increasing range of the projectile has effectively reduced the distance between countries, and the increased efficiency of warheads makes it possible to pack incalculable destruction into one missile, so that no nation any longer has an area it can protect. None can be unconditionally viable in today's world: each of them can exist only as long as the others so choose. "We can only continue to have a world of separate nations if none of them wants to upset the existing structure, for none can be defended" (*Conflict and Defense,* p. 273).

Boulding's perception of the shaky condition of the national state as an institution, an intuition based on moral and economic grounds in 1931, is documented in 1962 by a theory of conflict, and data about man's technical progress. When the range of the deadly missile is half the diameter of the earth, sovereignty becomes, in fact, a fiction.

The national state is not only obsolete, it is, in a way, in conflict with science and the scientist. In *Economics of Peace* (p. 68), Boulding says: "The accidental friendships and enmities of the destructive monsters that we call 'nations' may be important in their own right to the nationalist; but the scientist must be a servant of the truth rather than of his nation, and as truth respects no political boundaries, neither must he." The last article in *Beyond Economics,* written in 1967, suggests that "the conflict of values between the subculture of science and the subculture of the international system may well turn out to be one of the most fundamental conflicts of our age." These divergent values are spelled out as (1) secrecy vs. openness; (2) hierarchy vs. equality; and (3) power vs. truth. A vision of the state as the servant, not the master, of man is clearly Boulding's point of view. When an organization ceases to serve it should cease to exist and not be propped up with false legitimacy. "The nation-state can no longer be treated as a sacred institution; there must be a deflation of the emotions and values that attach to it, a decline, if you will, in the passion with which people love their countries and an acceptance of the nation-state and the nation-state system as essentially mundane institutions designed solely for public convenience." [3]

If one views war as the rupture of an existing social system, then it is wise to find ways to identify the stresses and strains that can lead to such a break. One such effort of Boulding's is his exploration of the theory that wars tend to happen when one country overtakes another in power, a factor closely related to the per capita gross national product. If this could be demonstrated, then the overtakes in GNP — which can be roughly predicted from collectable data — would give a considerable clue as to coming stress points. There are, no doubt, other kinds of data which could be used to greatly sharpen the effectiveness of this kind of prediction. And so Boulding has gradually refined the recommendation in that early pamphlet, for an international clearing house for statistics.

Quincy Wright's parallel development of the concept of a "World Intelligence Center" surely fed into this refinement.[4] Through interchange and discussion, the idea of what Boulding calls "social data stations" emerged. These would serve like a world network of weather stations, collecting and processing data on populations, rates of economic growth, surpluses and shortages, attitudes, tension levels, shifts in power relationships of classes or groups within a country, voting trends, images which nations have of one another — all sorts of social indicators which could be put together to identify social temperature and pressure and predict cold or warm fronts. Researchers such as Karl Deutsch, Robert Hefner, David Singer, and Bruce Russett have actively worked on the identification and measurement of such social indicators and the establishment of a central data file for their storage and disbursement.

Boulding urges the development of indices from this mass of information, comparable to the economic indices of prices and national income. With such indices, the direction of change could be identified early:

> The problem of the maintenance of peace is one of "conflict control." We are faced in international relations with dynamic processes of action and reaction in fear, armament, and in the images which nations have of one another which go either from bad to worse or from bad to better. If they go from bad to worse too long, the result is a breakdown of the system in war. The great problem of the maintenance of peace is how to identify these movements, to catch them young, and to deal with them before they become unmanageable.[5]

The situation at present, he feels, is so foggy that most international decision-makers do not know when they take a step whether they are going up or down, and the information from social data stations would at least tell them which way was up.

It is Boulding's repeated contention that decisions in the field of international affairs are made by folk knowledge, or possibly literary knowledge (using the Peloponnesian War, for instance, to make decisions about Vietnam). In the world of literary images, "reality testing is least effective and . . . the elimination of error either does not take place at all or is enormously costly. . . . For this reason . . . the international system is by far the most pathological and costly segment of the total social system." He suggests that the present system of information gathering (spies, embassies, cocktail-party and golf-course conversation) could hardly have been better designed to provide misinformation. The data collection and processing that Boulding proposes would help to equip the system to move into scientific knowledge; but there are other problems. International affairs is a world of small numbers of decision-makers, which means it cannot be treated statistically. Values, the learning of values, random elements, and the "heroic ethic" have to be taken into account.

Still, there are some points becoming clear about the "international systems" approach to building a body of scientific knowledge — the only hopeful way Boulding sees of getting intellectual purchase on the rusty bolt of the problem of war. These are summed up in chapter 3 of *The Impact of the Social Sciences.*

In the first place, such a system is Copernican. It is viewed as a totality, as if from the outside, not from the point of view of any one nation. Second, it is parametric. This implies the mutual interaction of a large number of variables rather than a simple cause-effect relationship. Third, it does not limit itself to equilibrium models but recognizes the dynamic and cumulative processes in operation. Fourth, it is institutional: the sociological and anthropological effects of organizations, symbolic elements, and cultural habits are taken into account, and a wide variety of behavioral principles allowed for. Fifth, it looks not only at the characteristics of the actors in the drama but also at the forms of relations and transactions between them. Sometimes it may even abstract so far as to look at the transactions as if the actors were not there. And sixth, it is aggregative; that is, it looks for ways to condense large masses of heterogeneous information into useful quantitative indices, as the economists have done with the cost-of-living index.

This kind of general theory of the international system is being developed by a handful of current thinkers, again a sort of "Invisible College." The ones closest to Boulding share his commitment to finding ways to establish and maintain stable peace; but there are others doing similar thinking on the strategic theoretical side, such as Herman Kahn and T. C. Schelling. The methods of looking at the material are similar; the main difference is in the choice of problems and in the constraints programmed into the stipulations.

At many points [Boulding has observed] peace research and national security research overlap. In these days, certainly nobody regards war as anything but a cost to be minimized in the interest of certain other values. Nevertheless, there is a difference between those who regard it as a tolerable cost and those who regard it as an intolerable one.[6]

The difference was embodied in the Center for Research on Conflict Resolution, as it carved out the field of peace research. Observers evaluating the twelve-year life of the center note particularly its impact on the growth of ideas and the formation of other organizations. Robert Angell, asked in 1972 what it had accomplished, thought a minute and answered, "Largely, that it's been copied. It's left its tracks in other places in the world." Political scientists Harold Jacobson and David Singer both pointed out that it had made peace research respectable, almost Establishment. Singer called it a worldwide symbol, the first university center for studying the causes of war and social violence. Jacobson even suggested that Boulding, in spite of his bludgeon method, had succeeded in shifting some political scientists' research perspectives. Boulding, asked to write an "Epitaph" on the center, summed up its research on the war industry, arms control and disarmament, quantification in the study of the international system, and conflict systems in general. Then he listed its direct or indirect offspring: the International Peace Research Association, the Peace Research Society (International), the Consortium on Peace Research, Education, and Development, and the Stockholm International Peace Research Institute.[7]

Kenneth Boulding is recognized, in his contribution to the *Journal,* the center, and the development of its thought, as one of the main reasons for the existence of the peace research movement. Certainly the ingredients were already there; he was not the first in the field, nor the major contributor of solid empirical studies. He was, in Singer's words, "the world's most indifferent, casual administrator," but also "a catalyst, reference figure, legitimizer" with "fantastic courage and gutsiness." His fiery enthusiasm created a general mood in which others were caught up. He may indeed have helped to set in motion one of those "quiet revolutions" that change the course of history.

5

Social and Political Allegiances

I have never quite been able to make
the grade as an anarchist.

— KEB, *Beyond Economics*

I

To speak about a personal ideology is to speak about the
development of identity. As Erik Erikson, the psychologist
who made the term "identity crisis" a familiar one, points
out, "the social institution which is the guardian of identity *is* what we have called *ideology;*" and again, "identity
and ideology are two aspects of the same process." [1] The
process of maturation at the point of identity-development
involves the young person's seeking out some elements in
his society which are already formulated into a pattern
that can give both a simplicity and clarity to his somewhat
confused gropings for meaning, and his finding a sense of
participation with something or someone good and great
and more or less powerful. But the essential quality of the
ideology chosen must match the feelings and ideas already
bubbling in the youth's inner cauldron — that is, must reflect what he already feels and knows to be true of the
world and himself. This matching or reflection is pictur-
esquely called "resonance" by another psychologist, Silvan
Tomkins, who has done much work with personality development and analysis:

> Resonance to an ideology is a love-affair of a loosely-organized set of feelings and ideas about feelings with a highly organized and articulate set of ideas about anything. As in the case of a love affair, the fit need not at the outset be perfect, so long as there is a similarity between what the individual feels and thinks is desirable and the characteristics of the object.[2]

In the same article Tomkins also describes the special case of the creative artist or scientist who may resonate in his youth to "that one ideology among those available which is closest to the ideology which he will later create."

Kenneth Boulding himself has given some attention to the matter of ideologies and how they are adopted. In *The Meaning of the Twentieth Century,* after defining an ideology as "that part of the image of the world which a person defines as essential to his identity or his image of himself" (p. 159), he speculates on how a person chooses this particular part of the spectrum of all possible world-images:

> What is it, then, that gives to an image of the world power over a man's mind and that leads him to build his personal identity around it? The answer seems to be that an image of the world becomes an ideology if it creates in the mind of the person holding it a role for himself which he values highly. New ideologies are therefore likely to arise if people feel that the roles which they occupy in the existing society are unsatisfactory to them or despised by others. To create a role, however, an ideology must create a drama. The first essential characteristic of an ideology is then an interpretation of history sufficiently dramatic and convincing so that the individual feels that he can identify with it and which in turn can give the individual a role in the drama it portrays. (pp.161–62)

There is no contradiction to Erikson and Tomkins here, but an addition of the dramatic role concept to their notion of seeking out something without that matches something (here, a need) within.

In thinking of the kinds of allegiances which drew the young and maturing Kenneth Boulding into social, political, and religious spheres, I would give considerable weight to his own analysis of the process, including the element of personal role in a drama. It will help us shape our thinking, therefore, if we consider his early years in the light of role-dissatisfaction and the appeal of a dramatic interpretation of history.

Kenneth grew up an inner-city child in the shipping and processing center of Liverpool, on the borderline between upper-lower and lower-middle class. His father, variously called a heating engineer or a plumber, was both an artisan and a small business man. They well knew there were people poorer than they (the family was surrounded by them), but the kind of money necessary for upper school fees, living in a less crowded neighborhood, or training for any kind of a profession, was just not available. It was by dint of hard work, a keen mind, and teachers who recognized his gifts, that Kenneth won the necessary scholarships to scramble up the educational ladder. There was, during his childhood, for the first time in modern English history, enough fluidity to permit a certain reshuffling of the arrangement, to begin to respond to the fact that, as he observes, "the distribution of skills is continually upsetting the distribution of roles" (*The Image,* p. 106). Yet the battle against the brand of class, his placement by society in a slot where he did not fit, left him with a lifelong scar. He still talks about being denied a job at Oxford some years after he graduated "because I was not one of *them.*" Even very recently in a conversation, he set himself off from economist Galbraith with the words, "We have quite a friendly relationship, although he's not my style; I mean he's a man of the world, he moves among the elite, you see."

His class struggle was most acute when he entered Oxford. There he found himself in a world where six young men could eat their meals for a week in a baronial dining hall in total silence and utter loneliness because they had not been introduced to each other — where the only people he could talk to, except formally in classes, were those who shared his status as a scholarship student — where he discovered that there were whole realms of culture not taught in schools, such as classical music, that he had never heard of — and where a Liverpool accent was roughly equivalent to having a black face in American colleges until very recent times. It is not surprising, then, that his search for identity would involve a placement in a kind of society ideally somewhat rearranged from the one he saw about him.

To what was he exposed? What were his alternatives in political ideologies? His father gave him the earliest. The day that Kenneth was born, he had intended to spend canvassing voters for the Liberal Party (at the time the major reform party): it was election day, January 18, 1910. When the returns were in, the Liberals had won (even without William Boulding's help), and the jubilant new father wanted to name his son "William Ewart" in honor of his personal hero, the great Liberal former-Prime Minister from Liverpool, William Ewart Gladstone. It was only because his mother objected to having two Williams about the house that they settled on Kenneth Ewart instead. His father continued to be active in canvassing during elections, and defended the Liberal point of view against one of Kenneth's uncles who was a Labour man, and another who was a Conservative, whenever the subject came up in family conversations.

The headmaster of the second grammar school Kenneth attended, who impressed him with a "curious combination of personal warmth and intellectual cynicism," was a socialist and an atheist. It was from him Kenneth learned one could question religious beliefs and economic systems. He spent a lot of time with Kenneth helping him prepare for his scholarship examinations, and while Kenneth never swallowed Mr. Lewis's doctrines whole, they formed what he calls a "creative tension" in him against the strong and competing doctrines he heard at home. As he moved into secondary school he found for himself several other similarly bright, similarly poor boys who began to consider themselves intellectuals. They read a great deal, particularly H. G. Wells and all of Shaw's plays and prefaces, and delighted in going to the playhouse and sitting in the balcony for sixpence to see each new Shaw play that was presented. It was in this school, too, that Kenneth was introduced to Gilbert and Sullivan, singing in the chorus of *Iolanthe* and *The Pirates of Penzance* in the school productions and feasting on each new opportunity to sing or hear a Gilbert and Sullivan operetta.

H. G. Wells's *Outline of History* was published in 1920. It must have been some three or four years later that Kenneth's mother and father gave it to him for Christmas and set in motion some powerful ideological forces. For it was reading this book — combined with his own encounter with the reinterpretation of English history from the point of view of an Irish school friend — that convinced him that history teachers were liars, that (as he later insisted in *The Image*) the narrow picture of history presented by one country's schools was a source of dissension and war. It was here, too, that he caught the vision of America as a new world, a world broken free of the old loyalties and the old traps of class and oppression. This was the beginning of his "long and stormy love affair," as he puts it, with this country.

Kenneth was suffering adolescence and seeking identity in the precarious decade between the Great War and the Great Depression. The trio of mentors he chose, Wells, Shaw, and W. S. Gilbert, were not the only voices around. Allowing for the normal lag between publication and general exposure, one thinks of Kipling, Forster, Galsworthy, Henry James — chroniclers of the order of things as they were — and, on the other hand, such writers as D. H. Lawrence and Virginia Woolf, plumbing human depths with new Freudian sounding lines. He did read Galsworthy and James, but even later in his life could never take to Lawrence and Woolf. It was evidently not the torment of human relationship that attracted and held Kenneth, nor the description of morals and mores, but the shattering of the social form. Shaw and Gilbert both attacked the foibles, customs, and expectations of society with penetrating wit and engaging humor; Wells, having pointed out its dangers and failings, was ready to remake it.

I I

When we look at the features that Boulding, then or later, shared with each of these men, the correspondences become rather startling. Like Gilbert, he has a knack for apt and perceptive topical versifying. While his poetry is sometimes very serious, he spills out cryptic, concentrated and often hilarious descriptions of people and issues almost as easily as someone else might doodle. (These have proved quite popular, often published with scholarly proceedings of meetings.) He won a prize in the lower sixth form for the best prologue (in blank verse, of course) for the school's production of *She Stoops to Conquer,* and there are notes and sections for several unfinished operettas, dating from secondary school days, in his files, with one for which the libretto was completed. Unfortunately, since he found no Sullivan, it was never performed. Later, by the expedient of using existing tunes for his lyrics, he overcame this deficiency, and a few selected gatherings were able to see and hear his compositions. For example, he was both author and actor in the parting celebrations at International House when he left Chicago in 1934 — "Julius Brutus, or Midsummer Night's Moonshine." The

Quakers at Pendle Hill were treated to a versified Don Juan in Quaker Hell at the close of a session there in the 1940s; at another session, they witnessed "The Pendle Pilgrim's Progress." And when Dr. I. Leo Sharfman retired as head of the Economics Department at Michigan in 1955, the staff performed in his honor a Gilbert-Sullivan parody "Ileolanthe," with Daniel Suits, Gardner Ackley, Richard Musgrave, and Boulding collaborating on the lyrics.

George Bernard Shaw, of course, is almost the symbol of the iconoclast. Where there were any idols of tradition, religion, moral code, custom, or belief, he sought them out to shatter them. He was not, however, without ideals, and it was these that he would put in place of idols. Here is Shaw, on his style: "It is always necessary to overstate a case startlingly to make people sit up and listen to it, and to frighten them into acting on it. I myself do this habitually and deliberately." [3] And here is Boulding:

> When one has to raise a lonely voice in denunciation of a respected object one has the choice of two methods. One can keep the bad news till the last and then make an exit before the tomatoes begin to fly, or one can apply the shock technique and stun the audience into insensibility by letting the cat out of the bag at the beginning. It is the second of these alternatives which I propose to follow. [4]

The shattering of icons or idols is closely related to the debunking of romantic stereotypes, the mischievous pin that pricks the child's balloon, or bursts a rainbowed soapbubble, frustrating the reader's or hearer's expectations. Such a pattern is evident in another set of Boulding productions, the stories he made up in response to a group of ambiguous pictures, an exercise in fantasy called the Thematic Apperception Test, or TAT. This is a projective test, which has many and varied uses in looking at personality makeup and motivation, to which Boulding cheerfully submitted in January, 1969. (Appendix A gives a fuller description.) A striking aspect of many of his stories was a romantic buildup suddenly replaced by the thud of dull normality. In one, for instance, a boy is dreaming of becoming a great violinist — but he will probably instead "turn out to be a mathematical physicist." In another, a girl is waiting for her lover by a street lamp in the fog under mysterious and emotion-charged circumstances — but when he comes, "they'll probably go off and have dinner and then to a movie." The anticlimax and the twist of skeptical humor remind one of Shaw.

That Boulding sees himself as something of a heretic may be guessed from a number of references. We are familiar with the disapproval he has encountered from some economists for straying off the beaten track. In *The Image* there is a possible foreshadowing of this: "There are many areas of experience which are not respectable for scientists to study and which they investigate with grave risks to their reputations" (p. 50). And again, more generally, after describing the restructuring of knowledge that he visualizes as essential:

> There can be little doubt . . . that, if the restructuring which I have suggested is in fact underway, it will eventually be recognized officially. Until then, the new structures, as new intellectual structures always have done, will have to live in an underworld, an underworld of deviant professors, gifted amateurs, and moderate crackpots. To this underworld, I invite my no doubt somewhat alarmed and bewildered readers. (*The Image,* p.163)

This style was probably reinforced by his experience as a graduate student under Frank Knight in Chicago, whom he found "thoroughly delightful . . . never dreams of talking about his subject [but] uses it as a peg to hang a chain of scintillating observations on. . . . He has come to the conclusion that there is no such thing as Economics, which is very disturbing to a professor thereof." (KEB let-

ter to Maynard Houston, January, 1933) John Platt at
Michigan remarked of Boulding, "If he can turn some
piece of conventional wisdom on its head he loves to: he
dearly loves a paradox." While Boulding has not been so
thorough as Shaw in tilting at all society's windmills, the
"shock technique" and the sudden twist of words to defeat
the expected have almost become his trademark. He and
Shaw are both entertainers.

And both are serious. Here, too, they meet on the
field of examining human ideals and their relation to
practice. One particular correspondence is the preoccupa-
tion they share with the conflict between vitality and artificial system. For Shaw, the life force is pent up in the dry
customs of marriage regulations and the expectations of
precise behavior. For Boulding, this conflict appears in
many guises. One is the flowing, dynamic, complex
human potential bound by coercive, restrictive governments, or dry, meaningless administrative requirements,
or the bonds of ignorance or poverty. Both men would
agree on a belief in natural goodness, the educability of
human beings, and the possible achievement of some kind
of earthly paradise.

Both, too, have seen themselves as alienated, as standing outside the world of other men. Shaw called himself
"a sojourner on this planet, rather than a native of it. . . .
I was outside society, outside politics, outside sport, outside the church" — but inside painting, literature, and science.[5] Boulding, not so publicly, has declared himself, in
being a Christian, an outsider:

> From childhood I was alien to my time,
> Because the moral soil in which I grew
> Was in a churchly pot, somewhat in lieu
> Of the open field of local place and clime.
> The air perhaps had a little local grime
> But the watering had a meed of heavenly dew —
> Only eternity, not time, was true,
> And Christly, heavenly loyalty was prime.

So have I lived loyal to a world not yet,
Or to a Kingdom not in man's time founded,
And in the bloody time by my life bounded
I bystand, loosely to the history's fret
Unfitted, dreaming loyalty to the Good,
Amid the roar of daily evil's flood.[6]

Yet the outsider may have a mission in interpreting what he sees from his point of view. Shaw has been described as making a moral analysis of contemporary civilization, as an "artist philosopher" conducting a campaign incursion (with his pen as his sword) into all areas of knowledge as a participant observer.[7] And Boulding, as has been mentioned, continually notes the crucial role of the eccentric or the prophet in showing society where it is and where it ought to be — the charismatic individual who brings change, breaks with his parents' standards, questions the sanctity of the "transcript" of experience handed down to him, defies the sanctions of his superiors and his peers. (See, for instance, *The Image,* p. 75.) He is more diffident about identifying himself with this role. He has called himself an intellectual middleman; but in *The Organizational Revolution* he equates the writer with the moralist and the innovator, "the creator and propagator of his own ideas and ideals, seeking not merely to describe but to change." [8] It cannot be denied that Boulding is a writer, and a moralist, and I read as an essential element in his identity this sense of his own mission, the creation of change by means of ideas. Preaching the attitude of moral and political realism, preaching the religion of creative evolution, attacking the illusions and orthodoxies of the past, and giving shape to the myths and orthodoxies of the future — all this has been said of Shaw,[9] and all of this could be said of Boulding.

And what of H. G. Wells? A lower-class boy almost two generations earlier than Kenneth, he fought his way out of several business apprenticeships and finally through a scientific education. (The urgency of refusing to be hemmed in by a static business position, even at considerable risk, was common to both Shaw and Wells. Boulding was never in quite the same kind of spot, though he once characterized a position he never held, a lectureship at Oxford, as a "comfortable fur-lined trap." Nevertheless, a like refusal to be hemmed in, even at the cost of his job, is evident at several points in his life.) From the specific, like Boulding, Wells moved to the general. While still a student he tried to work out a "Universal Diagram" from which all phenomena would be derived by deduction. Very early he realized that burgeoning communication was making all existing boundaries too small and tight, that men needed to move from a "localized" to a "delocalized" type of mind, and that he was on his way to Cosmopolis, to become a citizen of the world. A planned world-state was imperative:

> We are, as a species, caught in an irreversible process. No real going back to the old, comparatively stable condition of things is possible. . . . We are therefore compelled to reconstruct the social and economic organization until the new conditions are satisfied.[10]

Here is the sense of Boulding's Great Transition described in *The Meaning of the Twentieth Century* in 1964, although the content of the process is different. Boulding rejected the world-state early: he spoofs it in one of his unfinished operettas, "The Federation of the World"; in it strife was abolished by substituting rhyme for prose and banishing the Intellectual Advisors. But other Wellsian echoes may be found in his 1942 pamphlet, *New Nations for Old* (Wells published *New Worlds for Old* in 1908), and in the memo "Plan for the Establishment of an Order of World Citizenship" which Boulding developed around 1937.

As with Shaw, a number of phrases describing Wells's attitudes and goals could easily be applied to Boulding: Wells had a tendency to "get things ruthlessly mapped out and consistent"; history should become human ecology; there should be a worldwide "New Republic" of intelligent men (for Boulding, read "Invisible College"); he looked for a creative revolution by the cooperation of scientists, businessmen, financial powers, and news media, with self-consciousness and planning; "The Empire was a convenience and not a God" (for Boulding, read "the national state"); he set out, after his outline of history, to cover the rest of knowledge with an outline of biology and a review of economics and politics.

Wells, as everyone knows, wrote numerous novels both of science fiction and social comment, which Boulding did not; was an ardent supporter of World War I, which Boulding could never have been; engaged in a sexual life quite different from Boulding's, and claimed that he forgot a great deal, perceived less, and enjoyed less than most people — all states to which Boulding seems to illustrate a clear opposite. But probably none of these items were evident in the works which caught young Kenneth's searching mind and made him a Wellsian.

Certainly a Utopian thread is represented in all three: Gilbert, Shaw, and Wells. In Gilbert, it was the fantasy of the fairy world; in Shaw the transmutation of male–female relations or the creation of morally responsible industrialists; in Wells the dreams of science fiction or the hopefully realistic use of knowledge to transform society; in both Shaw and Wells the Utopian thread turned to Fabian Socialism for method. In Shaw, Wells, and Boulding, this hopefulness was based on a sense of the tremendous potential, the untapped resources, in the human being. Edmund Wilson calls it Romanticism:

> Certain writers with a strong Romantic strain like H. G. Wells and Bernard Shaw tried to promote through the new social sciences, in the teeth of the bourgeois world, the realization of those visions of universal happiness which had been cherished by some of the most individualistic of the Romantics, such as Shelley and Rousseau.[11]

Social science in the service of Romanticism, if such it was, carried many young intellectuals along in its wave. Wilson himself reported, "Shaw and Wells had been my gods at boarding school"; George Orwell wrote of Wells, "I doubt whether anyone who was writing books between 1900 and 1920 . . . influenced the young so much"; [12] and Walter Lippmann, an avid reader of Shaw and Wells, was acting on their ideology when he organized the Socialist Club at Harvard about 1910.[13]

Here is the drama — sufficient for even an ambitious boy — the creative evolutionary process of man, moving from artificial class and national bonds to the building of natural human ones all across the world, tied in with man's kinship with other living creatures and the whole earth. And here is a role for Kenneth: the one who sees and interprets the way to remake the institutions of society in this evolutionary direction, by penetrating their laws and presenting them with clarity and brilliance so everyone can understand.

I I I

Kenneth and his friends, in their final years at Liverpool Collegiate and their first years at the university, also thought of themselves as socialists. In fact, a letter to Aunt Ada in November, 1928, indicated the popularity of the movement: "Socialism is getting fearfully respectable. I think I shall turn Communist. There are far too many Socialists in Oxford." In the same month Kenneth heard the secretary of the British Communist Party speak at the Labour Club and was impressed by his handling of hecklers. "He certainly did not convert me to his pernicious doctrine of force," he reported to his parents, ". . . yet he certainly increased my respect for his personality."

In the election of May, 1929, Kenneth, like his father, was actively involved in politics — but not for his father's party. It was the Labour Party that carried his socialist banner. Campaign speakers from the three major parties were ranked as follows in Kenneth's letters home:

> The Conservative was honest, intense, and very sincere with a dogmatic, disagree-with-me-if-you-dare sort of expression. . . . The Liberal was a Perfectly Dear Old Man with a white beard and a mild dodder who quoted his friend Burke (Probably a contemporary). . . . But hardly the sort of man who would Do anything about anything. The Labour man was . . . difficult to put a label to: . . . with a semi-apologetic manner: but who spoke with a vision of a new world behind him and didn't utter a single platitude.

The Conservatives were inept, the Liberals "very wicked and most unprincipled" (there were charges against Lloyd George of bribery and corruption), the Labour Party "almost wholly composed of extremely nice people most of them with wings under their coat collars who wanted the people who made all the money to get their proper share in it, but the newspapers said that was very wicked because it was called Socialism." In the election in May 1929, he went about canvassing for Labour with great zest, ad libbing and arguing at doors in the villages around Oxford. Labour won, by a small margin, and (again in his letters home) Kenneth duly took credit for the victory, ending, "Best love to Dad. I'm so Sorry he isn't going to be a Socialist. But after calling me Ewart. . . !"

He was still a socialist at the next election, in October, 1931, and was quite appalled at the defeat of the Labour Party in what he felt was a "dirty election": "This disastrous election! The work of thirty years undone in a day by the stampede of unintelligent voters. It makes me weep." "The day of Social Reform is past: we have come up against the Rock of Private Property, and we or it busts, to put it concisely if ungrammatically." After the previous Labour victory, he had gone all over Oxford looking for a red tie, trying seven shops before he finally found one; but now that Labour was defeated, he bought a black tie and wore it everywhere. This seems to have practically marked the end of his political activities. The Liberals as well as Labour were set back, so he and his father could commiserate together, though they still had to agree to differ. Ten or twenty years earlier, Kenneth said, he would have been a Liberal; but the Liberals' work was done now.

Perhaps it was partly this election, but, according to Boulding, the credit for moving him gradually out of socialism goes mainly to Marx. About 1930, the young socialists at Oxford began publishing a journal called *The Plan: A Journal of Constructive Socialism,* edited by Bernard Ash, one of Kenneth's Liverpool friends. In issues four and five of this journal, Kenneth published an article called "Possibilities of Socialism in Britain." This is an interesting article because, while endorsing socialism, it suggested that there should be nothing sudden about the transition to the new mode of life but rather a long period of education to prepare the masses of people for the responsibilities and skills required in their new roles as decision-makers and full participants in a technological society. In a way, by advocating extreme gradualism, it indicates the beginnings of his movement away from socialism.

In June, 1929, Kenneth had left the science program for philosophy and economics and had begun heavy reading assignments in this field. In May, 1930, he made this comment in a letter to Aunt Ada: "I have been reading Karl Marx for days with the result that . . . my head is a wild and turbulent mass of Extremely ill digested Marx. . . . Marx is extraordinarily difficult but exceedingly fascinating." His attempt to digest Marx resulted in at least two papers in this period, "The Materialist Conception of History in Marx," and "Karl Marx's Theory of Value."

Boulding's current objections to Marx's thinking are concentrated in the same two areas as he chose for the topics of these student papers. His analysis is briefly stated in chapter 5, "The Marxist Dialectic," of his book, *A Primer on Social Dynamics* (1970). He does not quarrel with philosophical materialism but states its irrelevance by arguing that Marx fooled himself in calling his system materialism when the valuation of commodities, on which it was based, is a property of mind rather than of matter. Boulding feels that some of Marx's economics reflected Ricardo and Malthus and thus was not new, and some vaguely anticipated Keynes. He also feels that Marx showed "some fundamental confusions of dimensions as between stock concepts and flow concepts." (p. 76) Boulding's discussion, however, concentrates on Marx's interpretation of history and his theory of surplus value.

Boulding considers the labor theory of value and of production "midnineteenth-century social science," hopelessly outdated. Marx was wrong, he says, in thinking of the material commodity as primary and the acts of labor as its main input, ignoring the essential factors of organization and motivation that put the whole process together and are supplied by the capitalist. "Production seems to be something that is supposed to happen by people spontaneously putting a hand to a plough which somebody else has previously and spontaneously made." (*Primer,* p. 82) "The fact is that the process of production is essentially an organizational process, not a mechanical process of adding bits of labor to bits of embodied labor." (*Primer,* p. 83) Even the communist countries, he points out, have had to violate their own principles in recognition of this fact, and build in the motivational factors of price and income differentials. In addition, Marx failed to develop, Boulding charges, an adequate theory of distribution or to read correctly what actually happens with distribution under capitalism, and he failed to recognize that the forces of nationalism are far stronger than the forces of class in uniting groups of people.

But, for Boulding:

the principal villain would seem to be the dialectical philosophy. This places a premium on conflicts even where

they might be avoided, it provides a magnificent excuse
for the expression of aggression and hatred, and it diverts
attention from the solutions of problems to the winning
of victories. . . . The socialist countries, as long as they
are in the dialectical and revolutionary phase, develop at
an enormously high cost in terms of human suffering and
corruption. (*Primer*, pp. 92, 95)

He sees the importance of dialectical processes but considers them a second choice because of their great cost.
They work best, in his opinion, "when they are imbedded
in a large nondialectical matrix." The long slow upward
haul, as in his early article on socialism, still has his endorsement.

How much of a critical reaction flashed on him at the
time of his first reading of Marx, however, is a question.
His present recollection is, "I thought it was a bunch of
nonsense, and that cured me of socialism." It was probably not quite that sudden.

In June, 1932, he read a paper on Communism before the Oxford University Wesley Society. In this paper
he saw Communism's main fallacy to be setting up what
should be the means of life as its ends — a conflict of materialistic with religious values. But he responded favorably to Communism's ethical challenge toward justice in
distribution, which under capitalism looked almost impossible. A letter to a friend in November, 1934, contains the
sentence: "The past two years have made me much more
of a pacifist and much less of a socialist than I was before"; here the argument does not mention Marx, but
leans heavily on Kant, whose categorical imperative
seemed much more valid to Kenneth than Bentham's
utilitarianism — again a conflict of the materialistic with
the ethical. The letter goes on to recount in some detail
Kenneth's disillusionment with socialism:

As for Socialism; the collapse of the Labour government
in England in 1931 shattered any faith I had in the Labor

party, and Roosevelt has turned my mind still more away
from socialistic programs. The crux of the matter lies in
the reflection that socialism involves, in any of its forms,
a concentration of power, particularly of economic
though also of political power — into the hands of a single man or a single committee; and this is a thing which
I have come to detest. . . . Now, as an economist of
course I must recognize the unfortunate fact [that] Capitalism refuses to work without groans, shrieks, depres-
sions and constant and ever increasing breakdowns; . . .
the only thing wrong with capitalism is this regrettable
fact that it doesn't work. . . . I believe very strongly in
the *diffusion,* not the concentration, of power; and this is
most nearly achieved in a system of ideal capitalism. . . .
The horrid truth of course is that I am an individualist;
I believe in the infinite worth of the human soul and I
regard the personification of the state as the most crimi-
nal heresy that ever raised its horrid head.

It appears that it was not confusions in Marx's theories or
their unworkableness that turned Boulding away from socialism, but his realization that the materialism, the violence, and the power relationships involved in Marxism
were contrary to his fundamental values. Though Marxism had its fascinations, it did not fit the shape his convictions had already taken. He was ripe for another ideology.

Soon after Marx, Lord Keynes appeared on his hori-
zon. In November of 1930 Boulding heard him speak, and
in December he was reading his new book. At the same
time, the depression was looming as the dominant problem in the current world. Suddenly things seemed to fall
into place; Keynes with his *Treatise on Money* was "the
only man who really thinks he knows how Things ought
to be Run." The impact has lasted; a recent description of
the experience, an informal oral recollection, gives its
force:

You see, this was a feeling that *now* the world made
sense; history made sense for the first time; here was a

mind really at work, who was a *much* greater man than Marx, that is, a man who really had astonishing perceptions as to how you preserve the values of a free society and at the same time prevent this crippling unemployment. This was a — I would say it was a spiritual experience as well as an intellectual one.

He likes to quote Wordsworth in connection with this experience: "Great was it in that dawn to be alive, but to be young was very heaven!" [14] The excitement and power of this quotation carries the message that something in what Keynes was writing fit exactly what Kenneth was looking for. It was a logically acceptable, intellectually sound way of combining justice and freedom. Justice is what people ought to have (ideally, the paternalistic decisions of the socialist state supply this); freedom gives them what they want to have (ideally, free enterprise supplies this, but at the cost of considerable inequity and injustice). The combination of the market system supplying alternative choices, a measure of freedom, with enough government control through tax adjustment and financial policy to prevent destructive fluctuations of the uncontrolled free market, was a tricky balance but could provide a viable solution.

In a number of his books there appear discussions of communism and capitalism, or the ideologies of left and right. He usually points out the advantages and flaws in both, and ends up a little to the left of center. Regulation is useful for preventing disaster, for, in a way, making room for freedom. He has a doctrine of the "missed bus": "The bus for socialism comes along only at one stage of economic development"; if that time goes by without a revolution, and development proceeds, there is little appeal in socialism later.[15] In general, he weighs the efficiency of both socialism and capitalism as organizers of society and the values attained and lost by each, and suggests that both patterns are possible in the spaceship earth.

It is terribly important to Boulding that there be a number of possibilities for anything. This is part of his feeling for America. He thinks of the British class system as specifying one right way to do everything, and the Americans as breaking out of this. "I am convinced that if a thing is worth doing, it is worth doing wrong, or at least worth doing in many ways," he wrote in a recent article. He reports an extremely releasing experience he had one day some time back when he had to make a decision. He worried, prayed over it, and suddenly had the clear feeling that "God didn't care a damn" — it didn't really matter — which of the two alternatives he chose, either would be all right. From the "one right way" to the pluralistic universe has been an important direction in his ideological development. The need for many centers of power; the value of complexity; the "mosaic" society; diversity of ethical values — over and over in his writing we find commitment to plurality. He would like to see everybody leading many lives and having many identities and imitating many models. Even by 1928 he was drawn this way; in his first term at Oxford he wrote home, "It is a great pity that the political clubs [Conservative, Liberal, and Labour] all meet on the same night here. I should like to belong to all three."

His love affair with America was partly youthful idealism about a new, fresh world, partly a breaking out of the British class system (in America, "nobody asked us who our grandfathers had been, they accepted us as people"), and partly a rejection of narrow British nationalism, "to become something larger than English. . . . In a sense I became an American because this is as close as you could get to being human." It was movement from a narrow, restricted box to a looser, freer situation. When the narrow box of nationalism closed in on him in America, too, that was the beginning of the storm.

In America, Boulding, who was for some time a Democrat, broke with the Democrats over Vietnam, became a defiant nonvoter, and in 1970, though with some sense of anomaly, registered as a Republican. He became the faculty adviser for the Young Republicans at the University of Colorado, since he felt they were about the most constructive force around at the moment.

A move like this may startle some observers who are accustomed to thinking of Boulding as a radical heretic. He is a heretic, even among radicals. On the radical–conservative continuum he has always, since his Oxford days, had one foot on each side of the line (sometimes he stands on one foot, sometimes on the other). He has experienced the denial of the naïve expectations of capitalism's freedom by class barriers to jobs and the troughs of depression. Keeping in mind his repeated endorsements of innovation and radical change agents, we might look at some of his words about conservatives and liberals, government, and economic organization. In 1941, he suggested that if you trusted government you would likely be a socialist; if not, a capitalist; at the same time (it may surprise those who thought President Nixon had originated the phrase) he notes, "Governments, even democratic governments, tend to be swayed by noisy minorities rather than by silent majorities." [16] He was talking about an industry lobbying for a tariff. In 1953, he used neutral, favorable words on both sides when he described the conservative and progressive as the desire for purity vs. the desire for growth, or homogeneity vs. diversification. He also emphasized the importance of the conservative in society, as making for orderliness in the process of change. In 1958 he wrote, "It may be that the best safeguard against depression is radical policies carried out by conservative governments!" In 1963, "Government . . . may be a servant of freedom as well as its enemy"; in 1965, "The liberal is a man who does not believe in coercion at home, but who does believe in it abroad," and again, "I am not altogether opposed . . . to . . . legitimized economic coercion." In a conversation in 1969 he noted: "a frequent combination of conservatism and in-competence; they're not always the same thing but they do seem to form natural alliances."

Clues to and confirmation of the two major tendencies in Boulding's political and economic ideologies can be gar-nered by looking again at some of his responses on the TAT (the projective test consisting of stories told about a series of pictures). On the one hand, Boulding displayed the urgent need to burst out from the constricted to the looser situation, the need for alternatives and the freedom to make choices; and, on the other hand, balance, middle-of-the-roadness, the clinging to orderliness and a certain amount of regulation.

The need for autonomy is one of the strongest needs represented in Boulding's TAT stories. All the heroes act independently and take responsibility for their actions, except in one story where a family is working as a unit. In addition, five of the thirteen stories have autonomy as their major theme — three of young people going their own way, one of working alone creatively, and one being very simply a character breaking out and getting free from an intolerable situation. Though there are some negative results from independent action, the outcome is always positive in the end, and these five stories seem to be say-ing, "If you go ahead and do the thing you really want, you may find it easier than you thought; at least it will come out all right." They are straightforward incidents with definite outcomes (almost alone among the stories) and there seems to be more identification with the charac-ters in these stories than in most of the others.

The direction that action takes provides further evi-dence of the importance of autonomy. The four kinds of action most frequently used, representing 43 percent of the total acts in all the stories, are autonomous or dominating types of acts: over things, toward things, against people, or toward conditions.

One of the best clues to the extent to which the story-teller identifies himself with the characters is the number of behavioral levels he attributes to the character; for instance, whether he mentions his perceptions, his desires, his cognitions, or only his physical behavior. There are two similar stories, of a mother and son, and a father and son, in which the son has done or is planning to do something the parent disapproves of. In both cases, the parent forgives and continues to love the autonomous son. In the father–son story there is evidence of Boulding's identifying with both characters: there are four psychological levels for each. This illustrates the second ideological trend we have observed, the need for balance or the pull to both sides of the liberal–conservative continuum. The son represents the driving need for autonomy: he has either married an unsuitable girl, gotten into trouble with the law, or joined the Communist Party; he is surly, not sure of himself, but he has acted according to his own decision, and his political activism against the system certainly reflects some of Boulding's outlook. (The son in the other story is planning to go into the army or become a conscientious objector.) On the other hand, the older man is conservative, a professor or a banker, disapproving of his son's antiestablishment acts; yet Boulding also seems to identify with him. I can see these characters as the two sides of Boulding's conservative radicalism.

Five stories illustrate the conservative side of the struggle for stable values vs. an ambiguous world — they focus on reaching for security, making the environment less threatening, or putting down in some ordered form what is perceived and observed. A repeated pattern is the achievement of values, of clarity, order, and light, against the background of a dark, confused, rough or ambiguous world.

H. G. Wells described his life as a movement from

the narrow bounds of his backyard toward being a citizen of the world. For Boulding, too, the bursting out from too-small boundaries, world citizenship, the reaching for simple, unspecified, unstratified humanity — and indeed too, the heretical standing alone, the Shavian iconoclasm — may be the need for autonomy exploded to a world scale. But he could never quite make the grade as an anarchist; he needs always to have enough framework to organize chaos and legislate freedom.

6

Nonviolence: The Deep Root

Love is not enough. . . . Love without knowledge
will destroy us.

— **KEB**, *The Mayer/Boulding
Dialogue on Peace Research*

I

If any one article of Kenneth Boulding's faith and practice is completely consistent, utterly undeniable, persist-
ing throughout life, and coloring everything else he does,
it is the doctrine of pacifism or nonviolence. This is not
something, like socialism, enthusiastically adopted in
adolescence and replaced later in a more rational process
of examination; it begins much earlier and runs far
deeper. It is a positive affirmation of human life which
shows itself not only in resistance to war and anguish at its
increasing tragedy, but in his choice of the problems on
which to spend his intellectual resources, in his choice of
a religious community to belong to, in his conscious valuing of the loving relationship toward other people, and in
the actual qualities of patience and respect for the other
person — not necessarily patience with the other's ideas,
and not necessarily sensitivity to where he inwardly *is*, but
an absence of vindictiveness, superiority, or personal
power-struggle — that he brings to his contacts with peo-

ple in all the segments of his life. As far as I know, there was only one brief point in his life when he questioned this commitment, and though it has been sorely shaken it remains the deepest root of his identity.

At first glance, it is something of a mystery how he got that way. Neither of his parents was a pacifist; his church did not preach it (it preached love, but this can be defined almost as one wishes); none of his good friends endorsed it as thoroughly as he; none of his teachers taught it. Pacifism was a wispy, almost invisible thread in the culture he grew up in; yet as a young boy he found it and made it his own. I believe, therefore, the search for its origins needs to begin with his very early life. And, in accord with Freud's principle of overdetermination, as well as common sense, it is probable that a number of interacting factors led him in this direction. I think some, at least, can be identified.

Kenneth was born, as we have said, in January, 1910. His mother, a country girl, had always felt pent up in their row house in Liverpool without any yard, and some time in 1911, business seemed good enough for the family to move to the equivalent of the suburbs, "across the water" (the river Mersey) to Wallasey, where they took a house with a yard and a tree. They lived there for three years, with green things around them, salt air, and beaches for sand castles. Then on August 4, 1914, Britain was caught up in the conflagration of World War I, and so was this little family. In a few months, the decline of his father's business forced them back to the house on Seymour Street, which William Boulding had kept as his business headquarters through the intervening time. Both Kenneth and his mother were completely miserable at the move; it was a move from openness, freedom, and light to constriction, crowded living, and dirty pavements. It had, I think, immediate and lasting reverberations.

Kenneth's father volunteered for the army, but was not accepted because of a minor physical defect. His uncle, however, was conscripted and later returned with permanent damage from shellshock. One day, vividly impressed on the boy's mind, the uncle came home on leave directly from the trenches, crawling with lice. He went immediately to the bathroom, where he undressed and threw all his clothes into the courtyard at the back. Bessie, Kenneth's mother, took a hot iron out and used it to kill all the lice, no doubt with an open-mouthed small spectator at her elbow.

The war years were a series of shocking encounters — fine young cousins, friends, and neighbors, one day present for a festive meal, would be heard of next as losing their limbs or being killed across the Channel. The impact of this carnage on wives and families was well known to Kenneth; his mother would often be called on to comfort and console what was unconsolable. Once she took him with her to visit her aunt, who had lost her reason shortly after a son was killed. Kenneth would have been eight or nine. His mother describes it: "It was one of her bad days and it was terrible. The incident made a great impression on Kenneth and I think the memory of it, later on, helped to make a Quaker of him. Wars make tragic the private lives of ordinary people."[1]

Besides the casualty lists, the war was ever-present in rationing, the continual fear of zeppelin attacks, and the parades of soldiers with kilts and bagpipes, who, as his mother reports, started out fine and tall but were noticeably shorter and smaller as the war went on and the first ones were killed off. Liverpool was not bombed in World War I, but Bessie continually feared for the safety of her son and lost a good deal of sleep during the repeated blackouts.

Kenneth kept a diary during the year of 1918, and his daily entry began with a dating from the beginning of the war, such as, "1,478 day of the war." On January 6 the entry is, "The King ordered everybody to go to church twice today to pray for PEACE today and I hope it will soon come." The entry for November 11 is decorated with all sorts of flourishes and the big words, PEACE WITH GERMANY: "Peace day. We had a holiday from school. This afternoon and we sat in the front room window because there was so many people going done town and we are all very thankfull." As he remembers it now, "I'd rather be dead than khaki" is a good characterization of his feelings as a boy. If we think of a boy of four and a half when the war first took away the surroundings he loved and the happiness and contentment of the mother he depended on, forced him (according to his perception at the age of ten) into an inferior school, then plunged his world into a continued state of financial and physical anxiety for the next four years, it is not hard to see that the image of war would carry considerable negative emotional charge in that boy's life.

There were other factors working for nonviolence. One was physical incapacity to meet aggression. Here is an eight-year-old's diary entry: "There is a big boy in our street and his name is Harsly and he live at number 23 and when ever he sees you he starts fighting So Leslie and I thought out a way of dogeing him so we went to school by a different way up a street called hart street so we doged him easily." Kenneth was sick a great deal, not particularly well coordinated (described as "big and awkward" by a friend), and never athletically inclined. He didn't like games and would never let himself be "organized or dragooned" into games. So he found ways other than fighting to solve small-boy squabbles. One, evidently, was dodging. Another was verbal attack. The earliest memories of Leslie, his first friend (from the age of five to eight) include repeated arguments between the two; other school friends report that when Kenneth was indignant about something, he would never keep his mouth shut. And, at the age of eleven, he started publishing a weekly newspaper of one sheet, typed on his father's typewriter, which he peddled up and down the street. The main item of continued interest was the Seymourite Carolling Club and the rival club started by the "back street kids," with appropriate remarks about who was or was not a Seymour-ite. As he tells it today, "I found the pen was mightier than the sword: in my paper I could say nasty things about the boys I didn't like."

As far as I can determine, the discipline he received at home was gentle and reasonable rather than strict and authoritarian. He can remember getting only one spank-ing; his childhood friends describe both his parents as very kind and warm-hearted — perhaps capable of a whacking now and then, but they remember Kenneth as a child who rarely needed one.

There is at least one more factor in the picture. His mother and father were both deeply religious, active in, and committed to the principles and practice of the local Methodist chapel. While probably not more than one member of the congregation was a conscientious objector in that war, the teachings of Jesus were well known and often referred to in the family. Consideration for others was a paramount rule. Now certainly a logical little boy who thought a great deal (which is what Kenneth's friends report that he was) might figure out from pondering the Sermon on the Mount that "Love your enemies" might mean "Don't hurt or kill anybody, even if you don't like them."

Given, then, a boy who, for a combination of emo-tional, physical, and logical reasons, sets his face against war and fighting — where does he turn for support in a society to which that idea is strange or repugnant? He needs to find an ideology to fit what he has discovered in-side himself. So Kenneth did.

His first clue, perhaps, was a conscientious objector vaguely known to him during the war. His mother tells of a man she knew, a member of the Plymouth Brethren, who was a pacifist. The Boulding family used to pass him as he conducted open air meetings on Sunday evenings when they were on their way to the evening service at Brunswick Chapel. Perhaps she dramatizes: "He was quite young, but by the time the war was over he looked an old man. Englishmen could not understand why a man's conscience should interfere with his duty to fight when his country was in danger, or why love of God should come before love of country" (EAB). There was also one member of their church who was sent to prison as a pacifist and whom Kenneth remembers his mother defending spiritedly in conversation when others attacked his position.

From the time that Kenneth went to secondary school at the age of twelve, and probably earlier, if his own memory can be relied on, he really did not get into scuffles or fights with any of the other boys. He claims he can't remember ever even hating anybody. James Sculthorpe, a school friend of the time, recalls with some awe that Kenneth was "always on the pacifist side of things; there was only one time I saw him mixed in rough and tumble." This occurred when Kenneth, who had been made a prefect, was on stairs duty. A boy tried to go up the stairs, against the rules. Kenneth must have blocked his way; the other boy grabbed him; the two rolled down the stairs with their arms locked around each other. There was a room where all the prefects used to whack unruly boys; but James Sculthorpe is sure that Kenneth wouldn't have whacked anyone, or even give lesser punishments: he would simply try to talk boys out of their bad behavior. (Another prefect of the time remarked that Kenneth had the least effect of any of them because he avoided dominating the other boys.) He is certainly remembered as a nonviolent schoolboy by men to whom that seemed deviant behavior.

There were more public evidences of his pacifist leanings during those school years. When he was about fifteen, he published an article in the school paper attacking the military corps and defending the League of Nations Union. Even more impressive was the time (according to

James Sculthorpe) when he stood up to a military speaker in a school meeting and argued with the ex-army man as he expounded on the privileges and joys of being in the Officers Training Corps. (Boulding's own memory pictures the occasion less dramatically: he places it in a class, arguing with a teacher.) At any rate, wherever it occurred, this shy, awkward, stuttering boy of fifteen stood up and said straight out what he thought, to the point where the military advocate lost his temper.

At about that age — fifteen or sixteen — Kenneth made several institutional connections in the pacifist direction. The evidence is unclear as to the order of events, but apparently they fell in close succession. Kenneth was sent to a Methodist summer camp where the leaders so stirred him with a combination of religious fervor and intellectual acuity that he came to a distinct decision to become a Christian. At the same time, sensing the potential depths of religious life, he became more dissatisfied with the Methodists he had known and began looking for something other than Methodism. Either he stumbled onto the book *Conscription and Conscience,* by John Williams Graham, which started him looking for Quakers, or he began talking with a Quaker schoolmate who loaned him the book. The book was an account of the experiences of conscientious objectors in World War I, and Kenneth was deeply impressed by the strength of their convictions, the sufferings they had undergone, and the role of the Quakers in the issue. At any rate, the schoolmate, Robin Wall, recalls that Kenneth sought him out and asked him about Friends and their mode of worship. Robin invited him to come to meeting. From then on Kenneth attended the Liverpool Friends Meeting, finding there a direct religious experience in the silence, a people with genuineness, and a group which shared his convictions about pacifism. But through his high school and Oxford days, he also remained active with the Methodists.

This early decision for pacifism led him on a lifelong journey. In 1933, the Oxford Union passed a motion that "This house would not fight for its King and Country," and Kenneth was "frightfully thrilled" about it but he was studying in Chicago so had no direct part in it; he had left Oxford just a few months earlier. On his return to Britain (from 1934 to 1937) he got into a number of peace-related activities. During his years of teaching in Edinburgh, he did no electioneering but began making speeches at peace meetings. Much of his correspondence with friends in this period deals with questions about the soundest proposals for disarmament, restitution, reforming the League of Nations, and similar problems. He served actively from March of 1936 to October 1937 on the Northern Friends Peace Board, working on the same kinds of questions and publicizing the cause of peace. About 1935, he was asked by the local Edinburgh Friends Meeting to draft a letter for them to the Prime Minister, asking Britain to disclaim the "war guilt" clauses in the Treaty of Versailles, develop provisions for the revision of treaties, and move toward a "true, just, and generous" peace. By 1936, he was working with the Peace Pledge Union led by Richard Sheppard. In connection with this work he met both Richard Gregg (whose new book *The Power of Non-Violence* had impressed him as giving an intellectual foundation to religious pacifism) and Gerald Heard (whose proposals of techniques of meditation did not impress him nearly so highly).

After the momentous permanent move to America in 1937 (to be chronicled in detail in a later chapter), the contrast between the idyllic setting in which he was living and the chaos and conflict spreading over Europe weighed on Boulding more and more. In the teeth of Hitler's unbelievable affronts to human life and dignity, it became harder and harder for him to cling to his commitment to love his enemies. There came a point in May, 1940, when he felt almost overwhelmed by hate:

> I feel hate rising in my throat.
> Nay — on a flood of hate I float,
> My mooring lost, my anchor gone,
> I cannot steer by star or sun,
> . . . .
> Black are the fountains of my soul
> And red the slime on which they roll.
> . . . .
> I hate! I hate! I hate! I hate!
> I hate this thrice-accursed State,
> I'll smash each bloodshot German face
> That travesties the human race!

But suddenly something happened to him, something inward, like an illumination. It happened, he says, at a most inappropriate moment: he was drying himself after a bath. Something broke in on him, an experiencing, almost a vision, of the suffering that Christ had taken on himself for people no better than the Germans, no better than the Bouldings. He could see again the German boys he had known as friends, and sense again his kinship with all men, in suffering, sin, and hope.

> Hatred and sorrow murder me.
> But out of blackness, bright I see
> Our Blessed Lord upon his cross.
> His mouth moves wanly, wry with loss
> Of blood and being, pity-drained.
> Between the thieves alone he reigned:
> (Was this one I, and that one you?)
> "If I forgive, will ye not too?"
>
> My vial of wrath breaks suddenly,
> And fear and hate drain from me dry.
> There is a glory in this place:
> My Lord! I see thee face to face.[2]

All of his best friends who had joined him in pacifism in adolescence rejected the stand when war came. He had been very close at this point to doing the same; but something brought him back to the certainty that "though love is weak and hate is strong,/Yet hate is short, and love is very long."

The lines just quoted are taken from Boulding's one published book of poetry, *There Is a Spirit: The Nayler Sonnets*.[3] Beginning in 1940, and extending over the next several years, his struggle between hate and love was focused in composing these sonnets as something of a devotional exercise (and speaking of devotional exercises, Gerald Heard wrote the foreword for the book). They are based on the dying words of James Nayler, a Quaker who had suffered cruel punishment for certain excesses of enthusiasm in the 1650s. Boulding took each phrase of Nayler's statement about the spirit of love and built a sonnet on it, completing twenty-six exquisite and powerful expressions of the transcendence of the growing forces of life over the tremendous odds held by chaos, hate, and death.

Each of these sonnets has its special quality and direction, and I would like to deal, at a later point, with the imagery and form of the whole group; but for the expression of a position, I have chosen two which I feel are both impressive poetry and representative of the heart of the idea Boulding is working through.

No. 1. *There is a spirit which I feel*

Can I, imprisoned, body-bounded, touch
The starry robe of God, and from my soul,
My tiny Part, reach forth to his great Whole,
And spread my Little to the Infinite Much,
When Truth forever slips from out my clutch,
And what I take indeed, I do but dole
In cupfuls from a rimless ocean-bowl
That holds a million million million such?
    And yet, some Thing that moves among the stars,
    And holds the cosmos in a web of law,

Moves too in me: a hunger, a quick thaw
Of soul that liquefies the ancient bars,
As I, a member of creation, sing
The burning oneness binding everything.

No. 4. *But delights to endure all things*

How to endure, when all around us die
Nations and gracious cities, homes and men,
And the sweet earth is made a filthy den
Beneath whose roof black, belching vultures fly:
How to endure the darkness, when the sky
Is totally eclipsed by evil, when
Foul grinning Chaos spreads its reign again
And all good things in senseless ruin lie.
   Must we be hard as stone? It wears to dust.
As stiff as oaks? But they untimely break.
As pitiless as steel? It turns to rust,
And Time from Pyramids will ruins make.
In violence, decay, starvation, need,
  What can endure? Only the living Seed.

In the summer of 1941, Kenneth and Elise were married, and Kenneth took a job in Princeton with the League of Nations Economic and Financial Section, doing research into problems of European agriculture. Pearl Harbor, of course, came in December of that year, and in the spring of 1942, Kenneth and Elise, out of deep distress for the nations, drafted a statement, "A Call to Disarm." They showed it to their monthly meeting of Friends, who called it a seditious letter and strongly advised them against sending it out. Boulding showed it to his supervisors at the League of Nations, and they told him if he sent it out they would fire him. So he resigned his position and he and Elise distributed the letter. They were in total uncertainty as to what to do next; they expected the sky to fall in; but as Elise says, "You know we never had a ripple back from it — never so much as a *ripple?* We ought to have had a *little* bit of suffering and persecution, for all that!" Instead, Kenneth was offered a new job teaching at Fisk University.

In the spring of 1944, they composed another statement calling on all people everywhere to leave their allegiances to their earthly countries and join the universal Kingdom of Truth, which would not (as earthly countries did) call on them to "hate, kill, maim, burn, and destroy." Boulding evidently had some fear that this also might endanger his job. There is no sign that it did; he could have stayed at Fisk, but he chose the opportunity to go to Iowa State College at Ames. He did have a slight run-in with the college administration at Iowa in 1947 over using campus facilities and campus mail to call a meeting in opposition to the current national proposal for universal military training.

Boulding, though not yet a United States citizen, also had the problem of the draft to face. He had registered and received classification as a conscientious objector; but he felt that the work he was doing, and staying free to follow his "leadings," was more important than the work C.O.'s were being assigned, mainly on lands and forest projects in the Civilian Public Service. If he was called up he would therefore refuse to go into a CPS camp. He knew that would mean going to prison, or possibly being deported as an alien. He did not welcome the prospect, particularly as it would cut off his support of both his wife and mother; but he made the decision that he had to resist this intrusive coercion of government in the lives and consciences of people. He would, however, go so far as to take the physical exam. When he was called up, he stayed awake all night on the bus from Ames to the induction center in Minneapolis. He was lifted up by a strange sense of exaltation, not knowing if he would be coming back or not; and, somehow, all through the experience he felt as if he were in Meeting for Worship. Part of the physical was a psychiatric examination. The young psychiatrist who talked to him asked him about his reasons for refusing to fight, and he tried to explain the Quaker doctrine of the Inward Light, "the right of a person to do what he felt it was right to do." This involves a kind of waiting for guidance and clarity about important actions, and the belief that if one is truly guided by this Light (which is a potential common to all people of all times and places), this guidance cannot lead one to fight and kill. Such leadings, properly tested, take precedence over any temporal authority. The young psychiatrist was interested and somewhat puzzled by this, and took Boulding up to the office of the chief psychiatrist. After some introductions, the man leaned over the table and roared, "Do you ever hear the voice of God?" A Quaker finds this hard to answer in simple yes-and-no terms. Boulding knew the "right" answer was, "Oh, no!" but he sort of hemmed and hawed and said, "Well, not in a physical way," and tried to explain about the leading. As Boulding continues the story, "His face got blacker and blacker as this went on, you see, and finally he said, 'Get out of here!' and he scrawled a big X across the paper and I got a 4-F; so that was how I escaped the Second World War."

Perhaps the next major struggle in the Pacifist's Progress was his fight for citizenship. He had taken out first papers during the early years of his teaching in upper New York State, and waited out the required time. In 1947, after wavering a bit about the possibility of being a Canadian instead, he finally decided to proceed with American citizenship. The problem was the requirement that a naturalized citizen promise to bear arms for his adopted country; of course Boulding could not do that. The law had been interpreted somewhat equivocally, and it was not clear whether one could become a citizen without making this promise. The Bouldings hired two lawyers and brought the issue to a test. They thought they would have to take it to the Supreme Court. However, in the lower court, Boulding gave about an hour's testimony on the ground of the Inward Light, contending that he could not promise to do something he might not be able religiously to carry out. There was a question raised of some legal irregularity for which Boulding turned out not to be responsible — then the judge ruled in his favor and granted his citizenship. It was attained at the legal cost of $533, on December 14, 1948. When he wanted to affirm instead of swear the oath (another traditional Quaker witness), the judge had to instruct the clerk to leave out the phrase, "So help me God"; "and so," in Boulding's words, "I became a citizen without the help of God." [4] A letter written the day of the decision shows both his jubilation and his image of America:

> This country is wonderfully kind to heretics, and I was apparently able to convince the judge that at least I was not a dangerous heretic! It was, I think, one of the happiest and proudest moments of my life, and I hope I can prove worthy of the trust implied.

Less than a year later, Kenneth Boulding again had a new and more prestigious job at the University of Michigan. As Boulding describes it, "There have been times in our lives when we have made decisions of principle . . . but I am sure I'm not going to get much of a reward in heaven, because really — every time I've made a noble sacrifice, I've always gotten a better job!"

But this was not the end of the moral hurdles related to war and peace. In April, 1958, in response to continued nuclear testing, he initiated a "vigil" by the flagpole in the center of the University of Michigan campus, as a symbolic act of penitence and nonconsent. "I conceived the act as (for me) a moral obligation of citizenship in the United States." In 1960, he stood in front of the Pentagon in another protest vigil with a thousand other Quakers. In April, 1961, he turned down an appealing offer of a visiting lectureship in Hawaii because it required a stringent loyalty oath. In March, 1965, he helped to plan and conduct the first Teach-In on the Vietnam War, in which between two and three thousand students spent all night talking, listening, and debating. An observer, Rose Kelman, reports her memory of that occasion:

> The night of the first Teach-In — do you remember? — it was about 12:30, black night and bitter cold, and the bomb scare and everything, everybody out on the quad — and Kenneth was supposed to speak. And I can't remember anything else about it but these words: "I see a sneer across the face of America . . . and I don't like it." I don't know if I heard anything after that.

He found ways from time to time to reach into officialdom: to testify before a Congressional committee, to bring facts and moral issues about Vietnam to a talk with a governor. And, in the fall of 1966, the Boulding protest turned to the political process when Elise Boulding was asked to serve as a write-in peace candidate for Congress. She accepted the challenge and worked diligently (with Kenneth's full endorsement) in a campaign that was educational but not without bitterness and division even among peace advocates.

And the war went on. There seemed to be no way to reach the decision-makers.

The "love affair with America" had certainly gone sour. The violence of Kenneth's reactions to the war policies of the government is related to the intensity of his idealism about his chosen country in the early years. He had never fooled himself about the two faces of the national state, but he had hoped for better from the one state that had deliberately embarked on a path based on respect for life, liberty, and pursuit of happiness. In *The Organizational Revolution* (p. 195) he wrote:

> Toward its enemies . . . the national state is a monster, a liar, a thief, a murderer, a creator of orphans, a destroyer of cities, an immense machine to create pain, death, destruction, madness, famine, and intolerable woe. It is selfish; it cares for none but its own; its only objective is its

own power and its own defense; it is sadistic, ruthless, in-
human, diabolical. . . . The nobler the nation, the more
self-sacrifice it can call forth from its people, the more
likely it is to lay the world desolate and to consign to the
maw of war everything that the patience of enterprise has
built up.

And on a scrap of paper with no date are jotted three bit-
ter, incomplete lines:

> Don't love your country any more
> She's a bitch, she's a bastard, she's a whore
> She burns up babies, she roasts them slow

III

An irresistible, persistent nonviolence, though it may
bring despair, forbids Kenneth Boulding destruction and
revolution. Whatever the roots of his nonviolence, it will
not let him go. So he must part company with those who
despair of protest and feel the society must be destroyed
— the black militants, the Weathermen, the Communists,
the New Left. The costs of violence are always in his
mind; the costs of revolution — one, two, or three generations to get back to the level of living that people had before, the shattering of lives, the building of the habit of
violence: "Revolutions have a way of eating their own
children." [5] The counterproductiveness of uncontrolled
anger has been a repeated theme of his. An anarchist who
must have order, he is a revolutionary who cannot stomach revolution.

Nonviolence is a real and active principle in Boulding's life — it is logical, it is based on a sound conception
of humanity and of the will of a loving God (if such there
is). Nonviolence is perhaps the only way to steady the
shaky bridge between what is and what ought to be. But
the principle would be just as logical and tenable for
many people who have not chosen to adopt it. Why, then,
has he?

As social psychologists Smith, Bruner, and White have pointed out, attitudes or opinions serve several functions. We have referred to the first one: object appraisal as a cognitive activity, the apprehension and valuing of elements of reality. There is also a social function for an opinion as a vehicle by which we orient ourselves to membership groups or reference groups in our environment. The third function is psychological; attitudes serve partly as the means by which internal problems are externalized and acted out in the everyday world. A fear or wish may quietly influence which objects we perceive in our environment; and our positive or negative attitudes toward the objects we perceive are also influenced by fears or wishes often unknown to us.[6] None of these considerations determine the validity, the rightness, or the genuineness of an opinion: these qualities must be judged on other grounds. The more we can understand of the three functions, however, the better we can understand why a person believes and acts as he does.

The objective function of attitudes, as instruments with which to appraise reality, is illustrated by most of Boulding's writing. He chooses the problems that seem most important to him, and analyzes them in terms of values about which he is quite specific and open. But his attitudes have operated also in the area of social relations. His pacifism helped to determine the groups he joined. It partly came out of an intensification and purification of the faith of the Methodists, and it then led him to and was reinforced by his association with Quakers. Throughout his life he has found like-minded people with whom to ally himself, including his colleagues in the Center for Research on Conflict Resolution and, most notably, his wife Elise.

His pacifism may also have a psychological function as a defense against aggressive tendencies. Among the conflicts played out in his TAT stories, there is a group of five built around affiliation vs. autonomy, sometimes turning into love vs. hate, or helpfulness vs. hostility. These tensions spill over into the dimension of socially approved against antisocial impulses, the system vs. freedom, external strictures vs. internal drives, or conservative vs. radical, also shown in five stories. A closer look will show that the battle for freedom against nature or against the social system or against unspecified restrictions is permitted and approved, while aggression against individual persons, though allowed into consciousness if specifically stimulated by the picture (not introduced otherwise), almost never stands long or succeeds. A powerful and deeply felt ethical orientation built on respect for human beings seems to shape the rules of the freedom–restriction struggle and direct the flow of pent-up forces into nonpersonal channels.

Examining the details of the pictures, we find that cues to aggression are almost totally ignored. Though Boulding recognized the gun in one picture, he laughed long and heartily when I pointed out, after the test, that an indistinct object in another picture, usually seen as a gun or knife, he had called a "half-eaten carrot." In a third picture, what is almost universally perceived as a menacing dragon he saw as a harmless elephant. Aggression between persons is not introduced except where it is clearly evident in the picture; in two cases, this is in fantasy form, in each case quickly changed to a more acceptable fantasy (killing the father changes to becoming a surgeon; gloating over the death of an enemy becomes grief over a dear dead departed). The one story of actual aggression, a jealousy killing, is likewise quickly changed to a nurturant version—a husband caring for a beloved wife in her dying hours. In the variations, revision, and choices of stories, no aggressive act or thought is left to stand as the final version. It is simply not allowed through the value screen of his image: perceptions of aggressive motivations cannot pay the cost of entry. The cost of entry, for him, must be very high.

Nonviolence, the opposite of aggression, goes beyond a neutral, uninvolved position. It is a loving, caring relationship for other human beings. Boulding's persistent defense of nonviolence also involves a persistent image of himself as a loving and caring person (in an impersonal, nonsexual sense: Agape rather than Eros). It may be that this focus is related to his mother's Methodist talk of love. Certainly the family climate, though not without strain, discouraged the expression of hostility. Quaker theological language revolves even more pervasively around love for all. But his rejection of violence undoubtedly goes deeper than this.

Psychoanalysts suggest that the roots of human aggression are buried in the necessarily increasing separation of the infant from the mother in the birth process and the early months of life. Perhaps in him this feeling was intensified at four and a half, when his gay and lovely mother became depressed and miserable. If he conceived of her withdrawal as punishment for his own felt or spoken aggression, he could have been so threatened that any kind of aggression would be barred from his perception at later times.

Perhaps, then, there is something in him that he senses below the level of awareness — as there is in most of us — which would really like to rebel, to destroy, to shatter. His delight in shocking people with his rhetoric has already been discussed, but normally this is kept in bounds with humor. Indignation, however, sometimes almost gets away from him and he has trouble keeping it leashed. A 1929 letter to his aunt includes the phrase, "I feel sometimes as if I could smash things in a church." There are a number of incidents in his history when he spoke or wrote so sharply to good friends, or to associates in Quaker groups, that there were hurt feelings, sometimes even a break in relationships, although when these came to his attention he usually tried his best to make amends.

He is stirred at times by wrath of cosmic proportions — usually by cosmic causes. Once he came into his office after failing to convince a foundation of the desperate rightness of supporting research in conflict resolution, fuming at both the outward and the inward situation, and said to his secretary, "I am consumed by the moral disease of anger!" Several times a colleague, or his own later, cooler judgment, has stepped in to tone down a too-violent letter he had written when he felt some essential value subverted. Indeed, there is a passage in *The Image* (p. 51) on the high valuation we place on scarce goods, in which he states, "The violent make a religion of love." And one day in a seminar he reported this conversation: "Bob Angell asked me once, 'How is it you're a Quaker and so violent?' and I answered, 'If I wasn't so violent I wouldn't have to be a Quaker.'"

For such a man, the rebelliousness of youth, the developing dichotomy of our times, the looseness or freeness of life-style in resistance to the dicta of society, the overturning of the university and the world of rational intellect, the letting in of violence as a mode of behavior, could all serve as deeply unsettling movements to one who has held such forces in himself in tenuous balance over a long lifetime.

Despairing of protest, others have turned toward violence. He has moved in the other direction; he has turned toward knowledge. Peace research, rather than the peace movement, now looks to him like a wedge to crack the war system.

Since adolescence he has been active in the peace movement, sharing in its various phases — urging and criticizing and proposing — standing alone when his conscience compelled it, and working with others when their activities held promise. Some time in the last ten years, however, the misfiring of many efforts for social change, of which he had long been aware, and the growing negative reaction to peace protests of various kinds, have brought him to question the efficacy of the peace movement. In 1965, he published an article "Reflections on Protest," [7] which bears a striking resemblance to his 1931 article on socialism in its emphasis on gradualness. As that earlier piece marked his moving away from socialism, the later may have marked his moving away from peace activism. It is not nonviolence he is rejecting, but love acting without knowledge. In the time since then, we observe his debate with Milton Mayer in which he fought for the increase of knowledge rather than the increase of activism; a 1967 memo on the proposal of refusing to pay taxes as a protest against the war in which he carefully weighs tax refusal's effectiveness and makes a considered decision against it; and a number of heated statements about the misguidedness of recent student protests. But he has supported moderate nonviolent acts, such as the demonstration of students at the University of Colorado against the CIA in the fall of 1967.

His role, even in the Teach-In of 1965, was that of moderator, although he disclaims credit as a central figure in mediation. To the radical leaders he was "exasperating," yet with one foot in each camp he was turned to, both by university administrators and by the protest group, to bring the claims of moral outrage and professional responsibility together.

The Vietnam bombings had just begun, and, in protest, thirteen faculty members, their numbers expanded to forty-six within a week, had signed a statement declaring they would call off their classes to spend a day considering the issues of the Vietnam War. They called it a "work moratorium"; it was called by unfriendly critics a "strike." Michigan's Governor Romney demanded disciplinary action against the offending faculty members, and the State Senate passed a resolution censuring them. Boulding was sympathetic to the cause, but questioned the method and refused to sign the faculty statement. He and other leaders in the Center for Research on Conflict Resolution were consulted by Dean Haber in efforts to find an acceptable solution. They were meeting at the same time as, and exchanging messages with, the "strike" group's agonized all-night session out of which came the creative compromise which quickly took hold on other campuses as well: on the day of protest, classes as usual; but all night the classroom buildings would be kept open for the Teach-In sessions. Boulding served essentially as a middleman in this solution, a pivotal communication link.[8]

The compromise brought a campus-wide sigh of relief. Boulding accepted the protest group's invitation to be keynote speaker at the midpoint midnight rally. The administration gave permission with alacrity for use of buildings; dormitory girls were granted all-night permissions; the university dean and president issued immediate commendations of the concerned faculty group; and the number of faculty names on the final announcement of the program leaped to 216.

The dividing lines between Boulding and others who object to the war and repression in our society are twofold. One is the line between violence and nonviolence. This line he is not willing to cross even for changes that appear most desirable. He tried to explain this when challenged by hostile student militants during the Teach-In on Ecology at the University of Michigan in March, 1970 (described briefly in chapter 1). Love, for him, is a way of being — not a Utopian end-product or a method of achieving something — and to deny it temporarily for the sake of something better to come later is to deny all that really *is,* the process, the now, the only place in time where we can live. His respect for people and exultation in life does not have any quality of duty or goal-orientation as he expresses it, but is so foundational, so inward, so welling-up in him that it bursts and bubbles out in every contact. All through the Economics Building in his years at Michigan the staff always knew when he came in by his laughter booming through the old wooden halls as he greeted his colleagues and the office secretaries.

The second dividing line is more subtle and more questioned by peace movement activists. It is a matter of calculating results — of feeding in knowledge of systems — of choosing, his critics would say, in terms of expedience rather than conscience. This is a very difficult line to walk, especially when you have a lively appreciation, as Boulding does, of the absolute claims of conscience. It is also an application of discipline, and he criticizes even peace-researchers on this score. At a May, 1971, meeting of representatives of some fifty peace-research organizations, he declared there was "too much creativity in the peace movement and not enough discipline." He has always applied intellectual criticism — and accepted it, to a point — in relation to peace-action proposals, but this recent emphasis on peace research is a move to almost total concentration of his efforts in the knowledge, rather than the action, field. (Remembering the power of randomness, however, one cannot predict at what moment Boulding's conscience may require of him some new act of witness!)

The total ideological movement we have observed in this life can be described as two interweaving streams: the emotional route to expression and freedom, and the intellectual route to control (fig. 5). Three major cultural-historical factors impinged on him in his youth: war, British parochialism, and depression. Each was filtered through his own experiences of lower-class status and his own personal needs, particularly for autonomy. War and parochialism, both perceived as constricting, led through the emotional stream to pacifism, Christianity (as a way of being something larger than English), Quakerism (a way of being authentic), and America (a way of being human). Economic injustice and depression led him through the intellectual stream of socialism, to the adoption of economics as a profession, then to Keynesian ways of ordering

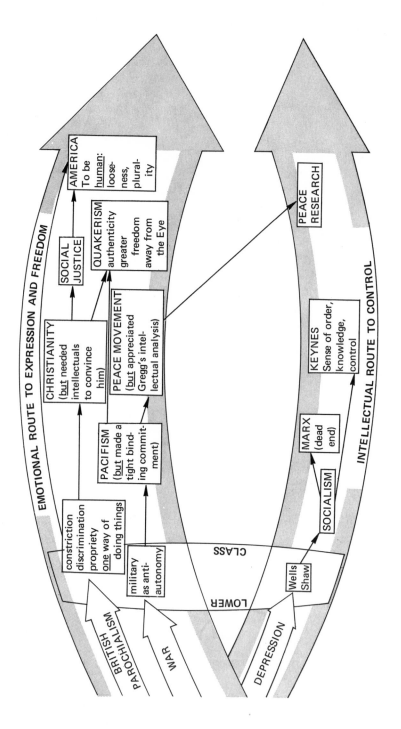

Fig. 5. Freedom and Control

society. But it took intellectuals to bring Kenneth Boulding to a commitment to Christianity, and his pacifism has veered from the emotional into the intellectual stream with peace research. Emotion and intellect, freedom and control, though they run in different channels, have never been far apart in his life.

7

Religion and Ethics: The Letter and the Spirit

The wearing of a halo is a balancing feat of some difficulty.

—KEB, *personal letter, 1936*

I

Religious and ethical ideas, as we have seen from the very first chapter, are interlaced with everything Kenneth Boulding thinks, says, and does. To try to look at them separately is to isolate only one aspect of an integrated whole. But analysis depends on abstraction; words and symbols by their nature chop off pieces of the fabric of experience; and we can only hope, in trying to communicate an immensely complex personality through words, to stitch the pieces together again at the end in some kind of fitting pattern.

The earliest religious symbol that young Kenneth stored in his memory came from a picture his grandmother used to have on her wall. It showed the Broad Way to destruction and the Narrow Way to salvation — a large and complicated depiction of the evils of carousing and pleasure, and the steep mountain track to heaven; over it all stood an enormous Eye, watching and judging. He got the feeling he could never get away from that Eye.

His grandmother, a kind and gentle soul, reinforced the feeling from time to time, as in her letter for his ninth birthday: "What a big boy you must be geting and I hope you are growing good as well but we cant be good onles we ask Jesus to make us and help us to be good can we." She praised him in another early letter for having read the Bible all the way through.

The Methodist chapel was the central core of the life of this little family. They went to church twice on Sundays and to Sunday school in between, at three in the afternoon. Kenneth's father was for years Sunday school superintendent, presiding in the same building where he had gone to day school as a boy. He was also a "lay preacher." The family often had the minister, a weighty church member, or an out-of-town visitor, over for dinner. Their social life centered around bazaars, harvest festivals, church concerts, plays and dialogues. Kenneth grew to like the hymns, which were his father's special joy, though he was bored by the long church services. But he endured them with some patience, sitting on a hassock on the floor, because the church was centrally heated and was the only warm place in the winter time. A particular red-baize-covered pew, about half way back in the central floor of the large amphitheater, was the one assigned to the Boulding family. The church was still collecting pew rents, though evidently not rigorously, for the revenues from this source are recorded as steadily declining.

Both his mother and his father had a simple, unquestioning faith in God all through their lives. This included the commandment to be kind and loving, and the belief that all things work together for good for them that love the Lord. His mother, cheering him up after the Labour defeat in 1931, wrote, "Thank God the future of the world is in His hands and not in mans." Many of the poems which she wrote all through her life center on the theme of discipleship to Jesus or the power of God's goodness in the face of discouragement or sad events.

137

We have already outlined the path that led Kenneth to the Society of Friends. Once introduced to it, he became familiar with the big, sparsely attended meeting-house, which was located only about five minutes' walk from where he lived, in an obscure alley behind the art gallery and the museums. There he reveled in the silence, the sense of freedom, the not being preached at or given "warmed-over fish" but fresh and living messages. This activity, however, did not separate him from the life of his parents' church. His attendance at the Methodist camp at Swanwick, in Derbyshire, continued for several summers, and his Swanwick-made decision to become a Christian was no doubt reflected in the note in his mother's diary for December 19, 1926: "A recognition service for new members was held at our church tonight, and Kenneth was among the number who joined the church." He would probably have been on the rolls anyway as a child of a church family, and he apparently never resigned his membership.

The records of Brunswick Methodist Chapel are almost untraceable. The stately Greek-columned and porticoed building in mid-city Liverpool (built beyond the edge of town in 1811) was bombed out in World War II. In the years since, the property has been sold and the congregation dispersed. Methodists, in any case, seem to be fairly casual about official membership, and if there *are* old membership rolls they are lodged in some obscure basement, or so I was told by the current District Superintendent in Liverpool.

Kenneth's membership as a Friend, on the other hand, is a little clearer. Although he recalls joining in 1928, the records of the Liverpool Monthly Meeting show that he was admitted there "as a convinced Friend" on November 25, 1931. This would have been in the middle of his last year at Oxford. In December of 1934, he transferred his membership to the Edinburgh Meeting, and later to other meetings wherever he was living. Dual membership in Friends and some other church is fairly unusual, and I suppose it made little difference after his interest in the Methodists lapsed later on, but it is strange that Liverpool Meeting allowed it, as I have been told they refused it to others in the same position.

However, membership is only the husk of religious life. Throughout his secondary school and college years, Kenneth was spending much energy working out what he felt and believed. This was an even more central part of his search for identity than his political and social explorations, and here, too, he chose his models. The most influential was probably T. S. Gregory, a mystical, humanist Methodist minister with a sense of the poetry of the Gospel, who was one of the leaders at Swanwick each time that Kenneth went. Gregory had a way of interpreting and expressing the living presence of divinity, which still flows, fresh and compelling, through the pages of a recent book of his. We could apply to him his own description of a man who has encountered the Spirit: "His life becomes magnetic and infectious with Christ." [1] The infection took. As a matter of fact, though we cannot necessarily read the opinion back forty years, there is a passage in Gregory's book (discussing the heritage from Charles Wesley) which could strikingly describe Boulding's approach to religion: "So the way lies before us to realize Love's almightiness by making trial of it. Our experience becomes as it were a research in the service of a heavenly science . . ." (*According to Your Faith*, p. 64)

Before meeting T. S. Gregory, Kenneth had already had experiences of true worship, both in the Quaker silence and occasionally in Brunswick Chapel through the words and music of one of the great devotional hymns of Bunyan, Watts, or Wesley. At such rare times he felt "lifted to the very throne of heaven," in touch with an entity much greater than himself. It is then that "the mind receives knowledge without the mediation of the senses, direct from the source," as he put it in a school essay. Now he was trying to fit such experiences into the framework of institution, sacred history, theology, and the broad world of general knowledge. The camp at Swanwick was not at all an evangelistic sawdust trail setting, but one of exposure to higher criticism, and examination of the flaws of Methodism, through lectures and reading and deep searching discussions long into the night. It was ideally suited for a boy of Kenneth's inclinations, leaning toward mysticism but critically intellectual; and it is easy to see how he would be drawn to such a man as the Reverend T. S. Gregory, intense and authentic, who exemplified a religion intellectually respectable yet alive with inner fire. It is interesting that a few years after Kenneth became a Quaker, T. S. Gregory became a Catholic — but, he claims, "without ceasing to be a Methodist."

Kenneth's allegiance was given to Christ and to the God the love of whom is love for all mankind, in a commitment as persistent and unshakable as his commitment to nonviolence — and certainly related to it. That it is still evident and operating forty years later is illustrated by Herbert Kelman's characterization of Boulding as a "real religious believer, yet so intellectually sophisticated" as to be a problem to those who could not reconcile intellect and religion. Pushed to the wall by boos and hecklers in the Ann Arbor talk for the Teach-In on Ecology in March, 1970, Boulding responded, "I'm sorry; I will confess I am a Christian — that's not a hopelessly bad thing to be." He added, "I am also a social scientist — and that raises difficulties."

During his Oxford years Kenneth moved from an appreciation of individual religious experience to an appreciation of the great body of truth summed up in all Christian experience. He and his Wesleyan friends hammered out together ways of living in terms of the truth they saw, exulted over conversions among the "tough set," even if accomplished by Buchmanites, and several summers they conducted "campaigns," in which they camped in a village, with the cooperation of local Methodists, and preached in the squares and the churches. He related recently:

> I remember one scandalous occasion on which I preached in a Methodist church and forgot to take up a collection, a cardinal sin in the Methodist Church; but fortunately the organist was a man of great presence of mind, and he turned the introduction to the last hymn into a voluntary, and quickly took up the collection. But these campaigns were quite important; the fact of trying to promote something forces one to examine what it is you are trying to promote.

He felt closer to the Wesleyans than to the Quaker students at Oxford, for class reasons, since most of the Quakers had gone to boarding schools and were of the elite while most of the Methodists were, like him, scholarship students. But he did attend Friends meeting, and, by 1932, joined in a Quaker group campaign with a purpose similar, apparently, to that of the Wesleyans: to present a living religion in a form to inspire and renew people.

From the time that Kenneth went to Chicago for graduate work in 1932, his break with the Methodists, except in sympathy, was fairly complete. He became a part of a lively group of Young Friends at 57th Street Meeting in Chicago, and began arguing with them immediately. (His first impression was that "American people are reforming rather than religious.") In the spring of 1933, he made a pilgrimage to Philadelphia as a Moslem does to Mecca, and heard Rufus Jones (a Quaker considered by many the greatest twentieth-century American mystic) speak. A letter from the summer of that year indicates that Kenneth was revolting against laboratories and the scientific method in favor of "the mystical and transcendental way of approaching things." He felt, at that point, that science couldn't deal with purpose and value, the important stuff of life, because "no experiment can verify a motive." His final evaluation of religion in America, after two years, made in a letter to his Commonwealth Fund advisers, was that it had little or nothing to offer.

> In Oxford Christianity is a living spirit; in Chicago it is a rattling skeleton. But . . . divinity may be starved but humanity flourishes. Among my friends in America I found more kindness, simplicity, and honesty, less pride, malice, or jealousy than I have ever found anywhere. . . . It is not that I am a particularly godly person myself . . . nor am I very conscientious about the practice of piety, but I do lay claim to a personal interest in and feeling for questions of religion, which to my mind is unquestionably the greatest adventure of the human spirit.

Back in Britain and teaching in Edinburgh from 1934–37, Boulding was solidly entrenched in the Quaker fold. "There is a very pleasant little Meeting here; two meetings, in fact, one a relic of the past and the other a hope for the future. I naturally belong to the Hope for the Future." He took a major role in the meeting from the time he came, starting a Young Friends group where there had been none, going to conferences and meetings of Young Friends and the Northern Friends Peace Board, and working actively in related groups such as the Peace Pledge Union and "Cosmops," a club of international students in Edinburgh.

One of the main Quaker adventures during his years in Edinburgh was a work camp which Boulding helped Ann Cumming organize. Ann had learned about work camps from John Hoyland, who pioneered the concept in England. She had given up teaching to live in poverty in London, and now had come to Edinburgh. Industrial Scotland was in a slump, as was most of the western world; in Holytown, the mining area near Glasgow, 90 percent were unemployed. What was worse, their houses were slowly sinking in a swamp, and it was Ann's idea that a group of young people could ease the miners' physical, if not their financial, situation, by digging trenches to drain the standing water around their homes, and perhaps extend a little sense that there was a small ray of hope and goodness left in the world. Boulding believed in extending hope, but was not so keen on digging as Ann was, so he modified the proposal to "Work and Talk: A Practical Conference on Unemployment." In a 1936 letter, he describes Ann:

> She is an astounding woman, aged 40, lives on 10 shillings a week and goes out charing . . . (scrubbing floors in offices and places) . . . a graduate of Edinburgh, speaks the most delightful English I have ever heard, wears an old cotton frock and looks like a duchess in it, and is one of the leading members of a kind of vague Franciscan movement. However, she believes in Salvation by Digging, whereas I tend to believe in Salvation by Talking: in this party we tried to combine the two methods . . . (Ann made us live on a shilling a day, which she estimates is about what the unemployed can afford to spend on food. This meant our staple diet was bread, margarine of doubtful quality, cheap tea and condensed milk.)

Young Friends of Glasgow and Edinburgh and young people from the Student Christian Union joined in the project at Carfin Hall, Holytown, in January, 1936. They spent the mornings digging trenches and building paths out of mine wastes — clinker and red ash — across the swampy tract to a tenement which housed twenty-five families. In the evenings they met with the unemployed workers for talks and discussions, with speakers (including Kenneth) presenting opposing points of view, Communist vs. socialist outlooks, and various schemes for improvement. Someone who was there has remembered for more than thirty years a young student's comment that he had "never known anyone who could keep his dignity and yet be so full of fun" as Kenneth Boulding.

As a climax to Boulding's activities with Edinburgh Friends, he was one of two young people sent as representatives from the General Meeting of Scotland (composed of four monthly meetings, with a membership of around three hundred people) to the Friends World Conference in Philadelphia in 1937. This proved to be one of the great turning points of his life, because, while he was in America, he was offered a job at Colgate University, and decided not to go back. Even at that time when he made the decision, he thought of it as emigrating, not sojourning, though he tried it for a year before he sent for his mother and moved her, also, to Hamilton, New York. (She never became an American citizen but did join the Society of Friends in 1942.)

He and his mother held meeting in their living room on Sunday afternoons, going from time to time to Utica or Syracuse for larger meetings of Friends. It was at such a meeting that Kenneth met Elise in 1941. By this time he was regarded as a very gifted minister and a very gifted religious poet, perhaps even something of a prophet. Ministry in most Friends meetings is the responsibility of all worshipers, whether by silence or by the spoken word, so that there is no official status usually implied in the word "minister," but only the informal recognition that some have a quality of religious life and a gift for communicating the Spirit which is not given to all. However, some meetings have a practice of "recording" ministers, which does make this recognition official. Syracuse Monthly Meeting, to which Boulding belonged, was one such meeting; and with the thought that it might be helpful in draft counseling, he was subsequently recorded as a minister by this meeting in October, 1943. The letter carrying this message bears the marks of much folding, wear, and patching, and was evidently carried about in his pocket for years.

Elise shared in Kenneth's spiritual sensitivity, and together they centered their lives in Friends meetings wherever they were, holding meeting in their home when there was no meetinghouse, actively moving and shaping the lives of these small Friends gatherings, and finding, in

144

their travels, a worldwide community of diverse but like-minded souls, both gaining and giving strength and joy and power. Kenneth in the early 1940s put more of his time in Friends activities, sought out and met with others, cherished and nourished the spirit of the Society, wrote and published more religious poetry, than he has recently. In certain circles it could be said, as one Quaker reviewer did in 1946 in a British Friends journal, "He is as well known as a poet as he is as an economist." Now others seek him out. He is invited to speak by Friends all over the world — but also by many secular organizations — and often flies to a conference and back again. Even in his home meeting he is present rather intermittently as his lecture schedule has occupied more of his life. But when he is there, he is fully there, and the hour of silent worship is still an intense hour of inner wrestling and outer sharing with all those present, seen and unseen.

"Traveling in the ministry" — an old Quaker term for visiting meetings and isolated Friends out of a concern to know them and to bring to them whatever message came out of one's own search for Truth — was something Kenneth did a great deal of before he was married. He and Elise did it together afterwards. They were particularly active in organizing Young Friends conferences on a regional basis to cut across doctrinal differences among Friends, in a drive for Quaker unity. They visited fundamentalist Friends and conservative Friends and pastoral Friends, enjoyed them all, and came to appreciate the whole as a spectrum, a pluralism, a diversity rather than a uniformity. ("It really runs the gamut, from the Nazarenes to the Buddhists.") Their "fit" was best in the small university meetings in Nashville, in Ames, in Ann Arbor "before it got big and prosperous," and now in Boulder; but they place a much larger importance in belonging to a world society which provides a spiritual community wherever one goes. "I don't think we would *go* anywhere where there wasn't a Meeting," Boulding remarked a couple of years ago; "or if there wasn't a Meeting we'd *start* one, because it is *so* important to have a central spiritual community."

In the first year of their married life, in fact, they did start one, not wholly without problems. Boulding's lively and biased account (from a talk in 1967) is as follows:

> We were active in starting the Princeton Meeting; as a matter of fact the Princeton Meeting thought it couldn't start because it couldn't get the Meetinghouse — there was a beautiful Meetinghouse at Stony Brook and this belonged to the Conservatives . . . and they didn't approve of this ragtag and bobtail in Princeton so they wouldn't let them use it. And Princeton Friends thought they couldn't meet, so we said, "We don't *have* to have a meetinghouse, we can just *meet*," which was a very strange revelation for Princeton Friends. However, we were eldered very severely for having a Negro couple to dinner; it was not done in Princeton at this time, and as the Meeting took a very dim view of this, we took a very dim view of the Meeting. . . .

A more congenial venture was the Friends Student Colony which the Bouldings set up in a big old house in Ames in 1945. From five to eleven American and international students lived with them there, sharing in the work, and keeping the house going even in the year the Bouldings were away at McGill. Silent worship every morning, Bible reading after dinner, and a devotional reading group once a week shared by other townspeople, were the framework of what they hoped could be "an island of healthy social tissue in the diseased body of the world," as they put it in their Christmas letter of 1945.

11

Boulding's Christianity, like his politics, is probably more conservative than many who know him would guess. The strain of orthodoxy which he brought with him from early experiences in England has remained to set him off from liberal American social-gospel or humanist emphasis. The sense of the *happening,* of something extraordinary that occurred in the Resurrection, is very much present to him.

> If you look at the Christian phylum as a great sort of expanding tree, through history, in a sense its life blood is the sort of hope that came into the world with the early church and the resurrection. . . . The great thing that Christianity has to offer is this practically indestructible hope — and, in addition to this, of course faith and love.

This very personal, almost inescapable hope is presented in a sonnet he wrote for Christmas, 1948 (quoted in part):

> For all that Reason in these troubled days
> Preaches so eloquently of despair,
> And dark prophetic faces everywhere
> Blanch at the future dread on which they gaze,
> I am disturbed by a perpetual blaze
> Of most unreasoning hope, quite unaware
> Of its immodest presence in the bare
> Black ruined fortress of our yesterdays.

Personally, the idea of immortality is not crucial to him, although he finds the orthodox tenet of resurrection of the body ("highly improbable but not demonstrably impossible") more tenable than that of disembodied spirits wandering about. He has never subscribed to a mind-body dualism, inheriting perhaps from Charles Wesley the vision of the corruptible putting on incorruption, and from George Fox and the great Christian "phylum" the faith in the Word made flesh. To this he has built his own parallel in the concept of knowledge or information embodied in physical form in the inventions, productions, and capital of a society. The sense of this fusion of flesh and spirit is well expressed in the first two lines of "Nayler Sonnet 13":

Creative Tension

My Lord, Thou art in every breath I take,
And every bite and sup taste firm of Thee.

The Christian hope for him is applied not to death
but rather to life, to the learning process, to man's continual enlargement toward goodness. Evil is only a defect in
the learning process: it is what is still unlearned, and is
yet a problem to alert us so we will learn. The greatest
sin, it seems to him, is pride; this interferes with our recognizing our failures and learning from them. The importance of humility for the learning process — the repeated
references to the meek (that is, the adaptable) inheriting
the earth simply through the operation of evolutionary
forces — are continuing emphases congruent with this
view of sin, but placing it in the secular causal relationship.

It is interesting to note that the three Biblical characters who most appeal to him are Jacob (a strong young
man, something of a rascal, but close to the Lord, and, in
fact, at one time wrestling with Him); David (particularly
in his aspects of fighting Goliath and the incident with
Nathan); and Job, who persisted in spite of all odds: "Yea
though he slay me will I maintain mine own way before
Him" — "wrestling," in Boulding's words, "with the randomness of the universe." In modern psychological terms,
the needs for achievement, aggression, and autonomy seem
to be blended in the characters of these three men. The
emphasis that comes through most powerfully is the sense
of their being very human but struggling against forces
that are superhuman, and prevailing in the end. This I
would judge to be more illustrative of the bent of Boulding's personality than of his religious attitudes per se.

In addition to the many articles in Friends periodi-
cals, the *Christian Century,* and other religious publications, an occasional poem which Boulding has published
in the same type of magazine, and the book of sonnets already discussed, there are three pamphlets in his religious

bibliography, all published by Friends. These are *The Practice of the Love of God, The Evolutionary Potential of Quakerism,* and *The Prospering of Truth.* All were given as invited lectures, the first in Philadelphia in 1942, the second in Melbourne, Australia, in 1964, and the third at London Yearly Meeting in the summer of 1970.

The first of these is a plea to redeem all lesser loves by the greater, the love of God himself. Its lyrical passages, intense imagery, and visual transposition of the experience of the Gospel bear a great deal of resemblance to T. S. Gregory's message and style. There is a very brief mention of science as one route to religious experience ("The pure love of truth is but a colder version of the love of God") but this piece is miles away from *Economic Analysis,* of the same period, and one would guess it written by a different man. Boulding *was* a divided man; the two main sides of him, the academic and the religious, each a powerfully compelling portion of his life, were not allowed to mix. He remembers from this period one occasion when he went to a faculty meeting at Colgate and "got into the Quaker mood — it completely upset the meeting. It was disastrous!" In his student days, it had been the same: a 1939 letter to an old Oxford friend confesses, "the shallow brilliance of the Oxford environment forced me to hide my deeper life in the Quaker and Methodist underworld . . ."

The 1964 pamphlet, *The Evolutionary Potential of Quakerism,* is altogether different. A certain combination of the religious and the intellectual occurs as Boulding, the social scientist, expounds his theory of history and applies it systematically to the issue at hand, the role of the Society of Friends in times past and to come. It is the familiar theme of evolution and mutation, with its main message that the Society of Friends has a great *intellectual* task ahead of it — to discover how love is learned — for the integrative relationship is the only one on which post-civilized society can be built. This would mean the ap-

149

plication of science to the religious experience ("the rules
of 'reality testing' which apply to ordinary experience
apply likewise to the religious experience of mankind," he
writes on page 23 of this pamphlet), and the role of religion is only that of a cautionary element to keep the scientist from pride, to keep the values of love and community
enough in the picture so that knowledge will not lead to
disaster. Religion is definitely subordinated; there is little
more communication of the spiritual in this second pamphlet than there was of the scientific in the first. Even the
Quaker mystical experience is described as follows (p. 15):
"The object of the Quaker meditation is not so much to
achieve union with the divine as to receive instruction
from the divine, and very practical instruction at that."

In the third of these pamphlets this combination and
conflict is brought to conscious expression. The bulk of
the work is devoted to a discussion of various aspects of
truth, or how we can know; the Image in the form of faith
or ideology enters in, and a strong emphasis is made on
the scientific method as a way of gaining knowledge of
complicated systems. But, in the last few pages, Boulding
expresses a sense of disquiet and doubt, both of himself
and of the Christian and Quaker institutions to which he
has given so much of his life. Both Christianity and Quakerism have failed to preserve the spark of revelation (however it may be explained) which clearly started their mu-
tant strains: and so, he feels, has he. Though he commits
himself to mechanism "as far as it will go," and to the scientific method, he clings still to the personal experience
of the Lord's power. And yet, recalling his successes in the
areas of wealth, family, and public recognition, he expresses the uneasy feeling (p. 45), "I may very well be further off from heaven than when I was a boy."

III

In most of his writings in the period from 1950 to 1970,
Boulding has insisted that the division of labor between

science and religion cannot be maintained — that each must penetrate the other for a wholesome interaction. He moved away from the inappropriate introduction of values — as for instance, the tone of moral exhortation in *Economics of Peace* — and from his earlier conviction that science was sterile because it had nothing to say to questions of value and motivation. He seems to have grown to a feeling of balance between the two, and achieved an integration and a blending, presenting ethical values in terms relevant to a scientist, and a scientific approach to religious questions, at least in the field of policy and goals. Yet he has always known that there are two poles in tension here, and the balance is precarious. A sentence in one of W. B. Yeats's critical essays gives vision into such a dilemma: "He who half lives in eternity endures a rending of the structures of the mind, a crucifixion of the intellectual body." [2] Boulding gives clues to this rending in himself in many ways. The intellectual–religious contrast pops through, for instance, in the words he uses to describe the Holy Spirit: "a Spirit neither learned, nor ingenious, nor respectable." [3] In one of his poems (1949) he describes the intellectual as having a roof of zinc, sheltering his spirit from the rain of Grace. And how could the tension be clearer than in this passage? —

> Communication between the intellectual and the religious subcultures is perilous in the extreme. It depends almost entirely on the doubtful abilities of a few individuals who participate in both. Society owes an enormous debt to those marginal men who live uneasily in two different universes of discourse. Society is apt to repay this debt by making them thoroughly uncomfortable and still more marginal. [4]

Boulding once used the imagery of the stalagmite and the stalactite to describe these two strains in himself, the religious and the scientific, the spiritual and the intellectual: one builds from the top down, the other from the bottom up, and they don't really meet; you have to follow both. "I do indeed lead parallel lives; my life is not really a whole." (He adds that he is quite cheerful about this.) On the other hand, after speaking of the compartmentalization of his behavior and modes of responding to people in the two communities, he goes on to say that the basic quality of the intellectual and the spiritual experience are the same. As further evidence along this line, his wife Elise is emphatic in her statement that he is *not* a divided man — that he carries the same warm, exuberant, loving self into every kind of situation. I would suggest that he perceives more keenly and feels more sharply than others the fragmenting that most of us experience without noticing, because he experiences so intensely the various segments of life, and strives so deeply for life's wholeness.

The perception of him as a man divided between the scientist and the humanist is not confined to Boulding himself. His close friend of Colgate days, Russell Freeman, remarked in a letter of 1942 (pondering whether Boulding should be classed as a genuine or a spurious prophet), "Of course there are other difficulties with you. When the skills and insights of an economist march parallel or not so parallel, I might suggest, with the demands of an intensely religious nature deep cle[a]vages tend to open." Some of his readers, too, catch the division. A personal letter related to *The Image* concludes, "Let me again say 'thank you' — particularly for violating the stern image of science which you presented but with which you did not conform." And a reviewer of *The Meaning of the Twentieth Century,* referring to another review which described Boulding as "materialistic, super-scientific, abstractly sociological, in short antihumanist" responds: "One can indeed discern such tendencies. Boulding at his best, however, is both humanist and humanitarian. Concerned with mankind as a whole, he stands, with a few saints, at some great universal center far from ethnocentrism." [5]

We have mentioned his difficulty in reconciling the

sophisticated mechanism of general systems with his strong feeling about revelation breaking into history, truly another order of reality: the system break, the random event, the mutation, the ultimate unpredictability of human affairs. He has described the experience of the eternal as one of the problems of the religious economist: "It may be . . . that the clamorous realities of the Communion of Saints actually unfit a man for performing the delicate and beautiful abstractions of economic theory." [6] Prudence, testing, calculation, and certainty stand on the one hand; on the other, the explosive, the unexpected, and the gloriously hopeful.

He has repeatedly characterized this spiritual–intellectual conflict in the terms "heroic ethic" and "economic ethic" (earlier he called it "prudential"). He gives a description of this paradox in *The Skills of the Economist*, p. 160:

> Below the stars, above the mud
> Man seeks to find his Highest Good —
> He's partly trader, partly hero:
> Between infinity and zero,
> He occupies a middle place,
> One foot in Sin and one in Grace —

The ethic of the New Testament is in inevitable tension with the economic ethic, as different as the mountains from the plains:

> There is an anti-economic strain in the teaching of almost all the prophets and poets. The careful, calculating, economizing way of life is neither prophetic nor poetic. It counts the cost; it asks for reward; it has no fine frenzies; it is humdrum, commonplace, even a little sordid . . . the gospel of "be righteous and grow rich," for all its truth and practicality, looks cheap and pharisaical beside the poetic vision of "sell all thou hast and give to the poor. . . ." [7]

In other passages, as in the one just given, Boulding displays a bias toward the heroic ethic, although sometimes he emphasizes its dangers of excess. For instance, in *The Skills of the Economist,* he describes the economic man as determined by the iron laws of society, but the poet, the artist, and the prophet as the determiners, those who break out of law and "unleash the forces of growth" (p. 185). Back in 1934, he was working over this idea and his place in it, and wrote to a friend, "It is not in me to be a fanatic: sometimes I wish it were, for the fanatics are the people who do things and really move the world; but I can't do it, and have accepted the fact."

But most often when he draws this contrast, he points out that each type of ethic needs the other. Though he has made many references over the years to the economic vs. the heroic, one of the most complete descriptions is in the 1958 book, *Principles of Economic Policy* (p. 433):

> Without the heroic, man is a dull dog, a creature of the counting house, a cold, calculating, earthbound creature. . . . Without the prudential, man is an impossible dreamer, flying to the sun and falling into the sea, ending in a nightmare of illusion and unreality. Somewhere between the dullness of the prudential and the madness of the heroic there must be an ideal human posture toward the splendid and dreadful universe in which man finds himself. Because of the basic incompatibility of these two ideals, however, *it may be impossible for a single individual to attain this ideal:* we cannot be prudentially heroic or heroically prudent. But perhaps in the larger framework of society these incompatibles may be resolved: the heroes break through the crust of the established order to set great dynamic processes in motion — these are *the prophets, the saints, the poets,* the conquerors, the revolutionaries. Then the prudent come along behind them and fit the pieces together into a new establishment; these are the priests and the popes, *the professors,* the politicians, and the business men.

I have quoted this at some length, and added the emphasis, to point out that while Boulding is suggesting that one individual probably cannot be both prudential and heroic, he is at the same time including himself in both categories — at one point as a poet or prophet, at another as a professor. Later, in 1969, he made this inner tension in one person specific: "Man requires both heroic and economic elements in his institutions, in his learning processes, and in his decision-making, and the problem of maintaining them in proper balance and tension is one of the major problems of maturation, both of the individual person and of societies." [8]

IV

To these conscious recognitions of tension let us add evidence from other directions. It is clear that Boulding values truth and beauty over the material or the merely useful. (He once wrote a letter deploring the paving of the roads around his house in Ann Arbor, preferring the ruts, dust, and holes that went with a sense of country to a smooth macadamized world.) In the TAT there was very little emphasis on the vocational area (in almost no stories are the characters absorbed in work or vocation), and a low regard for achievement insofar as that is understood as material success. His interest in economics is rather an interest in ordering experience, in finding pattern and truth as a means of control over a chaotic environment, than in the satisfaction of bodily, practical needs. Yet the blows struck for truth seem to land on the anvil of prudence, if every thoughtful analysis brings in royalties, every fight for conscience results in a better job, and he increasingly finds himself uncomfortably comfortable.

Relevant to this heroic-economic or mystical-rational struggle are several overall impressions to be gained from the TAT. One of these is the generally optimistic tone; nothing is really allowed to end very badly. This is matched in everything he publishes: a "cautious optimism" is almost a trademark. This kind of optimism is representative, I would guess, of this integrated tension: Boulding's basic Christian faith, tempered by his critical grasp of reality. As a part of the "happy-ending" pattern is a repeated sequence of daydream followed by anxiety followed by achievement of the dream in a modified form. Achievement may come through inner endowment or through effort, but the dream is always the first move. This sequence may be interpreted as the largeness of vision, then the recognition of evil or limitation, and, finally, a declaration of faith in good overcoming it, through determination and free will. But the limitation of circumstance, society, or reality does modify the vision. That the dreaming seems more essential than effort to the achievement points to a bias for inspiration or revelation — or maybe "Salvation by Talking" rather than "Salvation by Digging!"

A second pattern, previously mentioned, is what I call the punctured balloon. Romantic or extreme fantasy or behavior is followed by an anticlimax, either a replacement by normal behavior or a skeptically humorous remark. This is one form of a continual backing off from strong emotion in all his TAT stories — with the implication that strong emotion of any kind (love, hate, or despair) is destructive.

A third pattern is an overpowering sense of uncertainty; he seems always to be trying to find his way with inadequate clues, to keep looking for meaning, yet to hold himself back from total involvement, from letting himself go in making up a story. The fear of strong emotion, and the uncertainty and uninvolvement, I feel, all illustrate in another way the same conflict. They show an unwillingness to allow the full play of emotions — a looking for strings to tie up the package so it won't burst — a binding and ordering and control of a potentially dangerous, ambiguous, or explosive situation. Perhaps there is an echo of the Broad Way and the Narrow Way in his grandmother's picture. It is the fear of being carried off, the dike that must be raised against the flood, the effort required not to let the poet run away with the scientist.

Liquidity, fluidity, unboundedness may be seen again in the mystical experiences he records which are connected with water — the vision that struck him in the bath during the war, the title for one of his books that came to him in the shower. This could be read as a symbolic expression of joining the oceanic Infinite, with its elements of both fear and joy. Freud has said that water is a symbolic representation of birth, or a close relationship between mother and child. The mother-image here blends into the God-image. (Boulding's earliest memory is of slipping back into the water when his mother had dried him after a bath, and being unafraid, though his mother was anxious.) The water images in his writings are almost always positive: the mountain stream as goodness, the unbounded ocean as God. And we remember the prominence of the "watershed."

In a 1953 sonnet he catches the impinging fluidity of bodies and the need for solid incarnation:

> If I am not careful my whole world
> Will turn to Prayer, and be dissolved in Him
> From whom all comes: bodies, the lithe trim
> Figures of youth, the greening grass, leaves furled
> In winter branches, and the raindrops pearled
> In circles of light. O it is a slim
> Force that holds all things within a rim
> Of solid shape — and what if they unfurled!
>
> I cannot bear everything being everything,
> So stay incarnate, God, veil, hide, cage, prison
> Thy too unmediate self: In Christ be risen,
> But still in flesh! Thyself thou darest not bring
> Naked to thy creation, so beget
> Thyself, that we may love thee, and live yet.

On the one hand, Boulding senses that his whole being may dissolve; he needs to hang on, to stay within his skin and his individuality, or he will be lost in the flow. This body-boundedness, melted by divinity but caught again in a larger cosmic web, is the theme of the first Nayler sonnet, already quoted in chapter 6. It is expressed, too, in Sonnet 32 of *Sonnets for Elise:* "I thank God for thy body, and for mine, / That we are walled about with flesh and skin" — for if they were spirits only they would be lost in each other. On the other hand, Boulding recognizes the attraction of *being* lost in something greater than self; there is the need for freedom, looseness, and change. The very words, "the terrors and delights of dynamics" (into which the prophet shakes the static society) show his ambivalence about the shifting liquidity of things, his attraction to and his fear of being caught up in the flow.

We can read in many places in his writings the uneasy or unlikely balance of the forces of freedom and control — for instance, his insistence on the need for regulation to preserve liberty, or the need for indignation but the necessity for controlling it. In an unpublished paper of 1969 is the sentence, "The emotional steam which anger arouses may lead to power, but only if the steam is fed through a rational engine." The form of his poetry is another illustration of this tension; the sonnet is constricting and difficult, yet he has chosen it oftener than any other form to express his deepest feelings; for less important messages, he uses freer forms. He makes this explicit in the introduction to *The Nayler Sonnets* (p. *ix*):

> It may be wondered why in this age of free (and occasionally easy) verse anyone should bother to compress his thought into the archaic straight-jacket of the conventional sonnet. Nevertheless, as metal must be run into a tight mold before it can become a bell, so the intellectual and aesthetic effort required to compress an explosive idea into the formal limits of a sonnet may cause the truth within the words to ring all the more clearly.

However, in *The Organizational Revolution* he discusses at length how organizations, by their very form and rigidity, eventually kill the life that set them up.

Two or three unpublished poems set into startling clarity his own perception of this tension. The first, over which he labored long, was written around his nineteenth birthday, at the same time as he was struggling with the decision whether to continue in the physical sciences or slip over into the literary–philosophical world for the rest of his years at Oxford — and the rest of his life. It was called "The Sands of Egypt" and was submitted for the Newdigate Prize contest in the spring of 1929 — but did not win the prize. Its theme was a vision of vast empty sands, disturbed by the invasion of Life and Man: but the sands themselves were born of warring elements in passionate union, the whirling winds ("wild, all conquering energy of motion") and solid rock ("stern unyielding fixity of form"). Shifting images of the solid transformed into the liquid recur throughout the poem, and of the infusion of the Spirit into what was lifeless. Could the lifeless, the fixed, be science, and the looseness, the Spirit, represent the freedom and fulfillment he saw in literature and philosophy?

Then there are two poems, dated 1951 and 1952, which deal directly with the need for binding and controlling overwhelming inner forces — but also with the danger of death by rigidity that comes from binding too tight (the first I quote in part):

Youth is a disturbance, a taut binding
Of lines of force into a trunk, a tree;
It is an arrangement of music, through bonds, free, . . .

The final poem sums up the overwhelming impact of the boundless ocean of the divine, the temptation to let all bounds go, and the knowledge that this would mean disaster (we remember the greatest sin is pride):

O perfect Love, that put my fear to flight,
Embrace him too, and to thy purpose bend
His ruleless passion. He would be thy friend,
But knows not how, unless thou teach aright.
Without thee, he's my lord, and with cold fright
Congeals my limbs, and traitorously doth send
Aid to my foes, 'gainst whom he should defend
My earthly house, and desperate grows my plight.

Yet without him, thou may'st be overbold,
And leave me open too to treacherous sin;
I know the all-conquering power, but deep within
I know too that my thimble cannot hold
Thy abundant ocean. I must with thee plead
To leave me fear, harnessed to meet my need.

The evidence of repeated descriptions of the two ethics in his writings, his own admissions of his feeling of dividedness, the clear imagery of tension between freedom and constriction, the projective expression of the struggle for autonomy and conversely the need for order, and a life which shows a double stream of the mystical and the mechanical, with successful efforts at integration but a continuing sense of the conflict of the two — all these together build a picture of a man doing the impossible, standing as if with one foot on each of two drifting ice floes. Yet it seems to be the challenge of the impossible that draws Boulding to Jacob, David, and Job.

Freedom and control, which seem to be opposed in the mystic and the practical man, are both vital in fact, as Boulding has clearly recognized, to both the poet and the scientist. The wide range of creativity, of alternatives, of vision, the world's complexity, must be pinned down to a hypothesis or a form, then shaped and honed by critical standards. This conflict of freedom and control, which may be interpreted as the struggle of the primary processes and the ego, emerges as the major conflict, solved at different times in different ways, in Boulding's projective stories. It also seems to be the major personal conflict in

Boulding's life; and perhaps whatever makes it central in his person also makes him the person he is — the man who chooses the kinds of problems he does, who has the kinds of insights he has, who in wrestling with this tension is wringing usable patterns from an intractable world.

PART II
Patterns of Life

8

The Generations

All change may not be for the better, but it is clear that there can be no betterment without some change.

— KEB, *Beyond Economics*

I

It has been my position from the beginning, as I try to order and clarify the roots and the fruits of this life so freely thrown open to my inspection, that a great deal of the moving force for the mature adult comes from his own conscious choices. He is partly bound, it is true: he has been pinned to one time in history, surrounded by one set of opportunities, treated in particular ways by significant people around him, given one quota of biological endowment; and the combination of these forces has shaped the problems which are most troublesome for him, pointed up the environmental items to which he responds, and left him a share of motivations whose sources are unrecognized. But he is partly free. The ways in which he responds, his modes of handling problems, the items he chooses to magnify and minify in his environment — these he himself has carved and hammered out in interaction with the people, ideas, institutions, and physical objects about him from the very beginning. To explore this interaction we should look carefully at what Kenneth

Boulding was given, his genetic and cultural heritage; at what was done to him; at his physical and social surroundings, particularly in his early years; and at what was available to him, by way of ideas and alternatives. We have already begun to examine what he has done with problems and opportunities: what allegiances he came to, what attitudes he formed, what institutions he accepted and rejected, which difficulties he made the most of, and which he buried.

It is time, then, to look at his background, the class setting, the cultural complex, the interplay of personality in his family for the generation or two preceding him.

Both of Kenneth's parents came out of a working-class background, but on both sides there was some element of status strain, a slightly marginal feeling of having come down in the world.

Kenneth's mother's parents were George and Mary Rowe. They lived for most of their lives in the small market town of Chard, set in the softly rolling agricultural country of Somerset, in southwest England. George was the youngest in a family of ten, his parents illiterate agricultural laborers in Devon, who died shortly after he was born. George worked for at least four years in the mines near his birthplace, about fifty miles west of Chard, and probably learned the trade of a blacksmith there. After his marriage, he came to Chard and worked for almost forty years in a wheelwright's shop, shoeing horses, putting the iron tires on farmers' wagons, and doing the ironwork for the carriages the shop built for the more affluent. His work days generally ran from six to six, with occasional overtime for a few extra shillings; and Mary kept the family money in the proverbial teapot, feeling lucky when there was a sixpence left over after the few staples for the week were bought.

Mary's parents should have been in better financial shape, for her father was a veterinarian. In fact, they did live in a pleasant single-family stucco cottage up the road from the modest wooden-shingled row house where the Rowes lived. But unfortunately, her father George Austen was a "failed" vet (though he practiced, he had not succeeded in passing the examination for a license), and he was so fond of drinking that often he took his payment for service in a drink at the farmer's house; at other times his fees melted away at the Ship Inn tavern, his favorite haunt on Furnham Road. He walked about the country to make his visits; it was said of him that he drank up what it would have cost to keep a horse. Clearly he had tried but failed to follow professionally in his father's footsteps: his father had been a veterinary surgeon. All ten children in his family had to make their way at a lower level; the daughters were "put to service" or worked in the small collar-factory or lace-factories in town until their marriages to tenant farmers or transport workers. One son (perhaps the luckiest) was apprenticed to a coach-builder.

There was one strange thing about Mary's family, the Jane Austen myth. Kenneth's mother writes in her autobiography:

> Grandma was very proud of the fact, or so she believed, that her husband was the "great-nephew" of Jane Austen, the novelist. My mother was named Jane after her, and two of her sisters, Elizabeth and Emma, were named after two of Jane's characters.

This myth was pervasive and persistent. When Great-Aunt Emma died, in fact, the newspaper account described her unequivocally as "a great-niece of Jane Austen, the Victorian novelist, one of whose letters was sold at Christie's recently for £1,000." The connection was frequently referred to in family circles; a cousin of Boulding's still likes to mention his Austen literary heritage, though he knows its doubtful validity. Boulding himself told me the story as part of the first biographical interview that went into this study, and his mother kept it all her life as an element of her identity. When she wrote poetry or essays she liked to use the name "Ann Austen" as a pseudonym. Among the family it was sometimes assumed that this was the reason for Kenneth's astonishing intelligence. His mother describes it:

> My dear, gentle Mother was interested always in Kenneth's achievements and very proud of him, "He gets his brains from Jane Austen" she would say. Once a friend looked at me intently and said "WHERE does Kenneth get his brains?" I was not sure enough of Jane so I replied airily, "*I* think he gets them from ME and his Dad likes to think he gets them from HIM . . ." (EAB)

When we turn the cold light of fact (which I suppose only a biographer would do) on this legend, it seems highly unlikely. Jane, who lived from 1775–1817, never married. She had a sister who also died unmarried, and six brothers. A great-nephew would have to be the son of a nephew; but George Austen was born in 1823 of a father Thomas Austen, and there is no Thomas among Jane's brothers, nor any of their children who could have been old enough to have a child by 1823.[1] I am afraid there is no recourse for the connection except the misty possibility of a descendant of a great-uncle of Jane's — or, of course, some unrecorded illegitimacy. All of this makes any conclusion about genetic causation of Kenneth's literary talent a little feeble.

It is interesting, both that the family has hung on so tight to this myth, and that they never tried to verify it. In fact, the grandmother who was so proud of the connection could never have read any of Jane Austen's books; she could not even write her name. The tie to Jane was certainly a borrowed glory; there is no record that George Austen took any pride in it, but there was a lively awareness of it in the women in the family. Perhaps the pride in a woman's accomplishment in a man's world, and the cobweb thread tying them to a higher level of existence than the one they knew, kept the myth so alive. I cannot

Fig. 6. George and Mary Rowe, between 1920 and 1925 (*photo from Michigan Historical Collections*)

Fig. 7. The Rowe house in Chard, where Bessie grew up

help concluding that they did not really want the facts, suspecting they would come in conflict with their illusions.

There was at least one other class-leavening influence in Bessie Rowe's family. Her father, besides being a blacksmith, was the superintendent in the Sunday school and a local preacher in the Wesleyan Methodist Church. This meant he had to be very familiar with the Bible and with such books as *Pilgrim's Progress* and *Fox's Book of Martyrs* (well-thumbed and almost memorized in her childhood home, Bessie reports). Although, as Bessie was growing up in Chard, the local churches were stratified (the "Best People" went to the Parish Church, the tradespeople to the Baptist, and the factory and laboring folk to the Wesleyan Methodist), there was a yeasty movement inherent in the structure of the nonconformist Methodist Church. To use people in common walks of life as semiministers, conducting services in the smaller chapels under the supervision of the ordained ministers according to a regular "Plan," was a way of training, educating, and elevating the laity; and the Methodist Church was gradually becoming more and more middle class. George Rowe thus spanned the role-gap between a blacksmith and a preacher. As his father-in-law was a pseudoveterinarian, he was a pseudominister, and his sense of status-tension in such a tight society must have been enhanced by his double role.

Bessie went to the local "Board" school until she was fourteen, then was apprenticed to a dressmaker for three years. She tried to establish her own dressmaking business. However, she kept a book under her cushion when she was sewing, and whenever her mother was not about, the book would come out, and she would start reading. The family finally decided she would never make a success of dressmaking. So, at the cost of many tears (both hers and her mother's), she was sent off to an aunt in London who found her a job with a family, taking care of children. It was a pleasant family and a good year; she learned French along with one of the daughters, and attended the nearby Methodist chapel where she organized a little "string band" (having brought her fiddle with her from Chard). She even inveigled a lonely-looking young man into playing the organ to accompany them. In December, 1898, the young organist, William Boulding, sent a letter to George and Mary Rowe asking for permission to court their daughter.

William had been sent by his company in Liverpool to the London area three months before, to work on a job as a gas fitter. Though he had no family, his description of his qualifications must have counted for much with George Rowe: he had recently become a Christian, he was a local preacher, junior class leader, and Sunday school teacher. He added, "I firmly believe God has brought us together, and it is only after much prayer and seeking and in answer to this I have taken this step." The father's response was kindly but firm: Bessie (then eighteen) was too young to think about keeping company yet, but he might correspond with her "as a friend and not beyond that for a time."

William Couchman Boulding was then twenty-two. Since the death of his mother when he was twelve, he had had to make his own way in Liverpool. The choice of the trade of gas fitter was a natural one, since his own father, his stepfather, and his stepuncle were all gas fitters. As the era of gas lighting ended, this trade broadened to include the installation of hot-water central heating systems, general plumbing, and, eventually, electrical work, and, in time, young Will worked in all these areas. There is no record of his apprenticeship or training, but perhaps his stepuncle gave him some help when his stepfather, the story goes, threw him out on the streets. Up to that time, however, his schooling had been regular: there are yearly records of his promotion in the Brunswick Wesleyan School, with certificates for punctuality and attendance and several good conduct medals. The death of Will's mother came a month before his passing Standard VI, and this is the last of his school records.

The marriage that produced William Boulding was perhaps ill-starred from the beginning. It took place less than three weeks before Will's birth, joining William Boulding, son of a laundress and a butcher, and Martha Turton, daughter of an estate agent (equivalent to an American real estate agent). She was thirty at the time, and he was thirty-six. Martha's sister and her husband were the witnesses; Eliza was probably most concerned about her sister's prospects. The fathers of both Martha and William had died some time before. Clues are short on this section of the family, but there are some photographs. A picture of William's mother shows her looking rather grim, wearing a fairly simple cotton dress; Martha's mother appears in a silk dress, holding a book; and Martha's sister is decked out in gorgeous brocade. Martha's father, of ample girth, wears a frock coat and stands sedately holding what appears to be a Bible. William, in contrast, is thin, and sits casually and a little mockingly with his legs apart, wearing a loud checked suit, a wide-brimmed hat over his long curly hair. It would seem that Martha's family, financially and in status, was a cut above William's. She probably had a religious background that he may not have had. There is evidence that she attended the Brunswick Methodist Chapel when she was young; certainly her child was sent to a Wesleyan school, and she gave him a Bible on his twelfth birthday, though he was not baptized until his conversion in 1898. It seems likely that if it had not been for the pregnancy — whatever may have been the circumstances that brought it about — this marriage, which was evidently a step down for Martha, would not have occurred.

About William senior we know almost nothing more. His death, of a kidney infection, occurred when their son was a year and a half old. There was also a girl born to the couple, who died in infancy. After her husband's death, Martha married "Pa" Hardacre, the foreman in William Boulding's firm, and bore him two daughters in two years, and then a pair of twins who died. "Pa" is described by the son of one of those daughters as a "tartar," and apparently was a heavy drinker and openly loose with other women. In fact, at one time, he had two wives at once. Threats and beatings were his common modes of discipline. In such a setting young Will Boulding spent his early years, a chapter closed by the stroke that took his mother's life and sent him out to fend for himself.

Because Bessie's parents thought she was too young and that Will should have more money before he took on a wife, it was four years before Bessie and Will were married, in May of 1902. The only thing she is recorded to have regretted in later years about that day is that she wore a brown dress and her younger sister, in cream-colored silk, looked more like the bride than she.

In terms of personality, we know almost nothing about Will's mother and father; nor did Kenneth. Bessie's parents, however, had a more direct effect on him, for they lived until he was grown, and their last few years were spent in the Boulding household. Mary Rowe is described by Boulding as a woman of "unconquerable patience and sweetness." Somewhere, apparently (perhaps in reaction to her own mother's violent temper), she had found depths of faith and strength that kept her going as the balance wheel of the family, the buffer between a quarrelsome mother, an opinionated husband, and an impatient youngest daughter. Her motto was, "If you can't say anything nice about somebody, don't say anything." Though she appeared to a small boy as almost grim in her goodness, she had real tenderness for her family and a close relationship with Bessie, her eldest daughter. Her husband George Rowe was tall, straight, and handsome, deaf and cantankerous, a "furious worker" who did everything much better than necessary. He was given to moods of elation and depression, and Bessie remarked once that she thought he might have been more steady and contented if he had smoked a pipe, but unfortunately he "had no vices worth mentioning." He was suspicious and quick to take offense. Boulding has characterized him as a "wild horse, bridled by his sincere evangelical faith, . . . an austere man with a tightly controlled, but violent, temper." He has a favorite story of his grandfather's youth, when George was said to have been arguing with a local squire, asking him why he had a right to possess all those lands. The squire said his ancestors fought for them, so George put up his fists and answered, "All right, I'll fight you for them now!"

George Rowe was a forceful presence when he stood up in church to give testimony or to preach. At home each evening he would read to the family from the Bible before bedtime; and he went on preaching until he was over seventy. One early sermon of his is extant; the spelling and punctuation are imperfect, but the reasoning from the text is orderly, and the imagery is full of power, with echoes of the kind of figures in the sermon that sent Ishmael off whale-hunting in *Moby Dick*.

These were the heritages combined in the coupling of Bessie and Will Boulding — an obscure beginning for Will, and a sense that things had been better once upon a time but that life had to be made on his own from here on out; for Bessie, a fuller, more supportive family. Will had, from somewhere, strength: considering that half of his mother's children had died in infancy, he was lucky to be alive at all. What their genes carried in terms of unusual potential it is very hard to say. There was no one of eminence in their traceable past, only a succession of butchers, artisans, salesmen, veterinarians, dairymen, farm laborers, dressmakers, and maids. What they, their parents, or grandparents might have been, given education and opportunity, there is no telling. It may be that George Rowe, fighting his way into literacy, stubborn, hardworking, persistently religious, richly imaginative, brought an important genetic contribution to the making of Kenneth Boulding. Mary Jane Austen contributed, together with the Austen literary myth, a gentleness, serenity, sensitivity to beauty, and perhaps frightening saintliness — plus a feeling that by class, this was a family that should be better off than it was, that belonged in spirit to an intellectual and professional position that it did not, in fact, possess. Studies have shown that such a feeling may have more to do with determining attitudes, life-styles, and upward mobility than actual class level does.[2]

I I

Bessie, the village girl, was determined to make a life in the crowded, noisy city of Liverpool, secure in the knowledge that she and her husband were both devoted to the work of the Lord, and to each other. Will, the urban youth, had struggled from a supportless emptiness to carve himself a place in the economic world as a skilled worker, and in the institutional world as an active Methodist. He was now directed toward building the loving family he had never really had. When they knelt by the table for their first meal in their new home together, he broke down and cried.

Will's childhood must have been desperately difficult; he rarely spoke about it to anyone. Whatever insecurities this left him with, however, seem to have been caught up in his commitment to the nonconformist church, which was the main pillar of his identity from young manhood throughout the rest of his life. His baptism is recorded in 1898, but he was already giving sermons before that time. Will and Bessie's choice of a place to live when they were first married was near the Cranbourne Street Mission so Will could continue his active work there, bringing the light of the Gospel to others in this slum area, as poor and lost as he had once been. (The first time Mary Rowe visited her married daughter, she was upset by the neighborhood, and hoped they would soon move to a more respectable part of town.)

When the Cranbourne Mission was closed, Will and Bessie became loyal supporters of Brunswick Wesleyan Methodist Chapel, Will serving as a local preacher on the circuit and for many years as superintendent of the Sunday school. He had the gift of a kind of genial presence, preached sincerely and probably rather simply, and was particularly fond of children. For most of his life, he channeled a great deal of energy into an organization called the Shaftesbury Society and Ragged School Union. This was a carryover from the days when there were no schools for the poor in England except those growing out of charitable indulgence. At its height in the middle of the nineteenth century, the Ragged School Union, which had been set up to take care of children too poor and filthy to go even to the charity schools run by churches, had more than 17,000 day-school pupils; [3] but by the time Will got involved with it, its main activity was conducting religious services for poor and crippled children, and taking them for outings in the country. These outings were one of Will's greatest delights, and Bessie and Kenneth often went along on the trips to take a load of children to a seacoast home in Wales.

Will was a rather quiet man, not quick-witted or full of laughter like his wife, but not grim. "He was a dear," recalls Muriel Parkinson, a family friend of Kenneth's age. He was kind and gentle and loved to sing the old Methodist hymns. He and Bessie were both readers, and discussed many matters of world interest in their home; but he always seemed to be more awed by Kenneth's intelligence and achievements than Bessie, who simply reveled in them. Will's attitude toward Kenneth, as Muriel describes it, was, "What is this thing that's been hatched out?" while Bessie would simply say, "This is *my son!*" Still, he was very proud of Kenneth, and his conversation was full of Kenneth's doings, particularly when Kenneth was away from home. He built toys for him when he was small, brought home parts for his Meccano construction set when he came back from work, bought him Arthur Mee's *Children's Encyclopedia* [4] (the envy of all Kenneth's friends), and took him and his chums for outings on his motorcycle and sidecar. He turned his plumbing skills to his family's benefit, putting in a little window box with a fountain to try to ease Bessie's misery at moving back to Liverpool in 1914, piping gas and water to the top floor when Grandpa and Grandma Rowe moved in there, and installing a bathroom for the family when no one else on the street had one. He was a little rough, unpolished, unconcerned about clothes and appearances, and had practical, manual skills that Kenneth lacked. He was staunch, reliable, utterly honest, a little introverted but friendly, and humble; while Bessie was mercurial, warm and outgoing, girlish into maturity, usually sparkling and gay, but occasionally overburdened and depressed, though she would try to conceal this if she could. She made friends quickly and was tender-hearted. Neighbors and acquaintances sought her out in times of death or other troubles.

Those who knew them saw both as loving and caring, Will as neither dominant nor submissive, Bessie as slightly dominant in Kenneth's youth but more submissive as she grew older. In Boulding's eyes, his father was less submissive and more loving than his mother; yet he must mean by "love" a social concern, for he has said that he was much closer to his mother, and never really knew his father very well.

Will and Bessie were seen as models of goodness in their neighborhood, particularly by their neighbors, the Stones. Bessie, in turn, regarded the Stones in the same light. Leslie Stone told me a wartime anecdote bearing on this image. His father was called down to the police station one day because a shaft of light had been observed coming out of his window during a blackout, and Mrs.

Stone was beside herself with worry: "Whatever will Mr. Boulding say?" When he came back he was able to report with a chuckle that he had met Mr. Boulding at the police station, answering to the same charge.

Will was stocky, Bessie pert and petite. Kenneth towered over her at his adult height of 5′11″. As he grows older, his childhood friends are impressed by the resemblance of his body build and his shock of iron gray hair to that of his father.

Neither Will nor Bessie was quite traditional. Will was more interested in the work of the Kingdom, particularly for the young, poor, and downtrodden, than in the work of his business. The hundreds of weekends he spent in labors of love might have made his business solvent if he had used them in labors of wealth, but his life, I am sure, would have been much emptier. Bessie was more interested in reading, writing poetry, getting out of the house for a walk or a tram ride, digging in the sand or rowing in the park with Kenneth, or going to her sister's for tea, than in keeping her house spick and span. She was frank; she spunkily defended her broad Somerset accent in her first job interview in London, and permanently scandalized an elderly worthy in the church by announcing the fact when she was going to have a baby. She was impulsive; she cut off her eighty-year-old aunt's hair in a moment when her aunt said she wished it were short, before she could change her mind. She tried, at the age of fifty-two, to climb out on the roof with Kenneth and a friend when they were visiting Cambridge, but her recently-broken ankle, she recalled, "wouldn't let her." (EAB). She could enjoy, perhaps as deeply as Kenneth — perhaps she sparked Kenneth's enjoyment of — the soft green English countryside and the glorious ancient English cathedrals. Together the family made many trips in their little car around England and Wales, and practically made a collection of cathedrals.

The description of family background would not be

complete without including the larger family. Everyone, in the end, turned up in Liverpool. The Boulding household was so central, and the combination of sense of duty and enjoyment of company so strong, that other family members were taken in as a matter of course. Rosie, one of Will's half-sisters, lived with them a great deal of the time, and Will's other half-sister's children spent years at the Bouldings'. In 1920, Will made a flat on the top floor of their house for Grandma and Grandpa Rowe, and turned the basement into a blacksmith shop. Bessie's sisters Flossie and Ada were so much a part of the family that they were almost as likely to be found at Bessie's as at their own homes; and their husbands would have roaring games of checkers or dominoes in the evenings with Will.

Flossie's husband's younger sister came up from Chard to live with the Bouldings in Liverpool, and years later she wrote of the house on Seymour Street:

> It was indeed a House of Nonsense, and also something much more precious than nonsense, rather hard to describe, it was certainly a house for waifs and strays, and very few went empty away.

Flossie and her husband were both a little strict and proper, and believed in a neat house and clean clothes; but Ada was jolly good fun. She was dramatic, and loved to dress up; she would roll into the room with a grand entrance and a greeting for everybody. Once when the minister was calling, she went out and came back to the door dressed as a nun, asking for contributions for charity. She and Flossie and Kenneth put on wild charades at the family Christmas parties; one year Bessie wrote a play for the festivities. Ada had been an irrepressible child; she would never walk in the road if there was a wall she could balance on, and once scalded her leg severely by teetering on the flimsy top of a wash boiler. After she went to Australia, she ran a boarding house, and her letters to Kenneth were frequently decorated with sketches of stick figures. One showed a busload of people arriving for lunch just after the washing-up was done; another noted the "perplexity of the proprietress" with quantities of people coming for dinner after the mutton joint was much reduced in size. There is a note in one letter about a "dear lady" who would be sure to want something light for dinner; "If she does, will suggest a plate of feathers." She worked very hard, but kept joy about her. She was a second mother to Kenneth, and, eventually, a second grandmother to his children.

A word remains to be said about the economic level of the family as Kenneth was growing up. Will was a very good man, but not a very good businessman. After the prosperity of the first few years of Kenneth's life, the business gradually went downhill. Times were not good anywhere in Britain; England, clinging to the gold standard after its day was past, was in one long slump from World War I to the depression of the 1930s. There were continual coal strikes and other labor difficulties; and unemployment was even higher in Liverpool than in the rest of the country.[5] From having several men working for him in the early years, Will gradually came, by the late 1920s, to be working alone. He did a big heating job for a movie theater that went bankrupt and could never pay him. Perhaps from then on his head was never above water; but his bank and creditors, knowing his integrity, evidently kept supplying him, and not even his family knew that he was hopelessly insolvent until he died in 1933. He kept his accounts mostly in his head, and so his affairs were a little difficult to reconstruct.

Of course, his generosity contributed to his financial difficulties. We have mentioned his free giving of time and energy, and the sharing of the hospitality of his household. In addition, he probably gave money to anyone he felt was worse off than he. When George Rowe came to live with them, Will paid him several pounds a week for the work he did in the basement blacksmith shop, though he could not afford it, and could have done the work in half the time himself. He often did plumbing and heating work for churches, charging only the bare minimum. Far to the north of England, in Cumberland, I saw the hot water heating system he installed in Abbey Town Chapel in 1924, and, at family friend Dora Wilson's house, the estimate he had sent her father for the job, quoting a specially reduced price.

Bessie, of course, was aware of money difficulties all through these years, though she did not know the full extent of their situation. After her mother died, and her sister Ada sailed for Australia, and Kenneth was about to take off for Oxford, she thought she might augment the family finances by starting a little Methodist bookstore in their home. It is not really clear whether it was Bessie's project or Will's; both their names were on the letterhead. Boulding thinks it was his father's idea:

> but Mother did have to run it, because Father was hopeless at it. One time a traveler for Tucks, the Christmas card firm, came in and sold him about ten times as many Christmas cards as they could possibly hope to sell, and Mother had to send them all back.

Unfortunately, even with Bessie's help, the Methodist Bookroom proved no more lucrative than the heating business.

The house they lived in, though it is probable that Will owned it (although he was so far in debt that the bank essentially owned it in the end), was not exactly the mark of a substantial citizen. It was on a street which is marked on a map of 1934 as the border between one of the worst poverty areas in the city (so defined because at least one family in five contained individuals of the chronically unemployed or destitute type, often receiving public assistance, and many families lived in one room) and a district in the second-worst class (where more than one half of the residents received casual or small earnings, averaging less than 36s. per week, and many families lived in one or two rooms).[6] But in the voting list of 1925, in the Liverpool library, Wm. C. Boulding is listed as a juror, and the clerk there remarked when I asked, "He must have been of some fair substance to be a juror." There were a number of jurors listed on both sides of Seymour Street; perhaps home-owning was the criterion.

It is clear from the memories of Kenneth and his boyhood friends that the Bouldings did not feel poor (they were among the better-off in the neighborhood where they lived), nor did their friends regard them as poor (the father of one of Kenneth's best friends sold apples from a barrel) — "You could always get a good tea at Kenneth's house!" — but there must have been considerable insecurity about the ups and downs of the business, getting paid or not getting paid for a job, as the times got worse. The Bouldings were quite conscious of the layer below them, the ragged, hungry children, and the destitute Irish who either drank because they were poor or were poor because they drank (Kenneth was never sure which) — but they were also very conscious of the layer above them, the families whose sons were fee-payers at the grammar schools, or, at the next notch up, went to boarding schools and were assured of a place at the university.

The mix of poverty and near-poverty, with aspirations toward something better, which the Bouldings knew intimately, was typical of Liverpool. "In most parts of the city . . . families are to be found living near together but differing greatly from each other in social standing." [7] It was just one of the contrasts endemic to the world Kenneth grew up in, the noisy, colorful, crowded, ebullient city of Liverpool.

9

The Cultural Setting: Life in Liverpool

Everything is what it is because it got that way.

— KEB's formulation of
"D'Arcy Thompson's Law"

I

Modern Liverpool is still a city of contrasts. If you stand in front of the round-domed Picton Library, where Kenneth spent the better part of his Oxford vacations, you see on your left St. George's Hall, a great gray Victorian edifice built in Classical Revival style in 1854. Straight ahead and several blocks away, towering above the rose garden with its sedate and regular pathways, the old business buildings, and the board fence that hides a construction project, is the needle-slim disc-topped sky-high restaurant that is the new symbol of the city. And on your right, down toward the river Mersey, cheek and jowl with the old Town Hall and the approaches to the docks, is a confusion of cranes and entwined sections of elevated roadbed which marks the progress of the new tunnel and super-highway system for which huge chunks of the city are now being torn down. Where in the world but in Liverpool

Fig. 8. The Picton
Library, Liverpool

would you see a big lumbering city bus completely covered with contact paper in a pink, orange, and yellow daisy pattern?

Farther east, on a hilltop where the workhouse used to stand, is the ultramodern Catholic cathedral, looking from a distance laughably like its nickname "the Mersey funnel" but powerfully impressive when one climbs the long row of steps and catches the sunlight through its intensely blue stained-glass windows. In contrast to this radical architecture of the Roman Catholics is the ultra-traditional Gothic Anglican Cathedral, abuilding almost as slowly as cathedrals in the Middle Ages. The first stone was laid by King Edward VII in 1904, and the building process is still going on.

But architectural contrasts are only a sample of the contradictions in Liverpool. The city which opened a Philharmonic Hall in 1849 and has continued to support the Royal Liverpool Philharmonic Orchestra burst into public notice in recent years with the advent of its sons, the Beatles. They, with their new brand of music and poetry, and the blossoming of the devotees they attracted, suddenly made Liverpool, according to Allen Ginsberg, "the center of the consciousness of the human universe." [1] The split between the classical and the popular is currently highly visible, but not new. In spite of the twelve concerts a year being given by the Liverpool Philharmonic, the existence of two chamber music societies, and the weekly organ recital in St. George's Hall for an admission charge of 1d., a 1934 assessment of the musical situation drawn from interviews with a population sample was as follows: "Although concert parties and the musical entertainments provided at clubs and churches are not unpopular, the majority of the people have little taste for the straightforward musical performance." [2] Certainly Kenneth, though he listened for hours when he was exposed to a friend's records at Oxford, knew nothing of classical music in his days in Liverpool.

It is, in fact, a kind of contradiction that Liverpudlians should be occupied with such things as architecture, music, art, and books at all. Liverpool is a port city, the major harbor on the west coast of England, a working-class, merchant town. Its life was built around the shipping industry — shipbuilding, fitting, manning, victualling, banking and insurance, and the warehousing and processing of the goods imported and exported. Most of its population works at manual labor, or as sailors, clerks, and at minor commercial posts. It had a reputation outside Liverpool (in Kenneth's youth and until the Beatles) as a cultural vacuum — the kind of place from which an aspiring upwardly mobile young man would try to hide his origin. Yet the city *has* made opportunities for the broadening of the human spirit. It had its nineteenth-century philanthropists who gave museum and art collections to the city and built great gray buildings near St. George's Hall to house them, while the city council itself undertook in 1852 to provide one of the first free public libraries in the country. But in 1934, only about 16 percent of the population was using the library facilities.[3]

11

A kind of double thrust seems evident in the cultural sphere — the "elitist" approach from above and indigenous stirrings from below. We have already noted the classical music promoters vs. the strong ferment of original popular modes. In drama, as well, the first repertory theatre in the country was established in Liverpool in 1911, and its stage has provided sendoffs for such artists as Rex Harrison, Michael Redgrave, and Rita Tushingham. Boulding remembers Robert Donat and Diana Winyard playing there in his boyhood; professional plays were a staple of his youthful recreational fare. Professional music and drama have been supported by both private and public subsidies. In addition, Liverpool had, in the early

1930s, over fifty amateur dramatic societies. Other voluntary organizations at the time included twenty-three Learned Societies, thirteen for the promotion of literature, poetry, and painting, twenty musical societies, one hundred political clubs, and over four hundred churches, whose most popular activity besides the worship services was usually a literary and debating society.[4] Such a pluralism of grass-roots activities gives evidence of a yeasty setting, with a range of pursuits open and a lot of choices available.

Contrasts, at least in the period with which our story is concerned, have been endemic to Liverpool. One contrast which may be a cause of some of the others is the cosmopolitan flavor of its population. A port city naturally becomes the entrance wedge, and often the resting place, for various foreign nationals, and it is probable that no other British city except London has such a mix as Liverpool. The goods and passengers continually moving through its docks from every part of the world have left some residue. A number of Indians and Chinese, for instance, came as coolies on ships and took up residence there. For the Irish it was the easiest place to go. After the famines of the 1840s, a mass Irish immigration gave the city a distinctly Irish flavor, a high proportion of Roman Catholics, and a direct share in the bloody struggle for Irish independence. Only a slim peninsula separates Liverpool from Wales, so the Welsh, too, have their part in its culture. A Welsh Choral Union long performed regularly in town, while the Liverpool Welsh Society takes its place among the Merseyside Jazz Society, Lectures on the Catholic Faith, poetry reading groups, and adult education courses in the current offerings of evening meetings in the city.

To be exposed to differences, contrasts, and contradictions was Kenneth Boulding's heritage in Liverpool. It is perhaps not by chance that modern Liverpool has adopted the slogan, "City of Change and Challenge."

Creative Tension

Terms of contrast were adopted by columnist Alan Brien to describe Liverpool in a piece for the [London] *Sunday Times* of April 27, 1969 — the contrast of the sacred and the profane, the magnificent and the mean. Liverpool, he says,

> is the slummiest, chummiest, most violent, superstitious, traditional, spendthrift, bargain-conscious, youthful, capricious, Celtic city in England. . . . It is the creative tension between these rival qualities which gives the city its bouncy, opinionated, masculine vitality. . . . Nothing is entirely frivolous in Liverpool, and nothing is entirely serious, the two continually mix and blend.

And he notes the penchant of the inhabitants to protest by petitions or pickets whatever they object to: "The Liverpudlian by nature believes in shouting before he's hurt and considers himself someone to whom attention must be paid." Kenneth Boulding is a true son of Liverpool!

Viewers of the Beatles' fantastic masterpiece, *The Yellow Submarine,* could easily imagine there is something about Liverpool which produces discontinuities, leaps of wild imagination, ridiculous but reasonable extensions of analogies, and characters like Boulding and Jeremy, the Nowhere Man. The submarine's journey was one system break after another, from one weird world to the next; dropping through the Sea of Holes landed the adventurers in the Sea of Green; space rolled up behind them and time could be reversed by pushing a button. Unexpected objects kept emerging from prosaic-looking doors: the randomness of the universe was overwhelming; to open a door, or push a button, was to be transformed or transported in completely unpredictable ways. Then we have the absurd but fitting literalization of the "foothills of the headlands," the cross-fertilization of the fish swimming with arms, and the redemption of the world through music and love. Boulding's counterpart Jeremy, you will remember, was a misplaced nobody, who yet became somebody in the end. He was a botanist, a physicist, a classicist, a linguist, and a poet; he spoke in rhyme and wrote books incessantly, writing the reviews while he was writing the book. (Boulding in one of his prefaces gloated at the chance the preface gave him to write his review before the reviewers did.) He was a better mechanical fixer than Boulding is, and Boulding would never have fixed the half a hole to keep his mind from wandering, for his wandering mind is his genius; but remember how Jeremy overcame his enemies with love, and finally made the Blue Meany bloom?

So much for an excursion into the nonsense world, with whatever symbolic implications it can carry. We must soberly shift back to Kenneth's father's youth, when Liverpool also presented a time of change, challenge, and choices. The last decade of the nineteenth century was a period of major technological innovation. In 1893 came the construction of an overhead electric tramway along the docks. At that time, the tramways which provided the public transportation in other parts of town were horse-drawn, but they were converted to electricity with over-head trolleys in 1899. In 1897, the city started replacing the gas and incandescent lights on the streets with electric lights. At this point, an enterprising young gas fitter would have had to give some thought to expanding his skills to electrical work or going into central heating or equipping flats with "hot and cold water laid on." Will, though he apparently gained adequacy in all these areas, eventually concentrated on the installation of hot-water heating systems.

The first motor cars started appearing in Liverpool in 1896. A contemporary of Will's observed, "Of course those [motorcars] that are in use have to be preceded by a person on foot. . . . I should not think they would meet with a great success, not the same pleasure derived in driving one of these things as a nice horse, what do you say?" [5] Though car ownership was rarer in Liverpool than in the rest of England even in the 1930s,[6] William Boulding was one of the few, by the early 1920s, who owned a car, as much of his business took him into Wales and other parts of the countryside.

Around 1895, typewriters were beginning to be introduced into business offices, and telephone service was also used by some businesses. A "new and improved trunk wire service" installed between Liverpool, London, and Glasgow was celebrated by a conversation between the lord mayors and the strains of bagpipes from the north. Because of his business, Will bought a typewriter when Kenneth was eight or nine. Bessie's first contact with a telephone was in the second home where she worked, in London, in 1899. But she had more than enough of it when she had to stay at home to answer the phone from 1904 to 1910, while Will was out working during the day. Photography was spreading before the turn of the century so that the ordinary middle-class youth might become a camera hobbyist, although he generally had to develop and print his films or plates himself, and, of course, was dependent on a bright sunny day for good results. In the Boulding family casual photographs seem to have waited until about 1920, but Kenneth was an eager photographer, and by that time the ubiquitous Boots Chemists stood ready to process the films.

Recreational choices, for those who had the time and money, were also broad in the 1890s. Parks and public baths were available for swimming, bowling, cricket, and tennis. (Tennis in Bessie's youth was only played by the "best people," but her youngest sister Flossie eventually became quite a tennis enthusiast.) New Brighton, just across the Mersey, was developing its own version of the Eiffel Tower and Atlantic City at the turn of the century. Bicycling was becoming a popular sport, even for ladies. (Will offered Bessie the choice of a bicycle or a sewing machine for a wedding present; she prudently chose the sewing machine.) Voluntary clubs and organizations ca-

tered to all sorts of interests, from the Liverpool Phreno-
logical Society to the Young Abstainers Union. Evening
classes and social groups were sponsored by the YMCA
and many churches.

The choice of political allegiance could also be made
from many alternatives, but perhaps there was only one
natural choice for Kenneth's father. At the time Will was
growing up, cast out from his family, and seeking his identity, William Ewart Gladstone, champion of the under-
dog, was the great popular British hero of the middle and
lower classes. Four times between 1868 and 1894, Gladstone served as the Liberal Prime Minister of England.
Here, and in other government posts, he had improved
working conditions for dock workers, made efforts to aid
starving political prisoners, worked on the tax and economic structure, led in the fight to broaden the base of
suffrage (although he adamantly opposed suffrage for
women), attempted to promote disarmament, and long
struggled for reform and home rule for Ireland. His appeal to Nonconformists such as Will was particularly
strong because, although an Anglican himself, he put political decisions in moral terms and had an almost excessive anxiety to make his own conduct consistent and
Christian. To top all these qualities, Gladstone was a native of Liverpool, and returned there in 1892 to receive
"the freedom of the City." He made his last great speech
there in 1896. When the "Grand Old Man" died in 1898,
there was an oration given for him by John Dutton in the
House of Commons. A typewritten excerpt from the oration was still in William Boulding's wallet, along with
family pictures and other treasures, at the time of his
death in 1933:

> So it came to pass that throughout the civilized world a
> race or nation were suffering from oppression their
> thoughts turned towards Gladstone and when that
> mighty voice was raised in their behalf Europe and the
> civilized world listened. The breathings of new hope en-

tered the hearts of men made despearte [*sic*] by long despair.

The stamp of Queen Victoria, of course, was on all of Will's youth. Royalty was localized by fantastic celebrations in Liverpool, as, no doubt, in other cities as well, in honor of her birthday and her Diamond Jubilee: the firing of guns from the fort, fireworks and amusements, bands and parades. But 1901, the year before Will and Bessie were married, brought the close of the Victorian era. Bessie, in mild self-criticism, laments the short-sightedness of her diary from that period in her autobiography:

> Queen Victoria was in the last year of her reign but the only thing I have on record is that I fell downstairs on the day she died! I remember feeling that the bottom had fallen out of the world, but dear me, life went on as usual, except that we talked of the King instead of the Queen. (EAB)

Bessie worked in Liverpool for the two years before her marriage, and Will managed to save a hundred pounds to furnish the four rooms and kitchen into which they moved in 1902 on the back street near Cranbourne Mission. A year later, "Pa" Hardacre, Will's stepfather, died, and Will was encouraged to take over the gas-fitting business which had originally been his father's. He had spent all his savings fitting out his home, and the business was badly run down; but his Aunt Eliza Hall (the same sister who had stood up with Martha at her wedding almost thirty years before) loaned him ten pounds to buy the tools and equipment, and he went into business for himself.

A year later, feeling he needed to be in a more central location for the business (and meantime, the Cranbourne Mission having been closed), he and Bessie moved to a narrow row house at 4 Seymour Street, just off London Road, very close to Lime Street Station and the central complex of St. George's Hall, the art gallery, and the library. It was not a particularly "respectable" street, though it had been at one time. Small shops, factories, and professional offices had taken over some of the former residences. But this was exactly the kind of use they wanted to make of their home, and while the Bouldings gave a dutiful bow to respectability, it was never the overriding consideration in their lives; righteousness was far more important. Will had his workshop in the covered, paved back yard, and displayed a large sign in front of the house, "William Boulding, Heating Engineer." It was in this house, one room wide and three stories high, that Kenneth was born six years later; and 4 Seymour Street remained the center of the Boulding home and business as long as William Boulding was alive.

Born, then, under one set of a long row of chimney-pots on a busy street near downtown Liverpool, Kenneth was placed in time and space. Liverpool meant industry, docks, trade, and commerce. Playhouses, shopping, art, books, architecture and music, as well as places of worship, were all waiting in the space of a few blocks. Georgian and Victorian times were still alive, and the Queen, though mourned and gone, still looked youthful as she rode side-saddle on her stone horse in front of St. George's Hall. But the socialist movement was growing in the same town out of the strong Liberal tradition, whose memorial Kenneth carried in his middle name. His block held a mixture of Irish, Jews, Catholics and Protestants, poor and not quite so poor, just as the whole city was a racial, religious, and economic mixture. The Orangemen paraded once a year, going up London Road right under his nose with their drums and fifes, and sometimes clashing with the Greens. Though the Boulding house was a stronghold of abstinence, one door away was the corner pub, a seedy, dark, scruffy building from which the drunks came out on Saturday nights. Yet there were beaches for building sand castles, and at the end of a tram line or a ferry lay the country, fields and cows and ferny woods, cottages of stucco, brick, and stone, villages of crooked narrow streets.

Exposed to so many alternatives, one who was sensitive had to develop a taste and take a stand—either learn to resolve contradictions or live with ambiguity. Problems, diversity, aliveness, and a richness of opportunity surrounded 4 Seymour Street and breathed in the very fog that blew in from the Mersey.

10

Childhood: Experiences, Expectations, and Opportunities

The person or the nation that has a date with destiny goes somewhere, though not usually to the address on the label.

— KEB, *The Meaning of the Twentieth Century*

I

Will and Bessie had been married for almost eight years by the time Kenneth was born, and there was no other child who followed. There was, therefore, a great deal of love, attention, and hope focused on him. In fact, though she did not tell anyone about this for several years, Bessie had made a kind of pact with God in praying for a child — that if she were given a boy, she would do all she could to make a missionary of him when he grew up. When shortly thereafter she found she was pregnant, it seemed to her as if God was doing His part. Will, on his side, in naming the child Kenneth Ewart, endowed him with a certain politically messianic quality. Kenneth thus from the beginning was a special personage to his parents — preordained to work for the salvation of the world, religiously or politically, or both. There was also, of course, the odd literary predestination carried through the Austen family myth.

Kenneth was not only the only child, he was the only

grandchild in the family. Bessie's younger sisters Ada and Flossie eventually married and joined her in Liverpool, but neither had any children; so aunts, uncles, and grandparents, with a couple of "courtesy aunts" for good measure, all centered their lives around this one small boy, and all had high hopes for him. There seems to have been, after all, no real pressure toward his becoming a missionary, though there were plenty of admonitions about being good and loving in the birthday letters written to him by assorted relatives, and Bessie's diary records her praying when he was twelve that she would some day see him ordained. But the political and literary ambitions did not fade. In 1929, his Aunt Ada sent him a story she had written about his "becoming a great Politician, and Statesman, and finally Prime Minister of England." When I asked his Aunt Flossie what Bessie and Will had hoped for before their child was born, she said, "Well—they hoped for a son . . . and then they hoped he'd be brilliant." In 1930, his mother remarked in a letter to him about how easy it was for Randolph Churchill to get a hearing "with a name all ready made"; but "to make a name for oneself is far greater fun and much more exciting *I* think, so get on with it laddie!!" And a few months later, her mind on the same track, she wrote him after a visit to the library, "I had a look at the number of Poet Laureates since 1600 or something, there has been a Rowe and an Austin. I wonder if there will be a Boulding!"

As for the small boy himself, there may be a suggestion of precocity in this sentence in his autobiography, written at the age of ten, and referring to the time when he was between two and four: "There was no limit to my funny sayings in those days." But beyond this there is none in written records until some of his school reports, from about the age of nine on. However, when I talked to Leslie Stone, who was Boulding's inseparable friend from the age of about five to eight, and whose father was an optician in the house next door, he reported it was quite obvious that Kenneth's ability was miles ahead of other children his age. He learned to read "not far out of the cradle," before he went to school (Leslie recalled this because his own parents compared his progress unfavorably with Kenneth's); and although in school Kenneth was a bit "gormless" at times (vacant or daydreaming, not hearing what the teacher said), he had only to shake his head and look up, and the answer was there. Leslie remembered Kenneth as getting everything right without any effort. Kenneth confirms the early reading; but, like George Bernard Shaw, he can't remember ever learning to read, and concludes, "I was always able to read, I think." He thinks he used to read a book of sermons (but not understand them) at about the age of three.

The first school that Kenneth went to, a long block and a half from his house, was St. Simon's, a Church of England school. It was a forbidding two-story brick building, with doorways arched like a church's, and a tiny, paved courtyard at the back with a high brick wall around it and a great solid metal gate. Kenneth remembers his first teacher as nice, young, and "rather fluffy," though the teacher in the next room was grim and terrifying. Both he and Leslie remember being sent to the headmaster one day to be caned, but Kenneth howled so much the master couldn't do it. It was a slum school. Many of the children came in rags and had to have their first lesson on how to lace their boots; but it was near and safe to get to.

There are one or two mysteries about his years at St. Simon's. Try as he might, Boulding can only remember attending two years there, but his age and other evidence would indicate he must have been there at least three and possibly four years. His mother has saved no school reports from St. Simon's, though she religiously kept all the reports from his second elementary school and his grammar (or high) school. She does not even mention his attending St. Simon's in her autobiography, or anything about his first years at school, though his masters and schools loom large in the account after that time. Although Leslie is sure the teachers there recognized his brilliance, the son of a Boulding family friend reports that the headmaster at Kenneth's first school thought he was mentally retarded because he stuttered so badly, and they could do nothing with him. Another family friend, Lilian Shaw James, testifies that Kenneth's mother told her positively he did not start to stutter until he started to school. However, everyone else who knew him as a child seems to think he stuttered as early as he could talk, or as early as they can remember. No one can pin it to a positive time. Boulding himself cannot remember a time when he did not stutter; he thinks it might have started about the age of five, when they gave up the house in Wallasey and moved back to Liverpool, but he is not sure of this. Stuttering was, by general consensus, a very prominent trait all through his school years; but his mother, in the whole of her autobiography, says not a word about it.

His parents, in any case, must have had some dissatisfaction with St. Simon's. It is clear from Kenneth's diary that in January, 1919, he was taken to a better-known school for an interview but not accepted because of his stammering (this is the commonly used term in Britain). He was then taken to a specialist for speech lessons three times a week and a month later came back to the school. His speech was now good enough for the interview, but he apparently failed the long division sums on the examination. However, he continued the speech lessons and was admitted in the spring to Hope Street School, an excellent school run by the Unitarians, about three-fourths of a mile from his home. He won first place in his class the first two terms he was there, and the records from then on testify to the mutual appreciation between him and his teachers: "an easy 'first' "; "excellent abilities and keen interest"; "we are justified in expecting great things of him in the future"; "His ability is very much above the average and his general knowledge, the result of wide and careful reading, is most unusual in a boy of his age. He loves the acquisition of knowledge, and has a keenly inquisitive mind."

11

There is no avoiding the question of how and why the stutter began; but there can be no real answer for it either. Therapists and theorists in the speech correction field agree that even with cases of stutterers seen almost at the onset of the difficulty, the exact cause cannot usually be determined. Working across a vast gulf of time and space, therefore, with inadequate data, we must content ourselves with placing theories and evidence side by side, as far as either of them will go.

Explanations of the causes of stuttering can be grouped into three major types. The bulk of recent writing in the field suggests that each may play an important role in some cases, but none explains all. The first is constitutional: some basic physical difference predisposes the individual toward stuttering. The second is evaluational: the labeling of a child as a stutterer makes him into one. The third is developmental: events and influences in the life of the child trap him in an anxiety-situation of which the stuttering is the symptom, and against which it is the weapon of defense.

The two constitutional theories currently showing the most relevance are the cerebral dominance theory and the servo or feedback theory. Stuttering as connected with a shift in "handedness" (related to a mixup in cerebral dominance) had a vogue in the 1930s and 1940s and then went out of favor through lack of empirical corroboration. But it has now been shown that, although "handedness" is not as directly related as it used to be thought, the factor of cerebral dominance is extremely important to speech production. (Sometimes, but not always, left-handedness or ambidexterity is connected with lack of unilateral dominance.) Where neither half of the brain clearly takes over the organizing function, the motor sequences needed for speech interfere with and interrupt each other, causing stuttering. Results of brain surgery on stutterers (undertaken for other reasons) and a number of experiments in perceptual laterality indicate that "stutterers show coordinative deficiency in the timing of their speech musculatures." [1]

The other compelling segment of the physical-explanation theory relates to feedback. We ordinarily "monitor" our speech in subtle ways through messages from our muscles, and also by hearing, through the air waves and the bones of our ears, what we are saying. When auditory feedback of speech was experimentally blocked out in several studies summarized by Van Riper, stutterers became fluent.[2] This suggests that there is a mistiming in stutterers of the aural feedback mechanism and, perhaps, a lack of development of the proprioceptive feedback — a physical or neurological deficiency. This mistiming is overcome by the rhythm, beat, or emphasis in singing or reciting, which could explain why most stutterers can perform in these situations without difficulty.

The hypothesis is thus that the stutterer by constitution has a more fragile adjustment of the neural control and feedback mechanisms on which speech is built, and that therefore any kind of emotional or physical stress may be reflected in the disruption of these mechanisms.

We can cite pieces of evidence from Boulding's history which seem to be potentially related to physical causation. (By the nature of the factors involved, any measurement is a laboratory problem and, in part, a dangerous one.) His frequent childhood illnesses centered in his ears and respiratory tract, both related to the speech mechanism. There is, for instance, a diary entry of his mother's, from June 23, 1923:

> Kenneth has been home from school for 5 weeks, his ears have been very bad. I took him to a specialist last Monday and he talked darkly of operations and nursing homes . . . the abscess has disappeared thank God [apparently without treatment] and he is well enough to go to school tomorrow.

As for laterality, there is the gross peripheral indication in Boulding's admitted lifelong confusion about right and left, (which has even crept into the description of a diagram in one of his books). A number of passages in his diary at the age of eight are recopied, one in a small hand and one very large; he may have been practicing with right and left. His handwriting, in any case, has always been atrocious; it was the only school subject on which he got bad reports all through secondary school, and today it is almost illegible. His muscular incoordination and early inability at athletics might be related to insufficient laterality, but studies have failed to connect stuttering in general with lack of large-muscle coordination.

The evaluational line of explanation, developed particularly by Wendell Johnson, suggests several factors as possible contributors to the child's acquiring a "handicapping belief in the difficulty of speech." The anxieties and demands of the surrounding adults may be focused on communication, through perfectionism in child training, by expecting too much of the child (especially if he has spoken unusually early or well), or by either the mother or father's feeling a need for vicarious glorification. Experiences of failure in speech or language will also contribute to the potential for stuttering. It is others' reaction to the child's speech errors or hesitancy and the extent of their pressure on him about it that is crucial.[3] Both anthropological and social-psychological data bear out the connection of stuttering with competition, high standards of achievement, and a high premium on status, prestige, and competence in speech.

Fig. 9. Will, Bessie, and Kenneth in the yard of the house at Wallasey (*photo from Michigan Historical Collections*)

Fig. 10. Seymour Street, Liverpool

In a household of adoring adults with extremely high expectations, with a mother who has been described as a little high-strung, these conditions could well have been met. Boulding can remember vaguely his becoming aware of his stuttering problem when somebody shouted at him about it, perhaps an aunt. Language failures in the written record center largely around his spelling. His childhood vocabulary far outran his ability to spell, and there is an echo of this in the Seminar on Information that Boulding held in 1954. He is recorded to have commented on a paper on speech disorders that "the abominable English spelling causes a mild aphasia in all of us. It may very well be that the experience we had with spelling at an impressionable age produces some of the slight aphasia."

The developmental explanations for stuttering include the approach–avoidance model developed especially by Sheehan [4] and a number of psychoanalytic theories focusing on various repressed needs. Perhaps the most cogently spelled out is Glauber's.[5] Glauber dwells very heavily on the separation anxiety developed in the child when the mother herself has separation-anxiety problems. The male child in the oedipal period is particularly vulnerable. The act of speech, closely tied with the development of the ego, may come to represent to the child an independent separation-act, a kind of aggression against the mother, and carry all kinds of freight from the oral and anal periods which make it a frightening kind of magic. It then has both an attraction and a repulsion quality (the ingredients of the approach–avoidance dilemma), and the child both starts and stops when he speaks, in hesitating alternation, or stuttering.

With any of these theories, the experience of stuttering itself, once begun, is a vicious circle, frustrating, and anxiety-producing. Selective rewards and punishments for segments of stuttering behavior continue the pattern through reinforcement. Among the many kinds of avoidance behavior frequently developed as the stuttering pattern hardens are feigning stupidity in school to avoid reciting, developing large vocabularies as a result of substituting unblocked words for blocked ones, laughing a lot or playing the clown or fool "to allay [the stutterer's] hunger for social interaction," and trying on various dramatic roles or temporary personalities to negate the constrictive self-image.[6]

Putting aside speculation about the possible applications of the other items just cited, Boulding, unlike most stutterers, does not seem to avoid speaking situations (except for a dislike of the telephone), but rather, almost compulsively (and very successfully), seeks them out. But it is true that words have gotten him in trouble on a number of occasions, wounding friends and associates, and setting people against him. After one such experience, combined with a difficult bout with respiratory illness, he wrote in response to a writing request, "I think we need to do a good deal more practicing before we venture forth into the dangerous sea of words!"

It is possible that a subconscious reason for his choosing exact patterns with rhythm and rhyme for his poetry is *because* he is a stutterer, and such patterns become a releasing agent. Perhaps here even is a clue to the drawing power of form, or order, in general in his life. For the stutterer, the form of the metronome or the song actually can be the means to freedom from disabling speech blocks. But it is a limited, rigid pattern within which speech is free. Such a choice — saying anything one likes, but with hesitation and difficulty, or saying something by rote, smoothly and easily — could well be the analogue of his whole ambivalence about freedom and restraint.

As for the parent-directed aggression postulated in the developmental theory, there has never been any hint of hostility against his parents in any conversation, and he and all observers recognize that they were kind and loving and devoted to him. Yet in Boulding's TAT stories, the parents of the young children were more threatening than helpful, and the parents of the young men more disapproving than helpful. There are, also, many references in his writings to the upwardly mobile generation having to throw off the shackles of their parents — the sons specifically having to reject the mothers — and he does recognize that while there was a bond of love between the generations in his family, there was a great gulf of understanding.

Gertrud Wyatt offers a slightly different mother–child interaction theory, focusing on the critical steps in language-learning when the child needs the trustworthy feedback from the mother. The complicated process of symbolizing and structuring reality begins with naming objects at the earliest speech levels and continues through the time of putting things in relation, usually occurring at five to seven years. All of this is accompanied by a kind of "running commentary" for which the child needs correctional feedback from others until he is able to formulate internal feedback; and this need increases when obstacles or difficulties arise. If this repetition or feedback is interrupted, by separation, illness, or some confusion in the usual schedule, the child may revert to stuttering. At the same time, anxious about his difficulties in communicating and also about his mother's withdrawal, he may turn his rage and frustration against his mother. She, in turn, may respond negatively to both the stuttering symptoms and the child's hostility, increasing the anxiety and the symptoms it produces.[7]

We have already described, in chapter 6, the difficult move that the Boulding family made back to Liverpool from Wallasey when Kenneth was a few months less than five. (This is, of course, the traditional oedipal period, when the male child has to work through sticky problems of attachment to the mother and animosity to the father, according to the psychoanalytic developmental schedule.) This move could be seen as a precipitating factor in the stuttering, under either Glauber's or Wyatt's theory.

Trees and open spaces were very important to both mother and child. Kenneth's mother records that when she used to take him in his pram they sometimes passed a place where there were a few trees. In his second spring (at about fourteen or fifteen months) he noticed and was delighted with the new leaves coming out, and one of the first words he learned to say was "tees" (EAB). Then, after having a tree of their very own, they had to move back to smoke and pavements and city lights blocking out the stars. Bessie was very much upset, as we know since Boulding recalls her at the time sitting in the middle of the living room and weeping, and also from the following excerpt from her autobiography:

> We, especially Kenneth and I, left Wallasey very reluctantly and settled down to bricks and mortar again, I 'settled' with a very bad grace, and was unhappy for three months or more, it didnt help me either when Kenneth came in from a walk one day and put his little head in my lap and said tearfully, "Mummie, lets go back to Wallasey, the streets are so dirty here, and the people *so* untidy." It made Dad unhappy too, and he gave me 'A Good Talking To'. After that, I pulled myself together, and stopped wishing for the moon.

The specific time delimitation, and the fact that Will had to intervene (there is no other instance of such drastic action in her whole story), both point to a very definite disturbance of Bessie's normal pattern. Her relationship with Kenneth had been very close and supportive; they had spent happy days together with the sand and the rocks and the waves, or visiting relatives, or exploring the quarry near their house, or enjoying their little lawn and garden. Now everything was changed, and Bessie was too miserable to be the reflector and encourager she no doubt had been. At the same time, her withdrawal could have intensified her son's fears about his ambivalent needs for growing independence and close relationship.

Two other small pieces of evidence may point to this event as related to the stuttering problem. I have already quoted from Kenneth's autobiography as a ten-year-old the sentence about his funny sayings having no limit when he lived in Wallasey. This could be a somewhat veiled reference to the great limitation that was imposed on his communication later. A few sentences further, referring to the move back to Liverpool, is the phrase, "all my educational prospects were rent asunder." What could so violently have upset his prospects, with schools all about him in Liverpool, unless there was some event that shattered his self-confidence? His own memory, as I mentioned, connected the stuttering with this time.

We still face the problem of those varying recollections of the time he began to stutter, "as early as he could talk," "as early as I can remember," or "when he started to school." Boulding himself cannot be expected to recall clearly the time he started to talk, nor can anyone else I could discover. His next-door friend Leslie, who insisted the stutter began then, could not, in fact, have remembered Kenneth before the move back to Seymour Street; his other friends, of course, were also small children at the time, and most had not yet met him. The only adult still reachable who might have noticed and remembered, his Aunt Flossie, begged off the question on the grounds that she had been living in Chard during his early childhood and saw him only on visits. The single fairly definite statement is the secondhand one from his mother that the stuttering began when he entered school.

Nor is this conclusive. It is not unusual, but in fact is frequent in case studies, that the parents of stutterers insist there was no earlier occurrence of the difficulty when children are brought for treatment but subsequent evidence shows this not to be the case. There are at least two plausible ways an earlier onset could be reconciled with this statement of his mother. He might have had an episode of stuttering which subsided (again a common pattern) when the immediate crisis passed, but was reactivated at the time of going to school, in distasteful surroundings, among dirty, untidy children, and far from his mother. (It is recognized by Wyatt and others that the separation anxiety at the first school attendance often intensifies stuttering.) Or his mother may have refused to admit to his symptoms (her never mentioning it in all her writing would suggest a defensive denial) until they were forcefully pointed out by a disapproving headmaster. At that point, to say it was the school that started her child's stuttering would also serve to remove any guilt from her about her responsibility for it.

We do not know with certainty the time interval between the return to Liverpool and Kenneth's starting to school. The school has been closed long since, and the building has been taken over by a factory. The city library in Liverpool has no records from it, though they do have a school inspector's report that in the year 1914–15 the children just beginning school at St. Simon's included seventeen four-year-olds, thirty five-year-olds, and thirteen six-year-olds. When Kenneth was ten, he wrote that he started school at five and a half. My best guess is that he went to school for the first time some five to eighteen months after he came back to Liverpool. He remembers this as a rather confused time of unhappiness, with the war, and his father's business decline, the move, and the school all mixed in together. If he really did start school at five, he must have blanked out two years of memories; if he started a year or more later, then the school-trauma would have to be a reactivation rather than a single incident with the moving-trauma.

Actually the identification of a specific time of the onset of his stuttering is not necessary; the general pattern is very clear, and both Glauber's and Wyatt's theories of separation anxiety could apply at several points. The very strong mother–son bond in Kenneth's childhood is undeniable. His mother, from what we know of her, fits, in almost every way, Glauber's description of the mother who has never broken free of her own mother. We remember her tears when she left home to go to work. It was Bessie who was the favorite of the three daughters, and the one with whom the grandparents finally came to live. Bessie, too, was always measuring herself against her mother's code of behavior and wishing she could be more like her; she described her mother consistently in terms of perfection. She also, like Glauber's model, lived her life in large measure through her son.

Wyatt has observed that when a stuttering child was ill and nursed by his mother, the stuttering disappeared. We know that Kenneth spent a good deal of time in his early school years ill at home, though as an adult he has proved very healthy, with certain exceptions. His mother records a full nine weeks of nursing him shut up in quarantine when he had scarlet fever at the age of eleven; she wrote verse to amuse him. His wife reports that in the early years of their marriage he always seemed to get sick at Christmas time, and require as much care as a new baby. At times of particular tension and strain — soon after his father's death, and after he had taken on for the first time the responsibility for owning and maintaining a big house — he subsided into an illness of several months' duration. The first of these, spent with a collapsed lung in the infirmary at Harvard, was concluded shortly after his mother had wound up her affairs in Liverpool and arrived in America to join him. The second, a bout with pneumonia in Ames, ended in a trip with Elise, away from the house and the furnace and the winter, south to the mountains and the springtime. One could surmise that there was some special need that was met by being sick.

Other fears and anxieties usually expressed by the children Wyatt studied, suffering from the separation problem that led to stuttering, were the fears of their own rage at their mothers, fears of disaster, of being devoured, of losing autonomy. The son here, if we can take the evidence of the imagery in his poetry (treated in chapter 7), experiences a good deal of anxiety about separation and its correlate, incorporation (with the substitute love-objects of wife and God). The evidence from his life, of the personal distance he keeps between himself and others, the idealization but depersonalization of love, could also be a defense against the double fear of getting too close and being rejected.

It is possible that the need for autonomy, the need for boundedness, and the need to control aggression that we have noted in earlier chapters are all related to this mother–child separation problem. If these attitudes do all hang together in this fashion, there might have been another, much earlier separation crisis (perhaps at time of weaning, perhaps the universal experience of the birth and individuation process), of whose unresolved depths the later would have been an echo. At the very earliest dawning of the infant's awareness of self, there is a feeling of boundlessness; self and mother and the world are all one. Limitations and autonomy come later, and at some cost in rage and frustration of desire. If this leap is not made thoroughly, both autonomy and rage can continue to be a problem, and the "oceanic feeling" of boundlessness can be both an asset and a threat.

If, again, there is another unfinished crisis at the moment of trying to make sense of the world, to symbolize and systematize it in language, then such systematization could continue to be a powerful need. We do not really require additional illustrations of this need in Boulding, but there comes to hand a lovely example in a poem he wrote shortly before entering Oxford, coming out of "a sort of vision I had in Liverpool Meeting." These lines, in repeating the image of chaos that needs ordering and understanding, remind us of the creative uses of personal tensions.

> There is a realm I long to enter in
> For there the streams of understanding rise
> There the worlds welter has its origin
> And answer to the eternal question lies

There is the satisfaction of desires
The rightful pattern of the tangled net
There with unwinking blaze the sacred fires
Burn in the only cup untarnished yet.

Yet this domain by walls of polished steel
And towering adamant is bound about:
It lies within the unending cosmic wheel.
I, in the vast confusion, stand without.
But there are windows high in rampart face
Which throw small shafts of light among the cloud,
Where eager souls of men can sometimes trace
A hint of meaning in the surrounding shroud.

I know that somewhere, in the deceiving mist,
A wicket gate is set against the wall:
Therefore would I not faithlessly desist
From seeking to find reason through the pall.
For sometimes, in my clearer hours, I see
The glory shining through its golden pale:
And though I reach it not, I keep the key,
And hope that vision caught can never fail.

It seems very possible, as we try to pull all the theories on stuttering together, that on a base of subtle deficiencies in motoric facility and an emotional subsoil which places extra strains on the developing ego, the difficult process of learning speech could be disrupted. If, in addition, the surrounding adults demand quick perfection, the problem is intensified and the handicap may become permanent.

The cultural aspects of stuttering should perhaps be touched on. There have been so many famous British stutterers that an early quantitative study of eminent men and women found the "prevalence of stammering among British persons of ability" to be double that in the ordinary population.[8] A recent *New York Times* article calls the stammer a mark of the English gentleman. Perhaps the emphasis on propriety, which Boulding has noted with distaste, contributed to his personal incidence as well as to the general British incidence of stuttering. In any case, the *Times* article notes, "There seems little doubt that Britain is uniquely rich in affliction and affectation both." [9]

For Kenneth it is clear that what was an affliction was turned, not into an affectation, for he has worked hard to control and tame it, but into what is almost an asset. The speech lessons he received when he was nine may have helped him a little to get over the immediate hurdle, but he is remembered as stuttering very badly all through his school and Oxford years by those who were near him. He did not, however, let it keep him from speaking out when he disagreed with an argument or felt indignant over what he saw as an injustice or objected to on principle. It did keep him from taking part in school plays (except by writing the prologues), but when he sang in Gilbert and Sullivan performances (or hymns or anything else), the stuttering did not interfere. At Oxford, he gradually moved more and more into the forefront in the oral mode, giving papers for the Wesleyan Society and the Labour Club, canvassing during elections, and campaigning with the young Methodists in the summer — all this in spite of a tremendously handicapping difficulty.

Perhaps, feeling challenged by words when they set themselves up as blocks to him, he determined to conquer them, both on paper and in the spoken voice, and make them work for him instead of controlling him. Words have always held an extreme fascination for him. When he was fifteen or sixteen, perhaps younger, he had a game of sitting on his bed and holding a dictionary in his lap, letting it fall open, and putting his finger at random on a word. Then he would have to write a verse about that word. A number of these were published in a little typewritten literary magazine that he helped to edit at school; my favorite is this one, on the word "interpose":

> You can interpose a penny
> In a choc-o-late machine,

You can interpose with bene-
Fit in quarrels over keen,
You can interpose a wedge,
Between the window and the ledge,
When the Wind of all the Elements is
        undisputed Queen,
You can interpose with pleasure
In any dirty deed,
You can interpose some leisure,
In your working — When you feed,
You can interpose some meat, perhaps,
Between two bits of bread,
You can interpose a swearword
When you're getting out of bed,
But there's one thing I suppose
That you mustn't interpose,
Into other people's business —
That's your nose!

In the end he achieved in a measure his conquest over words. Before he was through high school it was clear he could handle the written language magnificently; the spoken took a little longer. He had some additional training with a teacher in Edinburgh between 1934 and 1937, who taught him how to relax the affected muscles. Now, though the stutter is distressing, it is seldom paralyzing. It forms, instead, an effective rhetorical device — the expectant pause, after which bursts out the devasting wit. "It disarms people," he confesses. "I can get away with things I could never get away with otherwise." By now it is so much a part of his style and personality that he would not feel himself without it.

III

But we have gone considerably afield from the small boy at Hope Street School. Mr. Lewis, the headmaster, and Mr. Clark, one of his favorite teachers, recognized his outstanding intellect and tutored him and his friend Ron

Shaw for an hour after school, giving them extra work to take home on the weekends. Kenneth was entered now in the scholarship race. This was the only route for boys of high ability but limited means to stay in the academic world. The end of school for a lower- or middle-class boy normally came at about fourteen, unless his parents could pay the fees for a grammar school, or he could win a scholarship.

The masters' faith was not misplaced; in June of 1922, Kenneth won the Earl of Sefton Scholarship to Liverpool Collegiate School, and Ron won a similar scholarship. About 30 percent of the secondary school pupils in Liverpool at that time were educated on scholarships;[10] but only six to ten of the "named scholarships" were awarded in the city each year. These boys were allowed not only fees but also about £9 a term for books and uniforms. It is a particular tribute both to the teachers at Hope Street and these two boys that they placed so high in the exam. A social survey conducted in Liverpool in 1929 showed a clear negative relationship between the number of scholarships awarded and the degree of overcrowding and poverty in a neighborhood: "Comparatively few children from the very poorest homes are found occupying free places in secondary schools." In a table (*The Social Survey of Merseyside,* p. 169) giving statistics for 1929–30, the wards in which Kenneth's home and school were located have the highest percentage of overcrowding in the city and the lowest percentage of scholarships awarded — in that year, none. The same source observes (p. 187), "Once entry has been gained to a secondary school, the *exceptional* child of poor parents has as fair a chance as the *average* child of parents in a better position to make a good start in after life." In confirmation of this, Ernest Dundas, another scholarship winner who became a good friend of Kenneth's at Liverpool Collegiate, describes what it was like:

> You had to rise socially, get better off generally; other places were having hunger marches; you saw what pov-

erty and unemployment could do. . . . You knew if you got to school and did all they told you, put yourself in their hands, you would emerge higher than you would have otherwise. I didn't feel oppressed or slave-driven; we took every night until Saturday doing homework — we had school Saturday morning — then Sunday there was extra heavy homework for Monday. There was just the expectation that you did this amount of work. The scholarship form had special standards of requirement all the way to the 6th form; you went on mercilessly to the end.

Before we let Kenneth go on mercilessly to the end, we should mention the other side of his life. His mother's account, his diary, and his memories give an impression of a rich child-life in his elementary school years: games on the street, golden summers at Grandma Rowe's in Chard with the freedom of fields and meadows, family picnics (it was tea, of course, that they packed in their basket) and trips to the country, endless sand-castle creations, sketching and painting, and many imaginative constructions with his Meccano set or stone building bricks in the attic room. A diary entry when he was eight reads, "I made a transporter bridge today with my meccano and it was such a big one I made the towers and dad made the rest but it only went very slowly and" (in letters twice as big) "was my own idea." Sometimes he and Leslie would hang up sheets and make caves and rooms of them, and once they were playing in the attic, Leslie remembers, when part of the ceiling fell in: "We sat in the middle of the rubble, like two great puddings. Mrs. Boulding heard the crash and came up the stairs like an arrow!" Outdoors, tops and hoops succeeded each other on regular dates; but there was some room for originality. They played Red Indians and burglars, and the game both Kenneth and his cousin Eddy remember best was when the bigger boys sat on the top of the front steps and made the little boys "Do Charlie" — that is, imitate Charlie Chaplin. (Eddy Wells was the son of Kenneth's mother's sister, and about Kenneth's age. He lived near London but spent some holidays visiting in Liverpool.) Kenneth and his gang apparently had their turn at evading the police, the year they formed the caroling club under Kenneth's leadership. The police were frowning then on small boys singing in people's lobbies; so the boys had to set a watchman when they went out to spread Christmas cheer.

Kenneth liked *The Swiss Family Robinson* and *Alice in Wonderland* and read them over and over. (Once at Oxford he went into a bookstore intending to get some economics texts he needed and came out instead with another copy of *Alice*.) He was curious about many things: the inside of a typewriter ("I wish I had a screwdriver"), smoke coming from a timber yard ("It was only two men with a wash boiler"), his father making water boil without heat when he mixed up whitewash. He recalls one summer when he and Leslie spent a great deal of time trying to make flypaper by smearing various sticky substances on paper. "Obviously we both had an experimental mind." He found the museum a fascinating place, particularly the model of the city of Liverpool in the 1600s, and the aquarium with the live fish. Leslie may even have helped Kenneth refine his scientific method by questioning his early dogmatism. His mother in Kenneth's eyes was the ultimate in people, and all that seemed necessary to him to give a statement truth was that she had said so. Leslie, however, would not accept this authority, and made Kenneth find other proofs for his statements as they thrashed out their seven- and eight-year-old's arguments.

After 1920, when Grandma and Grandpa Rowe came to Liverpool, there were no more summer holidays in Chard. But Will had a good friend at Brunswick Chapel whose brother lived up in Cumberland, in the north country; and from time to time the family would go up there for holidays with the Wilsons, and sometimes the Wilsons would come to Liverpool and stay with the Bouldings for a city holiday. Kenneth enjoyed bicycling and going to the seashore with effervescent, simple and genuine Dora, and remembers her father, a shoemaker, as an original source of folk wisdom. Dora for her part was always convinced Kenneth would be a great man someday: "You could tell he was brainy and would make out into something." But she added, "He was always terribly untidy — and would be yet, I should think; he was an awful case, you know!" And she laughed merrily.

In the years from twelve to eighteen, while Kenneth was at Liverpool Collegiate, he made a number of good friends, boys who shared with him a state of relative poverty and a high intellectual ability. There was Ron, and Ernest, and Francis Hogan, the Irish boy, who brought a new perspective to Kenneth's understanding of history. A third "named scholarship" winner, at the same time as Kenneth and Ron, was Bernard Ash, who also became one of his gang, though he and Kenneth were continually at odds. Ernest reports, "If Bernard and Kenneth agreed, that was lovely; there was nearly always an argument between them." Each, remembering those days, considers the other as having been very opinionated. Both stuttered; neither had sibling rivalry at home (gentle Ernest remarks, "The rest of us [coming from larger families] would have learned not to be so assertive!"), and neither would let the other get away with anything outrageous. Both were interested in social welfare, and together they organized a series of trips to various factories around the city. The group itself made a cosmopolitan potpourri, Scotch, Welsh, Irish, Jewish, and English.

The greatest joy of all these boys, in addition to arguing and having long talks about philosophical questions, was taking long rambles about the countryside. They would choose their direction, take a tram to the end of the line or a ferry across the Mersey, and start out on the narrow roads between hedged fields or along the grassy footpaths from village to village that England so generously provides. Kenneth, however, had a preference for trespassing "because the scenery was so nice that way."

Kenneth often led the way; he had always loved maps, and his mother in one flush moment bought him a whole set of ordnance survey maps of England, so he was well equipped for any jaunt. Several summers, the boys spent a week or two at a kind of hostel in Wales, camping, cooking outdoors, swimming, and climbing the high ridge that overlooked the River Dee. Sometimes they took bicycles for their outings. Bernard remembers Kenneth as a "very perilous" cyclist as well as driver:

> He was always doing peculiar things with bicycles; one afternoon he and I converged and collided in the midst of the road. He quite happily rode home on his bent wheel, going "Haw, haw!" every time it went around. Once he rode right into the back of a stationary car — they both glared at each other — neither said a word and they both went off. And once, with his father's old two-cylinder Rover, he was driving along and talking. He made a vast gesture to illustrate his remarks, and went into the ditch. He climbed out and said, "Haw, haw, haw!"

Kenneth's early friendships, and his love for hiking and bicycling, continued after the boys were separated. He arranged two summer bicycle-hosteling jaunts in Germany while he was at Oxford, and even after he was teaching at Edinburgh gathered some of his Liverpool gang to ramble with him in Scotland and Ireland.

I V

But the bulk of their time and their energy for those six high school years was spent in the towering, black, castle-like structure on Shaw Street that held their lives and their futures.

Kenneth had his points of issue with the school authorities, which are remembered better by his friends than by him. He was always careless of his clothes; one friend reports that he lost so many school caps twirling them on his finger on the way home that his mother finally sewed a strap on his cap to hold it around his neck. And when he was smaller, he and Leslie would go out to play together; Leslie would come home immaculate, but Kenneth's socks would be down around his ankles and he would be covered with dirt from head to foot. One of his Aunt Flossie's most vivid memories of his childhood is of the day she gave him a new cream-colored coat, and he immediately went and hugged a lamp post, getting the coat smeared all down the front. But it must have been principle rather than carelessness that kept him from wearing a tie to school. The tie and blazer were part of the school uniform; all the boys wore them as a matter of course; but Kenneth refused. It is reported that he was even told he would be made a prefect if he would wear a coat and tie; but apparently he won that battle, for he was made a prefect (even earlier in his school career than was usual) and also sang in the choir, still without a tie.

This was perhaps a minor skirmish in his personal battle for autonomy against conformity. The major battlefront was the classics master and vice-principal, W. P. Prideaux. (Boulding remembers that, as "V.–P.," Prideaux was always called "the viper.") He was accustomed to select the boys with high ability and draw them into his field, and he wielded great power in the school. "Most of us spent our life in awe of him," Ernest reports; "Kenneth broke free of him. . . . You had to be implicitly obedient to Prideaux, if he took you." When Kenneth went into the sixth form, at the age of fifteen, he had to decide between the classics and the sciences. He went into the science section. The English master called on Mr. and Mrs. Boulding to try to get them to persuade Kenneth to change to languages, saying he would be wasted on chemistry; and a little later, one of the mathematics masters called on them, saying they should keep him in his math and science form, as Kenneth would be wasted as a classical scholar. "I cant remember that we did anything about it," says his mother, "except to let him use his own mind" (EAB).

His own mind took him into science, though he had abilities in both fields, and Prideaux was probably more right than Kenneth admitted at the time. It was only after he was out from under this influence that he could make the decision for the literary side and have it be his own.

Liverpool Collegiate was the second largest school in the north of England, of excellent academic standing, and Kenneth was placed in the top scholastic level of the three "tracks" into which the school divided its pupils. With this kind of competition, of fifteen school reports which gave rankings, Kenneth was first or second in his class eleven times. In the subjects he took all six years, his average grade was highest in chemistry (98 percent), then literature, essay, physics, geometry, and algebra (80 percent). The first time he passed the Higher School Certificate he got distinction in math, and passed in literature, physics, and chemistry; a year later he took the exam in math, physics, and chemistry, and got distinction in all three. In the years 1927–29, only about one in nine secondary school pupils in Liverpool gained the Higher School Certificate, and more than half left school without gaining either this or the lower-level School Certificate.

After failing to win a scholarship at Cambridge in 1927, though he won one for Liverpool University, Kenneth stayed on at Liverpool Collegiate another year and succeeded, in 1928, in winning a science scholarship to Oxford. It was as a student in chemistry that he went up to New College, Oxford, in the fall. There were five boys that year at Liverpool Collegiate (a school of about 800 students) who won scholarships to Oxford or Cambridge, the largest number they had ever had. All four of Kenneth's friends succeeded in this high ambition, though not all the same year; Ron, Ernest, and Francis went to Cambridge, Kenneth and Bernard to Oxford. "Once he got this scholarship — his name in the paper and all," re-

Fig. 11. Liverpool Collegiate School

Fig. 12. The five scholarship winners in 1928: Kenneth Boulding, *third from left (picture on the wall of the vice-principal's
office)*

calls Kenneth's half-cousin, Robert Hendrie, "if his mother could have climbed to the top of the Liver Building (that's the highest building in Liverpool) and told it to everybody, she would — she was *that* proud!"

Luck, timing, hard work, and outstanding ability all formed part of the cluster of causes that brought these five young men from unlikely origins to the halls of higher learning, the traditional route to upper-level professions in Britain. The luck had come in the combination of parental encouragement and good teachers to channel and direct energies toward stimulating the interests, and motivating the work that led in this direction. The timing, in the short run, was against them. Kenneth and his friends belonged to the ten-year cohort of the population that formed, from their birth until they were through college, the highest percentage of the total United Kingdom population.[11] That meant that at every level — entering school, trying for scholarships, being ranked against other class members, winning awards, and finally hunting for jobs — there were more people at that same age-level in competition with them for the same goals than there were at any other age-level. There was no other cohort that sustained, as this one did, its highest-percentage rank through three censuses; it was an anomaly, I suppose, caused by the decimation of the war.

But in the long run, in the course of English history, they arrived at a very fortunate moment. They were actually the first generation which had a real chance to attain a university education in spite of adverse financial conditions.

Traditionally, it was not expected that working-class children should go beyond elementary school, and until the middle of the nineteenth century, not even that. It was only in 1880 (the year Kenneth's mother was born) that elementary education was made universally compulsory in Great Britain, and the facts did not immediately follow the law, since tuition was not free even in govern-

ment schools until 1918. In 1870, only 40 percent of all
ten-year-olds were receiving full-time education; by 1902,
100 percent of the ten-year-olds were in school, with the
help of government schools supplementing the previous
haphazard collection of church schools, and some provision for remission of fees for the poor; but even then, only
9 percent of the fourteen-year-olds were in school.[12] This
meant that education beyond grade school was still almost
nonexistent for any but children of the professional and
upper classes. For the others, there might be a couple of
years of trade school, and then apprenticeship, for a few
shillings a week, from the age of fourteen on — the vocational decision made, sometimes for a lifetime, in a casual
few days according to parental preference and what was
open at the moment.

It was only as the church and government schools
gradually became more or less standardized by means of
common examinations, and particularly as more public
funds were channeled into city and state scholarships
awarded in terms of these examinations, that opportunities began to open up for children of the underprivileged.
After 1902, a number of state secondary schools were established, and a certain number of places were reserved in
the privately operated secondary schools for children
whose fees were paid by the local education authority. Yet
even around 1920, "Secondary education . . . was still restricted to some 10 percent of the total school population
. . . [and] competition for . . . [free places in secondary
schools] was becoming progressively fiercer."[13] Substantial fees are still the rule in Britain's independent and di-
rect-grant secondary schools, but they have accepted (in
return for government assistance) a higher and higher
proportion of scholarship students, and, by 1945, the government had established totally free schooling in all the
schools maintained by local or state authority.

At the major universities prior to 1920, there had
been a few scholarships available through foundation

funds, but the system was highly restricted. It was only after the introduction of state scholarships in 1920, which were more generous in amount, that there began to be realistic opportunity for such an education for the boy who was poor. Even these were awarded only on the basis of rigorous examination, and carried tremendous prestige value.

For girls, the generation of opportunity had not yet come even in the 1920s. In 1895, girls numbered less than a quarter of the total number of pupils in endowed secondary schools. There were always fewer girls' schools than boys', and almost no secondary schools were coeducational until the 1960s. Ron Shaw had an older sister who had to fight her family's opposition to continue in school beyond the age of fifteen; she finally went to the University of Liverpool but could not have been admitted to a degree program at Cambridge, Ron's university, until 1948; Oxford began granting degrees to women only in 1920.

For Will and Bessie, therefore, whatever their abilities, it was practically impossible to do anything but enter a trade and settle, even if uncomfortably, into the upper working class. For Kenneth, the tight class system had begun to crack enough to let him squeeze through. After the small fees for elementary school, he never required support from his parents for his schooling. He was able to win, by passing examinations, enough to take care of his school expenses at a time when his father's financial state was becoming more and more precarious. He got very good at winning scholarships. There even came a time when he was to pay some of his family's expenses out of his scholarship money.

As a matter of fact, the stream of British life to which Kenneth's family belonged was almost a tide. The chinks in the class system had not come from the top. The whole movement of the Liberal and Labour parties — the agitation for universal education, the fight for better working conditions, for adult schools, and recreational opportunities for the common people — had been fed in large measure by the ferment stirred up by the nonconformist churches. These outlandish sects which began teaching servants and laborers that they had dignity and worth, and could even get in touch with the love and will of God, and which went so far as to train and use simple artisans, such as Kenneth's father and grandfather, to teach and help other people, were setting in motion forces that eventually cracked the system of privileged oppression. John and Charles Wesley taught that

> we are not mere objects of divine generosity, poor nothings till boundless grace elects some of us to sanctity and salvation. We are objects of divine *Love* and are therefore in our humanity worthy of it. . . . The member of a class was forced to become an individual. . . . So the conventional inertia, the conditioning assumptions, cracked under pressure of a supernatural and personal revelation. . . . [This message] opened a tremendous destiny upon the drab street. . . . It hammered the cake of custom in pieces. . . .[14]

Perhaps it is not surprising that Boulding lays so much stress on the power of the prophet and nonconformist to shake up society. Out of a generation of nonconformist working people, given a sense of self-confidence and hope for the future, arose a next generation of novelists, poets, members of Parliament, bishops, schoolmasters, industrialists, and government consultants. The wave for educational equalization has since rolled on so far as almost to erase any distinctions between abilities, or between children headed for higher schooling and those who are not. But the crest of the wave, where it has the most force, is just where it is breaking; and it was at that point, where education was just beginning to open up and let new talents and abilities through, that Kenneth's generation came along.

11

Into the World:
The Hurdle Race

The evolutionary process speeds up under adversity.

— KEB, Class lecture, 1965

I

The first year at Oxford was a cold and utterly miserable
one for Kenneth. Having had a status, not of popularity
but of recognized brilliance, at Liverpool Collegiate, and
a warm circle of good friends and loving family, he now
had to make his way quite alone. His grandmother had
died the year before, and Aunt Ada had sailed off for Australia, breaking the close family ties that had held since
childhood. In August of that year, his grandfather had
been injured by a car and died soon after; so that even at
home his foundations were shaken. And now he was
among men whose social expectations and very language
were quite foreign to what he had known, and many of
whom he felt were his intellectual equals or superiors.

The coldness was literal as well as figurative. New
College, through which he had his science scholarship,
was founded in 1379, and the massive stone building
where he lived probably dated from the fifteenth century.
He had a little room on the stairway just above the dining

hall; it was theoretically heated by a gas fireplace, but somehow the gas seemed to run out before it got to him. Kenneth regularly retreated to the nearby room of another student, which apparently was a little closer to the source of heat. What was probably his first published piece outside of his high school magazine was a poem written out of his physical distress and called "Owed to a Gas Fire." When he sent his mother news of its acceptance by the Oxford magazine, *The Cherwell,* he gloated, "I am an Author!" The accompanying "Portrait of Me as an Author" had a bald pate labeled "noble brow," a beard "a la Shaw," and a fat stomach "a la Chesterton."

The lonely student in the adjoining room was a Londoner ("almost a cockney") named Fred Watts. He and Kenneth had very little in common except good minds, a sense of humor, and their joint striving toward high ambitions from humble beginnings; but they became very good friends and, for the two following years, were roommates, adding to their circle of friends a number of other scholarship students. Kenneth seemed to have a knack for gathering variegated friends about him, as he had in secondary school, and it was the conversations with these men of widely diverse backgrounds (always excepting the upper-class level, with whom he had no informal communication) which he considers the major element of his education at Oxford. They used to study hard until about ten-thirty, then have a cup of coffee in somebody's room, and talk far into the night.

He and Watts were both trying to make their money stretch as far as possible, so three days a week they had a big tea and skipped dinner, eating Post Toasties in their room. His scholarship from Oxford, the "maximum emolument," amounted to £100. The state scholarship which supplemented it, apparently determined by financial need (Kenneth wrote in 1930 about the state scholarship "showing fainting fits whenever I get any more money"), was £135 a year for three years. These together did not quite come up to the £250 he estimated he needed for a year, so he cut corners where he could and made extra money by tutoring or by occasional prizes for essays or poetry whenever he was able. There was no opportunity or expectation for him to earn money in the summers; Oxford students are assigned major readings for the "long vacations" and he spent most of his summers, except for brief holidays, in the Picton Library.

It was here at Oxford, and especially his first year, that there was impressed on him so strongly that he never lost his hurt and indignation about it, a deep sense of the injustice of class discrimination. Purely on the basis of his background and origin, he felt himself shut out. In actual fact, just under 50 percent of all the students at Oxford that year were getting some kind of scholarship help, and, by the time he left, the proportion was just over 50 percent,[1] so he had company in his misery, but the lines between the upper and lower levels were evidently very clearly drawn. There may also have been a higher proportion of rich young men at New College than at some of the others, since its founder, William of Wykeham, had also founded a secondary school at Winchester, many of whose graduates continued on to New College.

Kenneth had never thought much of clothes or manners, though his mother made a few futile efforts to bring him around on these matters; here at Oxford, they were dreadfully important. And his speech, of course, had always given him problems, but here they were doubled; on top of his stuttering, he had to try to conquer his Liverpool accent and put on the Oxford accent that belonged to the cultured Englishman. Invited to dinner at the warden's, he had to struggle simultaneously with the right clothes (according to Fred Watts, a dinner jacket was de rigueur, but Boulding thinks he never had one), the right pieces of silverware, the right things to say, and the right accent to say them in. It was almost hopeless; and though he made light of these problems in his letters home and to

his Aunt Ada, he did admit to feeling homesick. "I suppose it is because I have not really fitted in with my
surroundings" — but the old spirit rises again — "and
somehow, I hope I never do. The studied inanities of the
upper classes wont do for me."

He was more miserable than they probably guessed.
He spent his days in the chemistry laboratory and at
lectures — sometimes cut a lecture if the day was fine in
order to recoup his spirits with a bicycle ride on the country roads — and wrestled with all of this and with where
he was really headed. This was the period when he was
writing, "under considerable emotional tension," the
poem "The Sands of Egypt," for which he hoped to win
the Newdigate Prize (this poem is discussed in chapter 7).
He kept to himself the reasons for his tension about it; he
was feeling torn between the science career he had chosen
and the literary career he knew he had talent for. If he
could win the poetry prize, it would be a kind of proof
that he should move in the direction of the humanities,
which was the way he kept feeling more and more that
he wanted to go.

When the results came out on the first of June, he
was devastated. A woman had gotten the prize. He dug his
bike out of hock at the repair shop, and rode and rode all
day, buying some cheese to keep him going, and a cycling
cape, as it "came on to rain. . . . And it did rain. It positively DID rain. I thoroughly enjoyed it, and battled with
the Elements for twenty good miles (Mostly uphill), and
got merrier and merrier as I went along, I got back to Oxford in a positively Jubilant mood and Had a Long Hot
Bath and Sang Lustily in it. and feel quite happy about
things . . . anyway, Those Women can Look Out next
year!"

His battle with the elements no doubt helped change
his mood; but the main thing that happened in the course
of the ride was that he finally decided, prize or no prize,
to shift his course from science to "modern greats" — the

School of Politics, Philosophy, and Economics. He would break out of what Fred Watts called the squirrel-cage of the chemistry lab into the widening horizons of thought and society. "Once there," says Fred, "he went off like a bomb — with absolutely no background at all in politics, philosophy, or economics, within the two years, he got his first class — it was a terrific act."

It was an achievement just to make the change. Comments about it from his friends who knew the situation range from "fantastic," "took great courage," to "possible but not easy" (accompanied by naming several Nobel prize-winners who had done a similar thing). Kenneth was somewhat in fear and trembling over it, since his scholarship was in science, and he had no idea whether it would be continued if he changed. He also did not know whether he could make a living in the new field. He wrote a letter to the warden asking him these questions and explaining his position; it must have been something of a masterpiece because the warden, he heard, was "quite impressed." The college agreed to change his scholarship, and he started jubilantly on his new course of study.

This was clearly a turning point for Kenneth, from constriction to freedom, and he felt it as such. A week later, as the college authorities seemed to be favorable, he wrote to his mother, "I feel like a dicky-bird let out of a cage." And a year later, a more sober resume in connection with a scholarship application read as follows:

> I have never had a single occasion to regret that choice; I found myself at home immediately in my new course and instead of a burden the more scholastic side of my life has become a joy, if not always a pleasure . . . it has meant more to me in the widening of mental horizons and a better understanding of the world in which we live than anything I have ever done . . . due . . . as much to conversation and intercourse with a circle of good friends as to purely academic studies . . . the reaction of so many minds so different in outlook from my own has, I think, helped me as much as anything.

One of his stories for the TAT, of a young man climbing out of the window of a dark room, making up his mind to get out and break free of an intolerable situation, could almost be a symbolic representation of this experience.

In the few days following this decision, Kenneth's high spirits broke out quite tangibly, judging from his letters. He and Watts one day piled up loose chairs and tables in another friend's room while he was out, and built a dummy of "piled-up clothes baskets with gowns draped about." Some nights later, they climbed the bell tower at eleven o'clock to see Oxford by moonlight, coming down and dancing through the moonbeams in the cloisters afterwards. "And then we found that the porter had locked us in the cloisters so we had to yell and shout and make a dreadful din before he heard us and let us out Most amusing." There were other pranks recorded in the following two college years, but none in his letters before this time.

The following fall, he and Watts took a double suite of rooms on the corner of the Garden Quad, directly overlooking the delightful green lawns and central mound of the New College gardens, which are thickly bordered with roses and dahlias and blooming trees and bounded by the ancient city wall of Oxford. They had many discussions but, Fred insists, no arguments (arguments, on the contrary, were what he had with Bernard Ash, who arrived at Oxford that year). Kenneth did contribute to strained relations for a time when, holding a cup of tea in one of Watts's treasured cups, he opened his hand for a gesture to accompany some statement, and the cup and saucer shattered on the hearth.

Kenneth usually set the level of the conversation on high generalities, politics or the historical development of a country, international problems and relationships, or the many meanings of a word. When he talked, it was as if to hear his ideas bounce back, to refine and shape his thinking, rather than really to get an answer, though sometimes he listened as another was developing a thought. He never tried to be brilliant in these intimate

circles; it was more a searching for the truth. "His motivation," according to Fred, "was not money, power, vanity,
or the admiration of women — rather the fascination of
the subject itself plus a sense of social responsibility. He
never thought deliberately to shape his career; having got
into PPE and discovering economics, he knew that this
was his subject and that he was going to be good at it." By
and large, though they might have started low, their positions were those of respectable conformists; at least this is
Fred's view. "I wasn't going to pull down society because
of our poor opportunities, but assist it in its evolution."

During these years Kenneth went rambling with
many friends, sometimes one, sometimes another, sometimes alone. He and Watts shared a bike tour of Germany
(which cost each of them a total of about £7) and an ex-
pense-paid trip to Geneva for the League of Nations Association (they quickly forsook the boring meetings of the
conference for the delights of bathing in the cold water of
the lake, walking about the town, and climbing a peak
early one morning to see the sun rise over Mont Blanc).
Explorations in music came as a happy surprise under the
tutelage of a gentle, cynical philosopher-friend. The summer after he discovered Bach and Beethoven, Kenneth's
family bought a gramophone, and he came out with this
gem in a letter to Aunt Ada in 1930: "I bought a new
gramophone record today: Fugue in D major, by Bach,
played on the organ of Salisbury Cathedral. Martha [the
girl who came in to help around the house] doesn't like
it: thinks it is too highbrow but I like it for it aint too
high for my brow — all together now — no it aint too
highbrow (too highbrow) for me"; this is followed by an
asinine jingle in the same vein, full of composer name-
dropping. And mixed in with Marx and Kant and Keynes
in his reading were Bertrand Russell's *Marriage and Morals,* now and again an H. G. Wells novel, Thackeray, Jane
Austen, a book of detective stories that he bought by accident, like *Alice,* and the masterpiece of historical spoofs,
1066 and All That.

Fig. 13. Kenneth in the Cloisters, New College, Oxford (*photo from Michigan Historical Collections*)

Fig. 14. Garden Quad, New College (Kenneth's room is upper left corner)

He found, as we have noted, a number of other outside interests — the Labour Club, the League of Nations Association, the Friends Meeting, and the warm fellowship of the Wesleyan students. One of the ministers who led the Methodist student group, who must by now be at least in his eighties and has not seen Kenneth since his Oxford days, still remembers him well. The Reverend Mr. Bodgener writes,

> Like most intellectuals, he loved an argument . . . he seemed to have an experience and awareness of life in advance of the general run of students. . . . He seemed free of the usual inhibitions. . . . "Openness" was an obvious characteristic, and strength of personal character as well as intellectual ability and strong social sympathies remain quite vivid impressions on my mind.

There were many hours of solid study withal, when the group of friends let each other alone, for they all knew they had to pick up extra knowledge, a breadth of viewpoint, that would have come more naturally with a more fortunate background.

In 1931, of the 130 students who qualified in politics, philosophy, and economics in all the colleges at Oxford, ten got first-class honors, and the best "first" in economics went to Kenneth. Bernard Ash (who might be biased, since he got a first in modern greats the following year) emphasized to me that to get a first in that school in Oxford it is not sufficient to have learned the material or done research. "They demand original thinking — they winkle out intellectual weaknesses." (When I looked mystified, he explained that when you eat winkles, you have to tease the meat out of the shell with a pin.)

Kenneth had also won the Webb-Medley Scholarship in Economics, which could be renewed for another year of study, so he elected to stay on for graduate work. That was sensible, for Fred Watts was looking all that year for work, and finally found a teaching post eighteen months after he graduated. But the sad thing about Kenneth's graduation was that the day before he was to receive his B.A., his mother was scurrying around getting ready to go to Oxford and slipped on the stairs and broke her ankle, so his father had to come alone for the ceremony. She was heartbroken at missing the great day she had looked forward to so long, even though Kenneth wrote her a description, with sketches, and made light of all the ceremonial fuss. In January of that year, he sent her an excited wire to say he had had an economics article accepted for publication; and he spent the £4 he was paid for it to buy new chair covers for her. In the spring of 1932, he was granted a Commonwealth Fellowship for study in the United States, which was something like a Rhodes Scholarship in reverse. It was a magnificent sum for two years' study ($3,000 per year), plus travel allowances, clothes allowance, and an interview with the Prince of Wales. (Kenneth regarded the last as a drawback, but his Aunt Ada was quite overwhelmed by the thought.) All of these honors his mother cherished, treasuring the many notes and postcards of congratulation that poured in.

Pride, joy, excitement, and dread of his leaving for such a long time crowded each other in his mother's feelings as she helped him buy new clothes for the journey and prepare to go off to America. It had been decided he would study economics at the University of Chicago, and "Chicago" in those days, if one's impressions were gained only from American movies and lurid news stories, conjured up images of gangsters shooting it out in the streets. Kenneth, I would guess, was buoyed up by a sense of guidance and perhaps destiny about his American dream. Dora Wilson, who was visiting in Liverpool that summer, remembers going to Friends Meeting twice with Kenneth during that time, and has been able to recall that he spoke each time in meeting on the theme of divine obedience. The first was based on Acts 26:19, "Wherefore, O King Agrippa, I was not disobedient to the heavenly vision"; and on the second occasion he quoted the verse of a hymn,

> To serve the present age,
> My calling to fulfil:
> O may it all my powers engage
> To do my master's will.

(Only a dear impressionable friend, steeped in the Bible herself and recalling the occasion whenever she reread the verse or sang the hymn, could have kept these details in memory for almost forty years!)

When the day came for him to sail, some fifteen or twenty loving friends and relatives were at the dock to see him off; at the last minute, his father rushed back to Woolworth's to buy each of them a yellow duster to wave as the ship pulled out. And with all the excitement, Kenneth left for America without his new hat!

II

Chicago was pure joy, "Jam with Nuts on it," as Kenneth wrote to a friend. His fellowship gave him plenty of money; the pressure of school work weighed on him very lightly, he found congenial men to argue with, both American and English ("There are a large number of Bright Young Men in the graduate school. We meet every week in a seminar to rend Mr. Keynes"), and, for the first time in his life, he discovered girls. "My time is divided up between eating enormous quantities of food, having violent arguments, economic and theological, going to innumerable parties given by innumerable charming young ladies, and generally enjoying myself according to the best Oxford standards." As for the rest of Chicago, there were parks, the lake, "whole counties full of slovenly slums, and the Loop — i.e. the centre of Chicago — which is stiff with skyscrapers, musea, Planetaria, Aquaria, Art Galleria, and so forth. It also contains, presumably, Gangsters, etc.

though these are so coy and retiring that nobody ever sees them and one suspects that they are invented by the papers to increase the circulation." Its main drawbacks were the climate ("just abominable"), the lack of places to walk ("there are two walks here: one to Washington Park and the other to Jackson Park: it is so nice to have such variety: there might, after all, be only one walk"), and the flatness ("Chicago is situated in the middle of a perfectly flat plain that stretches from the North to the South Poles in one direction and from the Alleggenys Allegennys Damn the word to the Rockies Good in the other").

The educational system he found less than inspiring, a series of classes, little tests, then forgetting all you have learned and going on to the next. To Fred Watts he wrote, "Many more quarters of the stuff that passes for education (Haw Haw) in this place would reduce my mental capacities to nil." Robert Shone, on the other hand, another Commonwealth Fellow from Liverpool, whose background was in engineering at Liverpool University, made good use of the courses and faculty and took an M.A. in economics in the years at Chicago. Kenneth, who worked for a while with some thought of a Ph.D., gave it up as too confining a program, and, a few years later, attained his M.A. from Oxford by sending in the required fee.

Kenneth and Shone became roommates and moved into International House for the second term. This was arranged for coed living (in separate wings) and it formed the center of many social activities. In the summer of 1933, the two of them teamed up with Bob Hall, an American who owned an old Buick, equipped themselves with a tent and camp cots, and set off for a grand tour of the West. As they drove they kept a journal (they started out taking turns at the writing, but Kenneth ended up writing most of it, up to the point where he had to leave the others), and they sent off quantities of postcards from every picturesque spot. Kenneth completely lost his heart to the West, and wrote reams of purple prose about it, interspersed with his usual hilarious quirks: "Madison . . . has a Capitol, very much like the one at Washington, which apparently gave birth to an enormous number of kittens at one stage in its career"; "North of Baribug (Bariboo, Bugaboo) there is a curious country most of which has been removed, leaving chunks of it standing straight up out of the plain"; "I have made a Great Discovery about prairie. Prairie, in fact, is the American equivalent of Moorland" — but Bob insisted it was not prairie, only land, so from then on Kenneth wrote "Prair?e," explaining this was pronounced "Quairie." He was reported by Shone to have a "magnificent and unflagging desire to do everything memorable."

In the midst of all this gaiety and freedom, in August, while the three were at the Grand Canyon, a cablegram reached Kenneth that his father had died. Even in her very condensed message, his mother had included "Don't fret; best love." They had known since 1930 that Will had diabetes; he had been controlling it with diet, but from time to time got so tired of boiled cabbage and "sawdust biscuits" that he would go to a restaurant and buy himself a proper meal. He was getting more and more tired, and probably more and more worried about his financial state. The week he died, he had been on a business trip and it was extremely hot; he collapsed at a friend's house, was taken to the hospital but went into a coma and died at just about the moment that Bessie, rushing down to Worcester by train, could arrive.

As soon as he got the word, Kenneth started for home. He took a train to Chicago, then, hoping to save time, a plane from there; but instrumental navigation was not highly developed in 1933, and the plane was forced down by bad weather in Columbus. The ensuing mixup missed him the fast ship he had hoped to get, and he had to wait three days in New York before getting another, so it was almost three weeks after his father's death before he arrived home. Of course friends and relatives had rallied round his mother, and providentially Aunt Ada had been in Liverpool on her only visit during her stay in Australia; but it was a bleak prospect that Kenneth and his mother had to face. Kenneth had had word of financial difficulties in the spring, and had turned over all his Liverpool bank account to his father and sent him $150 from his Commonwealth money; but now they learned Will's liabilities amounted to about one and a half times his assets. "Never mind, mother," he comforted her, "I'm as good as an investment" (EAB). Their house and furniture had to be sold (though they kept a few sentimental pieces like the glass cupboard that had belonged to Bessie's mother and the lamp stand the church had given to Will after thirty-two years' service as Sunday school teacher and superintendent). When all was settled up, the trade creditors were paid 14s. on the pound. Bessie moved in with a relative to try to gather herself together, and Kenneth, in less than a month, sailed for America again. He was depressed, but could muster enough good spirits to write Dora Wilson, who had worried about his leaving his hat behind the year before (in Cumberland dialect), "I 'av me 'at this time!"

He spent that fall at Harvard, working with Schumpeter, but wrote no glowing notes about Boston or Cambridge, and about the first of December, he was hospitalized with a leak in one lung. His mother arrived in Boston just before Christmas, armed with his cautions, "Be sure you don't mix up a $1 bill with a five or a twenty, and be *very careful* in the traffic!" — and a week or so later Kenneth was well enough to go with her back to Chicago. There they found a small apartment, and Kenneth picked up some of his activities with his old friends again, for the one remaining semester of his Commonwealth Fellowship.

He was working harder, and a little less available for festivities now that his mother was with him, but he found time to write and act in a skit put on by the British group at International House at the end of the semester. The cast called for a philanderer (played by Kenneth) and two women; but there were not two British women there, so the tall, slender American social secretary of the house took the other part. Somehow, Lucinda looked so lovely in the Elizabethan costume that Kenneth suddenly realized he was smitten, and almost immediately — about a week before he was to leave for England — proposed to her. He had known her, of course, for almost two years, but did not know until he talked to her of marriage that she was already engaged to someone else.

Females, except for his mother and aunts, had played no great part in Kenneth's life up to that time. Until he came to Chicago he had never met a girl he was romantically attracted to, though he had some good friends through family connections and had taken them out from time to time. Girls scarcely existed for him, as every school he went to in England was for boys only. (In his elementary school there was a girls' section, but they were taught in separate rooms and had separate playtimes in the courtyard.) In his very young days in the summers in Chard he had a girl playmate; there was a sister of his uncle's who was around a good deal when he was in high school, but she was being actively courted by someone else; he enjoyed biking and rambling with Dora on holidays in Cumberland, and he had a lot in common with Muriel Parkinson, the daughter of his parents' old friends. But except for these girls he knew as people, and treated like his male friends, females, in general, were just a lower order of beings to him. When he was at Oxford, the Friends group and the Wesleyan group included girls; a man who knew him there reported that he would completely crush the girls with his overpowering way of making statements or deriding something he thought was foolish. His mother and Aunt Ada, through his Oxford days, had supported the expectation that it would be a long time, and there were many more important things to do, before getting interested in girls. He had always been scornful of people who fell in love, and insisted he would not marry until he was in a position to make a living; and, as recently as the preceding fall, had written his mother, "I have no possible prospect of marrying before thirty."

But now he had made up *his* mind, an upset was pretty hard for him to take. He tried to cover the hurt with humor, as was always his way. A letter to Muriel about a month later tells the story, "The little god with the arrows scored a bulls eye in those last few weeks at Chicago, though I am afraid on the whole he has bungled the business very badly, and I have crossed him off my visiting list from henceforth." It was some years, however, before he crossed Lucinda off his visiting list.

I I I

Back in the "dirty hick town" of Liverpool, "close, cabined, and confined" (as he described it in contrast to the clean freshness of the American West in a letter the fall before), Kenneth and his mother had to scrape up something. They lived with relatives for the summer, as one after another ephemeral job prospect disappeared from his grasp. He had come to the end of the scholarship road, and had now to make a living; and it was 1934, the depths of the depression, and no one was making a living. Finally, toward the end of the summer, a post opened up at the University of Edinburgh, and his "best first" in economics stood him in good stead. He was hired, for £250 a year (the same amount he alone had lived on while he was at Oxford), and he undertook to establish a home and support his mother on that.

Renting was impossible. He had a little savings from his Commonwealth money, and they bought a second-floor flat overlooking the Firth of Forth, and he went to work in the dingy old medieval buildings in what he considered a medieval economics department. The house they lived in had been built by two brothers, who later found their wives couldn't get along, so one sold his flat to the Bouldings. They had not bothered in their halcyon days, however, to divide up the yard. To be respectable in Edinburgh you had to have a front door and a back door, a flower garden and a clothes-hanging garden, and making this division was a source of some amusement to Kenneth. They worked it out, "but," he said, "the Polish corridor was nothing compared to the land problem at our house!"

Constriction seems to be the word to describe the conditions of the next three years. There was not enough money; there was no lively conversation with congenial minds except for Will Baxter, the one good friend he made in his department; there was an oppressive hierarchical structure to the teaching staff so that there was almost no communication among them; the whole Scotch atmosphere was stiff and dour and formalized; and the teaching in the department was bound by the conventions of years before — Keynes had scarcely been heard of, and the mathematical approach Kenneth had learned at Chicago was off limits. It was just *not* his cup of tea, and it was not surprising that something boiled over.

The difficulties were compounded in the summer of 1935. In the spring of that year he heard that Lucinda had broken her engagement and planned a trip to England in the summer with her father. He wrote her a rejoicing, boyish letter about all the things he wanted to show her when she came; but her visit in July was only a brief weekend in Edinburgh, and a walk together on the windblown park at the top of the city, and her answer was no.

In addition, two fellowships at Oxford were offered that summer, and Kenneth tried for both and got neither. The second rejection left him with a very bad taste in his mouth, because a friend who had a hand in administering it had written urging him to apply, and he had assumed that was practically an offer of the job. He was then asked to come for an examination, which he felt was asinine and humiliating for one who was already teaching and had published articles; and, after all that, they decided not to award the fellowship at all. At this point, all the humiliation he had suffered as an undergraduate at Oxford came flooding back. He wanted to shake Oxford's dust off his feet and never return. He was convinced that they had not hired him because he did not come from the upper class.

The blows to his self-esteem, personal and professional, were just too much. Nonviolent resistance he endorsed, but docile submission he did not. He had no weapon but angry letters with which to attack Oxford, and with them he managed to collect his travel expenses to Magdalen College for the exam. Lucinda was across the Atlantic, and he still felt a fondness for her; but his feelings boiled out against the system he was caught in, and, unfortunately, that was also the hand that fed him.

It seemed innocent enough; he was asked to speak in a program on university education, held in April, 1936, by Cosmops, the club of international students which had been one of his side interests. It was a weekend gathering, including students from Edinburgh and Glasgow Universities, and was not supposed to be a public lecture. In his speech he let himself go in a rather informal manner, his pictorial style enhanced by a good deal of emotion, about the Scottish universities. Unfortunately, a newspaper reporter was there; and in *The Scotsman,* Edinburgh's sedate daily newspaper, there appeared an article on the conference on the main news page, with the headline pulled from Boulding's speech: "Scots University Education 'Sitting on its Haunches for Past Fifty Years' ".[2] After an introduction about the conference, two paragraphs describe Boulding's contribution:

> Mr. Kenneth Boulding, who has had experience of American and English Universities, and who is at present

Fig. 15. Boulding at the Cosmops Conference (*cartoon
from Michigan Historical Collections*)

Fig. 16. Boulding and
his house in Edinburgh
(*photo from Michigan
Historical Collections*)

Lecturer in Political Economy at Edinburgh University, said that Scottish education had a staggering reputation in England, but he thought that must be founded on its standard of 50 years ago. He found that it had apparently been sitting on its haunches for the past 50 years.

Mr. Boulding described Scottish University education as "something which has simply got ossified," and added that if there was not a big explosion it was just going to die on its feet. While admitting that he could not diagnose the trouble, he criticised the lack of touch between professors, lecturers, and students, and said there was not enough scope for original work in the Scottish Universities.

Sir Alexander Gray was the professor of Boulding's department. Professors in Scottish universities (there is only one in each department) are only a little lower than God; their wives don't meet socially with ordinary lecturers' wives. When he was considered a bright young student, Kenneth had gotten away with a good many aggravating remarks. We remember his controversy with Professor Knight at Chicago (chapter 2). However, Knight had been a man who did not pull rank, but joined the battle in verbal argument and the pages of journals — a field of equals — where Kenneth enjoyed the challenge. Here, on the other hand, at the point in his career when he considered himself a professional, doing original thinking, publishing in economic journals, and deserving recognition as such, he was seen only as a young insignificant lower-echelon lecturer who could not even say a sentence without incapacitating stuttering, and whose views or ideas certainly could not be taken seriously. Insubordination, which came naturally to Boulding from boyhood, was a capital crime in this well-organized system, and Boulding had already tangled with Professor Gray more than once. Earlier, when his brilliant friend Albert Hart, from Chicago, was visiting, Boulding had taken him in to see Sir Alexander. Afterwards Gray fumed (I am told by

Kenneth's friend and Edinburgh colleague, Will Baxter),
"Those two young so-and-sos were trying to teach *me* economics!"

When he saw the article in the paper, Gray was furious and lost no time in writing a very severe letter to
Boulding, which Boulding felt required in response an
offer to resign. Gray mellowed at the measure of humility
displayed (this was one of the times Boulding rewrote his
first draft before sending it), and with a fatherly gesture
pointed out that times were so bad he had better hang on
to the job he had and not leave hastily.

There was a set of limericks published with sketches
of the conference speakers in the Cosmops magazine, *The
Cosmopolitan,* in the summer of 1936. The limericks are
unsigned but have a similar stamp to countless verses
Boulding has produced at countless conferences since.
Strangely enough, the one below his picture reads,

> There once was a *Scotsman* reporter
> Who said what he didn't quite ought 'er.
> But, instead of a scolding,
> He got Mr. Boulding
> A feminine fan and supporter.

Boulding was not so humble and mollified as not to
say another word. A year later, an anonymous article "by a
University Lecturer" appeared in the university student
magazine,[3] beginning "In Scotland . . . professors form a
race apart," pointing out the "purely hypothetical case" of
a professor who does not work well with his staff, mentioning the "slum conditions under which work is carried
on in many departments," and asking for paint, a fire, or a
thunderbolt for the university. "In the educational battle
paint may be more important than professors, and we
have plenty of the latter." The printed article, with a
typewritten manuscript copy, is in Boulding's files. Who
the author is we are left to surmise.

His appointment, in any case, was for three years,

without any tenure. It seemed fairly clear that Boulding would not be rehired in 1937 when his term was up. There were no jobs hanging like plums on the trees that summer either; and he had no real prospects when he went to Philadelphia for the world conference he was sent to by the Scottish Friends. It is almost surprising that he said no when he was telephoned there by someone he had known at Chicago and offered a job at Colgate; but the salary was $2,000 — two thirds of what he had received as a student — and after three years of penury he could not quite see supporting his mother on that. He spent a weekend at another Friends gathering, and Colgate called him again, raising the offer to $2,400. That swung him; he got the feeling that at last somebody wanted him, and he made the decision for America. Nothing succeeds like failure; he had failed as an Englishman, so he became an American.

12

To Work and to Love: The Garden of Eden

Safety is for the slave, not for the free:
So will I walk with danger, and with thee!

— KEB, *Sonnets for Elise*, No. 36

I

Once settled in the village of Hamilton, in upstate New York, Boulding found his world opening up again. He had felt alien at Oxford, and alien in Scotland, but he never felt alien in America. There was a circle at Colgate of young bachelors like himself whom he found congenial and whom he still cherishes among his friends. With one of them he bought a car, neither being able to afford a whole one. Dividing the car was something like dividing the land around his Edinburgh house: they worked out a complicated system of rotating days of the week on which each would have use of it. After a year, he found a little house and sent for his mother.

The next few years he recalls as a microcosm of paradise. They lived in a lovely village in a rolling, green peaceful valley; he had interesting companions and a job that developed his powers. He was working, through these years, on writing *Economic Analysis,* the book with which he made his name. But it was the people — the warmth and acceptance and friendliness of the people — that struck him most. Later he recalled them as "a people who opened the doors of their houses and their hearts to a wild, black haired young poet-economist and made him their own." His mother, simple English countrywoman that she had always been, was immediately taken in by the women's clubs that met in the afternoons, given a forum for her poetry and her gift for recounting incidents, and appreciated for her gaiety and friendliness. All the children about began calling her "Auntie Boulding." Boulding insists that there was absolutely no malevolence among the people of that town. This means, I think, that both he and she had finally found people who accepted and appreciated them and did not put up barriers of class, manners, or social status to shut them out. Even four years of teaching at $2,400 without a raise did not tarnish too much the image of pristine goodness, openness, fulfillment, and joy that hung about that setting. The one major tension of those days was the contrast between their idyllic surroundings and the catastrophe gathering about their friends and relatives and untold innocents in England and the Continent at the same time.

He saw Lucinda from time to time on a friendly basis, and occasionally pressed his suit with her. It was not until 1940 that he was finally convinced her continued negative answer was both irrevocable and for the best. She lived in Maine, and that summer he and his mother drove up there for a short visit. They could hardly believe their eyes when they saw the elegance of her house, a maid, period furniture "in the best style and taste" (as Bessie recorded it years later). Lucinda's father was very American, very New England, her mother very kind; but Kenneth suddenly felt the great gulf between his background and hers as an irreconcilable barrier. Bessie's diary entry at the time was very brief: "June 27. Lunch at Lucinda's in great grandeur. Lovely ride afterwards along coast. (Cried nearly all night!)"

On May 5, 1941, the first copy of Boulding's book arrived from the publisher. It was a labor of inspiration and intellectual challenge, but also a labor of love; its dedication was "To Elizabeth Ann Boulding." Kenneth had worked for a pittance for seven years; he had promised his mother he was as good as an investment when she was left penniless, but this was the first real return on it. His undying faith in himself was finally paying off. We can imagine how proud and pleased Bessie was.

But the day before, on May 4, an event had occurred that was to shake the roots of her life. Kenneth had been in Syracuse for Quarterly Meeting, and there had met and shared the afternoon sessions with a tall, blond, Norwegian-American girl who was in her first year of graduate school and had just applied for membership in the Society of Friends. Her application was to be considered at monthly meeting the next weekend in Hamilton, so Kenneth invited her to stay at his house when she came. She, in turn, was in a state of agitation for the next several days because he had not informed her whether her weekend hostess would be his mother or his wife, and coming rather newly to Friends circles she had no idea whether he was married or who he was except that he had sat on the facing bench in meeting for worship and given a message she disagreed with.

It was very soon clear, however, that Boulding was not only not married but moving very rapidly toward changing that state. He contrived respectable ways of spending both the coming weekend and the following weekend with his new friend, Elise Biorn-Hansen, and the week after that he visited her every day. His love-gift to his mother, the achievement of his life, was turned into a love-gift for Elise, with a sonnet written for her and pasted into its flyleaf when he presented her with a copy. Along with it, nineteen days after they had met, he asked her to marry him. About three months later she became his wife, and his mother's exclusive place in his life was gone.

Sociologically, marriage for him at this point was not surprising. He was 31; the average age for males at first marriage in England and Wales at that time was 26.8 years.[1] But one who had had a number of years of graduate school would be likely to exceed this. Several of his Chicago friends, but few of his Liverpool and Oxford friends, had married by that time, and some remained lifelong bachelors. (Although he could not have known it, the average age at marriage of his male ancestors in his father's line for six generations back was also 31, ranging from 26 to 35.) He had now finally attained his goal of minimum security: with book royalties assured, he could feel secure about supporting a wife. But the inner elements of the decision are more interesting.

Boulding wrote a rather astonishing group of sonnets, mostly in that summer, though a number were written in 1944 and a few between then and 1957, when he had them privately published under the title *Sonnets for Elise*. They are full of tenderness and devotion, emphasizing the spiritual but not ignoring the physical comforts of love, and, like the Nayler sonnets coming out of nearly the same period, are a door opened on the inner life of a richly imaginative and deeply feeling man. The first, compelling in its image of love and fear, follows:

> Timid, I wondered how my love would come:
> As violence in the blood, tempestuous flame,
> Half shining ecstasy, half smoky shame,
> A song, half calling clear, half mumbling dumb?
> And so I starved, for fear that some small crumb
> Of love's good bread might choke me, and I came

To fight with love, resist his every claim,
With a cold armament of senses numb.

But not in tempest, lightning, fury, heat,
He came upon me: these I learned to shun;
But as the still beams of a kindly sun
That drew me into life, full and complete.
I knew from books that love could cast out fear,
But not in truth — until I found you near.

We can see, in this one alone, the echoes of hurt, the tight
control of emotion he imposed on himself, and a parallelism with the image of the "still, small voice" in this experience of finding Elise. When we look at the whole group
more closely, five major pairs of conflicting elements come
into expression: quietness and light vs. dark, strong emotions; perfection vs. imperfection; life and freedom vs.
death and rigidity; fullness vs. emptiness; and structure
vs. chaos. In each pair, the first is the positive factor, and
the one with which Elise and their love is identified; yet
we again see here some of the same strains within the man
that we have found before. Quietness can become dullness
and emptiness, and part of the value of fullness is danger
and freedom, adventure and accomplishment, which can
border on the frightening strong emotions that have a
negative cast. Again, the familiar valuation of life against
death, freedom against rigidity, stands in opposition to
the valuation of structure against chaos. Boulding's
radical–conservative struggle is revealed here all over
again.

In the Nayler sonnets, the first two of these opposi-
tions receive the most emphasis, light against dark (love
against aggression) and perfection against imperfection
(good against evil, God's greatness against man's small-
ness). The mountain peaks, the seed and the flower, the
boundless sea and the snow-fed brook; tangled strings and
nets and looms; wombs and their harvest; candles, stars,
and suns; and shapeless black winged monsters — all find

their place in both these sets of poems. But strangely enough, when we think of the intensity, the verbal aggressiveness, the independence and sense of autonomy that have so characterized Boulding all through his life, the image of Elise that comes through the love sonnets is almost entirely one of being strong, dominant, and powerful, in contrast to his submissive role. She holds him as a slave; she is the alchemist who transforms him; she is his teacher; she is the musician who plays upon him, the instrument; she is the wind, the air, his sustaining medium; she is the magnet that directs his confused particles to a unified goal. She is the sun; she is the fire; she is the unbounded sea; she is pure love and goodness and almost God. (The sun and flame and wind and sea are all used as images for God in the Nayler sonnets.) The only sonnet which gives the opposite image, in startling contrast, is Sonnet 29, in which the conflict between freedom and control is brought to a head; he faces the dangers of overwhelming emotion (the candle-flame that burns down a building, the river that floods) and promises to be the channel to control her passion.

Sex was not talked about in Kenneth's circles as he grew up, but in this area, like others, he is quite willing to shock people by inserting unexpected words in unlikely contexts. His biological analogy of social artifacts becomes sometimes quite specific: "We do not find the First Baptist Church having intercourse with the Second to produce a Third." [2] Yet he has some strange hesitancies about the topic.

It might be helpful to set beside the poems whatever evidence we can find in the area of love, sex, and marital relations in his TAT stories. There seems to be, in general, a very negative attitude expressed in these stories. Sex (male–female romantic attachment) is introduced where it is not obvious, in five stories, making six of the thirteen which include a love or sex involvement. All except one of the pictures where sex is introduced show grief or a conflict situation, and out of the six stories with sex involvement, only one is a positive relationship. The others concern either unfortunate choices of partner, or loss, or interpersonal tension. The one positive sex experience is treated anticlimactically.

In no case does a lover turn, in loss, from one love object to another. There is unyielding fixation on one, with total hate or despair at disruption of the relationship, or total grief at the loved one's death. Strangely enough, however, there is no mention of marriage except at its earliest stage (the death of a *bride,* or *planning* to marry an unsuitable girl), except for the final, most respectable version of picture 13. This shows a man, his hand over his eyes, turning away from a bed on which lies a partially covered naked woman. Boulding's first version is a jealousy killing, but in the second, the pair are pictured as husband and wife, presumably of some years. But here also the outcome is grief, since the wife has just died. All the rest of the couples are in the "lovers" stage, and every one has a hard time because of it; even the happy couple have to suffer for their enjoyment by waiting in very bad weather. The other sufferings range from separation from father or mother over choice of wife, to death of the loved one, to violent jealous aggression or irreparable despair at a quarrel.

On the other hand, as we found with the "aggression" cues, some specifically sexual items in the pictures are not mentioned. The sexual implications of the naked woman in picture 13 are ignored; a woman in another picture is often seen as pregnant, but not by Boulding; he does not mention that the man in a third has no clothes on. The romantic male–female relationship is apparently triggered in his mind by a suffering situation, but any reference to physical contact is missing.[3]

This negativity toward sex may be read in terms of the classic oedipal conflict. The trauma in his early life between the ages of four and five could be seen as contributing to the nonresolution of his oedipal strivings, and the early death of his father and complete dependence of his mother on him as symbolically fulfilling the oedipal myth. This makes rather a neat psychoanalytic package, if one wants to interpret it so. But there are other ways, too, of wrapping the package.

It does seem clear that the area of love and sex, as reflected in these projections from his TAT protocol, is a problem area. There are no healthy, happy, long-term male–female relationships represented, nor even short-term ones, seriously treated. It is a stereotypical black–white (mostly black) view of romantic love. It is saying, "If you fall in love, that will bring unhappiness." To all appearances, this view is in marked contrast to his own long and happy marital relationship, characterized by mutual respect and real affection, though with considerable independence on both sides.

But his general attitude toward the male–female experience is that it is one in which people are the unwilling pawns — are exploited by each other or by the environment (including, of course, their internal drives). Corroboration for this view is given when we look at the two times in his own life when he was attracted to a girl. Both were very sudden, impulsive acts. The first time he fell in love was described thus in a letter to a close friend: "The slope was slippery and my heels were greased." The attack by Cupid's arrows, already quoted, was also from outside, beyond his control. And his active pursuit of a surprised and hesitant Elise he wrote up under the title, "The Viking Conquest, or How Kenneth Fell."

It is not particularly surprising that he had no well-developed role relationship with girls as girls, for his childhood and youth had not exposed him to any. In the main, his relationships with boys fulfilled his needs for autonomy and self-development. They played at building houses or bridges with toy bricks or Meccano parts, went on hikes or bicycle trips together, talked over ideas and philosophical questions, encouraged each other in learning and passing examinations, listened to music together. If in contrast he saw the sexual relationship as one in which something unwanted or unexpected was happening *to* him, where he was not ordering and making sense of things, it would be understandable for one so full of desire for autonomy to consider it a negative experience. The flood of aggression, and the flood of sexual emotion, might be seen as deeply threatening.

As he tried to sort out his feelings about sex, at the time of his approaching marriage, he worked out, or rather, suddenly saw a connection of the act of sexual union with the resolution of two major opposing tendencies, toward homogeneity or absorption (the oceanic oneness of everything), and toward separateness or autonomy. Sex thus becomes the vessel, as he dimly recognized, which holds most fully the unfinished conflict from his childhood, the continuing pressure both to unite with and to separate himself from the mother who represented the world.

Perhaps he also had a sense, from long exposure to a talented mother who was held down by the needs of the home and the expectations of society, that the sexual relationship is an exploitive one, particularly of women. While Boulding views the environment as exploitable, nowhere do we find that he feels *people* are exploitable; and he may have been reluctant to enter such a relationship. Certainly, from the beginning of his own marriage, he was more than traditionally open to the possibility of his talented wife's finding fulfillment in the society outside the home — though he did little to lighten her home burdens and clear the way.

There is another piece of evidence we can place beside these. All through his 1942 pamphlet *The Practice of the Love of God* (again, written in nearly the same period as his marriage and the two groups of sonnets), there runs the theme that man can love other people, his family, his nation, his small group, but that these loves are cancerous and destructive unless they are subordinated to the greater love, the love of God. This is summed up in the phrase in *The Organizational Revolution* (p. 86), "the worst enemy of the greater love is the lesser."

If we combine, then, the deep fear of overwhelming emotion carrying him where he did not choose to go, the shadow of potential over-identification with his mother, the fear of hurting or exploiting another, and the religious conviction that nothing must get in the way of the love of God, it seems reasonable that he had to cast his love in terms of devotion to a God-like figure too strong to be hurt, who would make him purer and better. Even more, it was seen as a love that was sanctified by God and dedicated to His service. There is some confirmation for this in the fact that he could not write sonnets to Elise when she was with him, only in her absence (the idealization was easier then).

There are also, unavoidably, masculine elements in this controlling image of Elise, and corresponding feminine elements in his image of himself. In Sonnet 41, the image of the literary creator as giving birth is made very specific. Written to keep Elise from despair after several years of childless marriage, it contains the lines, "Rejoice that in my womb thou dost beget/ These spiritual children undefiled." I think it is true that the traditional masculine–feminine separations do not hold in his concepts. He is not afraid of identifying himself with love and gentleness; he rejects masculinity when it means destructiveness and cruelty. He developed this parallel in an article on revolution in which he said,

> Revolution may be compared to the sexual act, which fertilizes the egg of the new society and in which overtones of violence are frequently present. The growth of the egg, however, requires an entirely different situation. It requires the warmth and security of the womb, which is the most nonviolent place on earth.[4]

257

He chooses the "feminine mystique" of development over the "masculine" violence of revolution. Economics, whose name is derived from the word for "household," a feminine pursuit, is preferred over the "masculine mystique" (his word) [5] of the international system, with its secret power plays, cloaks and daggers. When he played "mothers and fathers" with the little girl who lived next door to his grandmother's in Chard, Kenneth was not the father but the baby, and Marjorie played the mother or older sister.

It is interesting that his family is traced mainly through the female line, his mother and his mother's mother. There is an obvious reason for this: both his father's parents and his maternal grandfather's parents died while their son was a child, and there was little memory of them carried down in the family. Kenneth's father, in turn, died much earlier than his mother. This might suggest a simple physical strength carried through the females which would predispose a son toward identifying with them. These connections are illustrated by the selection of family portraits hanging on the wall in the Bouldings' living room. In contrast, Elise's family portraits are just the opposite: her father's parents and her father's father's parents are there; and her mother died some years before her father.

Both, then, have transcended the traditional limiting role-categories, and their marriage has made room, for the most part, for two people to grow as people, not just to relate as male and female. Elise would sometimes say, when their daughter Christie was baking bread, sewing, and doing the shopping and cooking, "It's good to have a woman around the house." Kenneth could not really be called "a man around the house"; he doesn't fix mechanical things, wash the car, carry out the garbage. Both partake so much of intellectuality and abstraction, Elise of determination and Kenneth of eternal childlikeness, that they cannot be sex-typed in the normal mold.

III

From the beginning Elise refused, and Kenneth did not wish her, to sacrifice herself on the altar of "nurturing his genius" as she was urged by friends to do. His genius would do all right without her, and she had a job nurturing her own. But they have found real companionship in discussion of ideas, in the shared commitment to worship and service, in learning from each other, in being able to laugh at the same things. Here is a sample spontaneous inanity, in their shared office at the University of Colorado:

> *Elise:*   I'm sorry, Kenneth, but we're going to have a sociologist for supper.
> *Kenneth:* Well, I'm sure he'll be delicious!
> *Elise:*   Yes — do you want him with onion sauce or mushroom sauce?

She has been buoyed up by his high spirits, and he by her continuing love and care; both have served for the other as a sounding board for ideas.

There have been echoes from time to time of Kenneth's early male–superiority cultural orientation, or perhaps simply of his overriding personal autonomy. He could never be persuaded to take any responsibility for care of the children when they were small, and when Elise wanted to take graduate work, she had to juggle this by herself. She has served as coordinator and administrator of the household, he as provider and entertainer, stimulator and joint enjoyer. Pursuing his inner gyroscope always, whether it leads him to build castles with his children's blocks, recount funny stories from a recent trip, discuss a complicated concept, or go out and buy a piece of land because it has a waterfall on it, his life keeps spilling over into the lives of the people around him, paying little attention to where they are, but carrying them along (if they are willing) in his joyous stream.

To retrace the historical steps — after six childless

Fig. 18. Three Bouldings, 1947 (*photo from Michigan Historical Collections*)

Fig. 17. Two Bouldings, 1941 (*photo from Michigan Historical Collections*)

Fig. 19. Seven Bouldings, 1969: *from back, left to right:* Elise, Kenneth, Christie, William, Philip, Russell, and Mark

years, Elise waiting and hoping and busying herself with interracial groups, voting issues, and the teasing, beckoning academic world (without a social science course in undergraduate school, she achieved an M.A. in sociology at Ames), their first child was born in 1947. After that, at regular two-year intervals, four more arrived, all boys except the middle one. Elise fitted in a life of Quaker activity, scholarly activity, and motherly activity around them, and afterwards went on to her Ph.D. in sociology.

The family has always been a household of individuals, with mother, father, and all five children leading active lives of their own. The children universally reported to me that each was encouraged as he grew up to be and do what he wanted. They knew, however, that their parents liked some things they did better than others: they liked it when their offspring initiated activities, particularly in the cause of peace, social justice, or nonconformity to middle-class pride in dress or money; they liked it when they did well in school or showed special talent in speaking or art; and they didn't like it if one of the children was indifferent, apathetic, or insensitive to the needs of other people.

But it has been a unified family, too. Rules were made in family council meetings, by consensus (though William, the youngest, sometimes felt what he said didn't count for much). Holidays have been family times. Christmas is a happy blend of Norwegian and English customs, with Kenneth doing all sorts of unnecessary things like making candles, decorating the cake village that became a family tradition, and cutting out paper figures for the Twelve Days of Christmas. (Christmas had always been a party time for him, with his mother usually inviting in all the neighborhood children, and Kenneth devising the decorations and games.) Mark particularly remembered the many kinds of Christmas stories they used to have from all over the world. It has been a family of more music making than listening, with Kenneth and Elise breaking out into Gilbert and Sullivan over the dishwashing, or Russell playing his guitar for the family to sing, or Elise her cello and Philip his violin and Kenneth his recorder.

I asked each one of the children what they liked best about their father, and what they would change if they could. Some would like it better if he didn't go off traveling so much, or if he had more patience with some of his children. Almost all of them found the reflected fame an asset, but some felt it would be better if he didn't make so much money, and they lived more simply. His standing up for what he believes in counted heavily; but his perceptiveness, cleverness, breadth of vision, knowing so *much* about *everything*, was mentioned more often, with more appreciation, than anything else. Russell, at twenty-two, was far enough past childhood to be able to say that what he admired most was "the fact that he's never grown up, and I don't think he ever will! . . . I don't care about being famous and speaking and conferences and writing books and things like that, but I do want to be able to maintain the type of just joy of life that he has."

There should be room somewhere, and perhaps it is here, for the last sonnet in the group written for Elise. For her birthday, after sixteen years of marriage and five children, Kenneth presented his image of the joint process, the strains and the hopes, of producing a marriage and a family:

> God, in His evening of creation, saw
> That it was good, and as I think how we
> Have through time made each other, I too see
> That it is good, and with a kind of awe
> I see in us the whole creation's law.
> For I in you, and you, my love, in me
> Have shaped the daily clay that needs must be
> Molded towards perfection or to flaw.
>
> And there will come a Sabbath, when we rest
> From this long battering week, and others take

The burden of creation, and we make
A Holy Day, and move from good to best,
And in that Sabbath we shall come to know
As flower, the seed that now in us must grow.

13

The Boulding Personality

My pleasure was not unalloyed
In being analyzed by Freud
For though he taught me quite a lot,
Some of it's true and some is not.

— KEB, Conference on Total Societies, 1965

I

It would be nice if I could lay out, simply and clearly, a neat, well-rounded description of the personality of Kenneth Boulding, all wrapped up with good solid explanations as to why he is the way he is. Though I will try to gather up the loose ends of his attitudes, activities, and personal impact on those around him, the life will always slip through the mesh of words. I must lean in wholehearted agreement on psychologist Robert W. White:

> The faithful student of personality must often postpone the satisfaction of discovering laws. Above all, he must avoid the pitfall of waving complexity aside, as if it were merely a surface illusion that would ultimately dissolve into a few clear-cut principles. Complexity is inherent in personality. It is no surface illusion; it is a stubborn and inescapable fact. When we forget this fact we embark upon one of those foolish ventures in oversimplification which end by impeding the understanding of human nature.[1]

264

Perhaps, then, complexity is as good a place as any to begin, for this is one of Boulding's values, and a brief review of the elements of thought and behavior toward which he is drawn should form a part of our picture of the man. Under the rubric of "openness to alternatives" we can classify a number of his preferences. The fight for heterogeneity, the pluralism which keeps alternatives open, pervades his views on economics — as illustrated by the market system — and politics, in which he endorses the continuing dialogue. "The thing that is most fatal to the political process is conclusions; when once the train of thought has reached a terminus, everybody might just as well get off it." [2] It spills into aesthetics (he doesn't like a drab uniformity), morals (each man has to act in terms of his own value system) and religion (there should be many kinds of churches to fit every brand of spiritual experience). Even his views of truth and personality are pluralistic, and his mode of development of a subject (as in *Economic Analysis* or *Conflict and Defense*) is to begin with the simpler and more abstract case and add greater and greater dimensions of complexity and variability. The plurality of points of view, in fact, was the burden of an essay he wrote when he was fifteen: the child may look stupid to the professor, but the professor, concerned about irrelevancies, is stupid to the child; and nations look stupid to each other. If behavior is fundamentally subject to choice, which is what he calls "an economist's way of looking at the matter" and is certainly his chosen way, then there must be alternatives in order to have choices.

One of the reasons he has always opposed world government, even though it may seem to present a way out of the war system, is that it unifies, homogenizes, and does away with alternatives. Where in the world would you go, if you couldn't stomach the system in the world state? Perhaps the glimpse of alternative cultural systems that he had in his youth through reading Wells, and tasted in his experience at Chicago, helped him resist the stifling system in Edinburgh and eventually move out of it to an alternative which suited him much better. There is a passage of Kurt Eissler's which underlines the creative potential of society's providing alternatives:

> The climate of certain historical periods favors the evolvement in certain personality types of above-average talents . . . [but] it may happen that many a subject's potential genius remains unrealized because the culture of his time does not provide that frame into which the subject could fit the creations of his particular skills.[3]

A man cannot move to another time, but moving to another place may provide a different cultural frame, as long as there is a plurality of cultures.

The value of instability is related to the rejection of inevitability and rigidity. "Complete rigidity in the image prevents the growth of knowledge altogether," he insists; not only that, but uncertainty itself is fun; it is the "race between learning and disaster which makes the present age so exciting." The importance of slack, impurity, and loose ends as growing points in a culture is part of this concept, as is surprise. "Surprise is an essential element in information. It is only by unexpectedness that knowledge increases." Cousin Eddy has described Kenneth, and also his Aunt Ada, as "more receptive to new ideas than the rest of us," and "jumping at the opportunity for new experiences."

Complexity and uncertainty are part of the whole vast area of conflict. It may surprise some who think of Boulding as a peacenik to learn that his ideal is actually a "perpetual state of unresolved conflict"; that he believes "Conflict conducted in a decent and responsible manner is essential to any form of progress." Conflict is creative; evolution and learning could not take place without it. But though conflict need not be resolved, it must be managed to be creative, both in society and in the person: "The problem of balance is crucial. Pure altruism is no more desirable than pure selfishness." Economics is one reconciler ("it is corrosive of ideologies and disputes that are not worth their costs") and another is the recognition of the good and evil mixed in all of us. After a kind of litany of the positives and negatives, the good and evil, of human creatures, Boulding concludes, "The truth is that each of us is on both sides." Carolyn Hamm, a perceptive young friend who lived with the Bouldings in Japan for a year, observed, "I think Kenneth has a sense of the yin and yang of life, and that's why he doesn't get tangled up in guilt feelings about anything." This conflict between selflessness and independence, between affiliation and autonomy, was the theme of three of his TAT stories, and all three ended in a balance; autonomy won, but affiliation did not lose. It was specifically pointed out as needed by both society and the individual in a passage in *Principles of Economic Policy* (p. 139):

> It is not the business of this work to resolve the moral tension between selflessness and independence — perhaps, indeed, this is a tension that should not be resolved. Creative individuals and creative societies may be those in which these opposites are held in tension; it may be that when the tension fails to maintain itself the society — and the person — falls either into tyranny or anarchy.

This is the tension involved between the exchange system (promoting independence and rational choice) and the integrative system (promoting self-sacrifice for the good of others). Boulding has observed that the exchange system by itself does not produce the qualities of character that are needed to maintain it.

It is at least a plausible hypothesis that the theme of conflict resolution has been a central one in Boulding's public work partly because it is a central theme in his own life: the balance of forces, the control of emotions, the managing of tensions, may be one of the roots of his own creativity. A support of this thesis is in what may or

may not be a very personal reference in *The Meaning of
the Twentieth Century* (p. 147):

> A troublesome question, which is again worth asking
> even though we cannot answer it, is whether man needs a
> certain amount of trouble, difficulty, challenge, or even
> pain in order to stimulate him to that constructive activ-
> ity which is necessary to prevent him from going to
> pieces. . . . It may well be that evolutionary potential al-
> ways emerges out of some kind of crisis situation.

Ambition, or the push for self, certainly played a part
in Boulding's rise in the academic world. He never tried
to hide from himself or others the fact that he wanted to
be noticed. His advisers, indeed, assumed this; he was told
to concentrate his energies on producing a book because
this would have more status value than a diffuse series of
articles. He exulted when Frank Knight attacked him in
print, for it made him more visible. Discouraged about
the progress of his writing after he came to Colgate in
1937, he wrote to a friend,

> If it wasn't for knawing ambition, I could settle down in
> this transatlantic arcady into a very charming and com-
> fortable rut . . . I shall have to decide whether to seek se-
> curity and oblivion in Hamilton, hiding away in the un-
> breakable peace of these frozen hills, or whether I ought
> to break out of it.

At various times, in private references to his works in progress, he dropped such remarks as, "I hope of course that
it will make me famous when (and if) it gets published";
"[I hope it] effects the Copernican Revolution in Economics"; "It turned out to be something that in scope
almost tries to be another Marshall — a grand systematization . . ." Even in 1946, when he was totting up the
relative advantages of two universities in trying to decide
where to locate, "prestige" was one of the items on the
list. (To be fair, I must state it was one of twenty-eight
items, and its valuation was contrary to the final decision.)

On the other hand, the push for selflessness or altruism has always been present too, originally arising from the standards of his family. At the age of ten or eleven, he was collecting pennies and shillings for a missionary fund, apparently from all his relatives and whoever came to call, including a donation from himself. The five shillings that he and his gang of "Seymourites" raised by singing carols was given to the Sunshine House for the Blind. At fourteen, he sent a donation of two shillings to the Fresh Air Fund with which his father was so active, along with a letter remarking on how he was struck with the benefit to the children when he went on an outing as a helper to his father. And when he was in Oxford he engineered an elaborate excursion of young working-class men and women from a mission in the London slums to both Oxford and Cambridge as guests of the Methodist students there, with the Londoners conducting the evening service in the university town, and a return visit of the students to preach in the London mission on a later weekend. A newspaper clipping from the time, the spring of 1932, concludes,

> Since a young student — Kenneth Boulding — first thought out the great advantage to both by such a demonstration of comradeship, over a hundred Clublanders have lived memorable days in the company of new-found friends. . . . The expenses of the trips were paid by the students.

He carried on the drive for good works at Edinburgh, as we have related, with the Carfin Hall workcamps, and again at Colgate by organizing students and faculty into community service projects, cutting firewood and shoveling snow for the incapacitated. The Friends Student Colony that he and Elise established at Ames was a variant venture meant to benefit others.

Yet, in addition to the family pressure for good works, there must have been a real appreciation for the potential in others coming from within Kenneth as well, for we have evidence of more personal interaction expressing this. A fellow-student at Liverpool Collegiate, who was not among the brilliant scholarship class, reports that Kenneth would frequently help him with his math. "Kenneth used to work it all out, show me how it was done, then rip it up and throw it in the fire so I would do it myself and remember how." (His sons have said they get the same kind of attention when they ask for help with their school work.) Kenneth's friend Muriel Parkinson credits him, during his high school and college years, with broadening her viewpoint and perceptiveness about political subtleties, historical developments, and the nuances of architecture.

> He treated me as somebody worthwhile, gave me the sort of encouragement that didn't come from others. . . . His ability to express himself and help us to express ourselves had a direct influence on my brothers. He helped all of us to think more clearly, didn't force or overwhelm us. He was a good teacher.

Martin Hoffman, a young student when Kenneth was teaching at Ames, who lived in the student co-op in their house, feels that his whole thinking about social problems, war and peace, and relations with other people, has been very much influenced by both Kenneth and Elise. "Kenneth is the kind of guy in whose presence one feels *better* about oneself; an evening or afternoon or a day with Kenneth is a potent psychological shot in the arm, an exhilarating experience intellectually and emotionally." Similar testimony is given by another former student who lived at their house in the Ann Arbor years: "He lights people with hope and the ability to carry on and carry through."

The extension of independence to others, as one cherishes it for himself, is indeed a resolution of the tension between selfishness and selflessness, which Kenneth has found. From his earliest years, as we have remarked,

Kenneth has been violently opposed to any kind of exploitation or oppression. Ernest Dundas reports him in his high school years as "either full of jollity or else flaming indignant over anything tyrannical or authoritarian." Bernard Ash, summing up Kenneth's mellowing over the years, and recalling his compromising on some minor prohibitions he used to consider important (such as an occasional glass of wine), added, "But the toleration of human misery Kenneth will never grow old enough to compromise on."

Related, perhaps, to his own class struggle, he has made a fierce identification with victims of discrimination. He wrote a satiric, almost Swiftian letter on race prejudice to the newspaper in Ames in 1944, describing the exclusive, debilitated society of "Pinky-Grays." Another letter, in 1939, was an icy response to the dean of men at a Quaker college who had suggested that a prospective student of Jewish-Quaker parents would find admission easier as a Friend than as a Jew. Boulding wrote a poem called "No Room," arising out of this incident, about a Jewish boy of obscure parentage, whose father's name was Joseph, who was refused admission to a liberal arts college because "The Jewish quota's full as it can go." The poem was not accepted by the Quaker journal to which he submitted it, "partly because of its length and partly because of its content," the rejection letter said.

The "infinite worth of the human soul," as Boulding put it in 1935, people as ends, not means, as was his argument in 1953 and 1966 articles in *Beyond Economics,* and his recent extreme reaction to the name-calling of the militants of right and left who lump people together with derogatory terms — his strong opposition to the denial of the quality of humanity to *anyone at all* — are all of a piece. They are all an extension of his own intense need for independence and autonomy, to allow for the same need in everyone else.

To be able to disagree with people without over-

whelming them with his own views, however, is a facet of
respect for people which he has not always achieved. His
ridicule of something he thought absurd has, again and
again, caused lasting hurt feelings; but an opposing idea
which he admits to the ring provides him with a good
sparring match. "To be able to like and respect people
with whom you violently disagree," he wrote in 1934, "is
perhaps the pleasantest of all intellectual delights." That
he has sometimes succeeded may be judged from the comment of one of his co-workers at Michigan who describes
him as "one of the few really moral men I have been able
to tolerate in a positive way, because he didn't impose
that on others." He has not imposed on his children any
specific expectations for their future, only that they become what they are led to become (yet one could point
out, in each of them, qualities they seem to share with
him). He has not imposed on his students a particular
body of theory, but tried to open them to a wider range of
possibilities, and to their "inward teacher."

An aesthetic sense and sureness of taste has served
him better in some other contexts than when it leads him
to laugh at someone's ideas. One of his friends reports that
sometimes they would be walking together and Kenneth
would stop short in front of a building and break into
loud laughter over some architectural anomaly. He writes
in his letters incisive and delightful descriptions of buildings he sees wherever he goes, and has a much deeper sensitivity than most people to color combinations, form, and
detail of construction. This sensitivity and decisiveness of
taste extends also to other activities, musical productions,
for instance, and books. When he was quite young his
mother records that he would often say "This is a good
book to disagree with"; and his reading notes from his college years often have critical comments in the margins.
His cousin Eddy remarked on this quality as much as any;
from boyhood he had felt that Kenneth always was quick
to "choose the better part": that even when Eddy pre-

ferred something different, or he was praised for his behavior and Kenneth scolded, Kenneth still seemed the one who had chosen the most important or deeply satisfying activity, and he had the feeling that Kenneth knew from somewhere inside what was really best.

Complexity, plurality, and alternatives for choice, independent action and furthering the independence of others, and aesthetic appreciation have been described as some of Boulding's values, from observation of his writings and the reported experiences of his friends. We will remember from earlier chapters his commitment to nonviolence, religious values, and world-mindedness, as well as his radical–conservative stance. The characters with whom he seems to identify in his TAT stories represent almost the same range of values: need for autonomy, resistance to and upholding of the Establishment, nurturant care and affection, disapproval of violence, glory through artistic achievement, and a recognition of a responsibility to truth, that is, the difficulty of adequately representing reality. Even though he professes love as one of his highest interpersonal goals, when the theoretical choice is given between an activity for others' benefit and, for instance, an intellectual project, he is likely to choose in favor of the intellect.

We cannot, with certainty, weigh the contributions of the individual, the family, and the culture to these values, but we can make some guesses. His family supported and encouraged his intellectual bent, which must have rested on his own natural gifts. His family church taught the valuing of the spiritual over the material life, but something in him also reached out for deepened spiritual experience. In the aesthetic realm, it was he who opened the door for his parents, introducing them to classical music, art, and architecture: here his contacts with other students and his perceptive sensitivity to the larger culture transcended his family background.

Being English, I think, made a high aesthetic evaluation easier for him than if he had been born American. One growing up in Britain and occasionally visiting the Continent must have a far greater sense of the majesty of the work of man's hand than a child in an American city. Stonehenge and Salisbury, thatched cottage and castle, Oxford and Liverpool, all present multiple and awesome architectural images in time and space. In addition, the low valuation of the economic, and the high of the aesthetic, strikes a tourist in England everywhere. A narrow road winds in among the stone cottages of an old village; totally missing are the gas stations, hamburger stands, and motels that line the approaches to every four corners in America. Although the almighty pound was a powerful force that overrode humanitarian and aesthetic concerns at the beginning of the Industrial Revolution, the development of consumer goods appears twenty years behind today. (According to Boulding's analysis, this is the cumulative product of a very slight difference in the rate of growth of per capita income between the two countries since their days of rough equality, the early years of the twentieth century.) [4] Only in London is advertising as blatant as the American pattern; and either ecological care is far ahead of ours, or littering is also twenty years behind. The government is interested in the preservation of every tree and every historical building: the owner must get a special permit to cut down a tree in his yard or remodel the kitchen of a seventeenth-century house. The continuous existence of the monarchy, an anomaly in the modern world, must be cued, in part, to the joy of the spectacle. And the amount of time devoted by almost every English householder to the cultivation of his garden — a feast for the eyes of neighbors and passersby — would seem an almost unthinkable diversion from useful occupations to most Americans. There is a cultural emphasis which weights these two values of the aesthetic and the economic, I would guess, in the opposite direction from the way they are commonly weighted in the American society.

We turn now to an examination of Boulding's unconventionality, which Bernard Ash labeled his "profession." This quality was mentioned by his friends whom I interviewed, almost without exception. It shades off, on one side, into deliberate rudeness to get people's attention, on the other, to complete unselfconsciousness in pursuit of his own absorbing interests, and, somewhere in the middle, is a simple refusal to accept any higher authority for anything. "Noisy and troublesome people," he wrote in 1966, after a lifetime of observation, "get attention; the quiet are ignored, even when they are wise."

The quality of unconventionality seems to have come to the fore in his personality some time after his early school years. Leslie, who knew him earliest, does not really mention it except in terms of Kenneth's quiet withdrawal into himself. Muriel, whose family moved away from Liverpool in 1912 and back there in 1924, saw him for intermittent visits when he was seven or eight and remembers him then as very sober and shy, never laughing. This would have been during the difficult period at St. Simon's School. (A picture of his first class at Hope Street School, at about nine, shows him looking a little frightened.) But by the time he was fourteen, she recalls he was entirely different — self-confident, careless of his manners, and totally unembarrassed. It is possible that the faith in him which his Hope Street masters expressed, and his growing faith in himself through the intellectual mode at which he found he could be successful, and perhaps a measure of energy actively turned toward overcoming, ignoring, or defeating the handicap of his stutter, had combined to turn him outward by this time. This was in the developmental period called "latency," when the child's task, according to Erikson,[5] is to solve the problem of industry vs. inferiority, to gain skills in using the tools of the society he lives in. It is a time when the conflicts of early childhood are temporarily in abeyance, to give way shortly to the storms of adolescence; and Kenneth seems to have drawn on his resources and used these years to master this hurdle in good form.

By adolescence, then, he had become a rebel against authority, a fighter for reason and justice, and a good-natured, high-spirited provocateur, sometimes with intent to sting, sometimes not. As high school friends describe him, "He was always extremely hospitable even at the height of being extremely rude; he would never act spitefully but would be overbearing and dogmatic. He knew he was rude and enjoyed it; he didn't hate people, there was something impersonal about it." He did not follow the crowd: "He was never a joiner, but never looked down on anybody." He resisted authority: "He would never pipe down or shut his mouth for anybody over him." Even when he was made a prefect, as we remember from an earlier chapter, he refused to wear a tie, and he laughed at the ridiculousness of the special cap with the long gold tassel that was a mark of the prefect's uniform, on top of his always unruly hair. He would say outrageous things about the administration of the school; and his mother, who herself had little tolerance of rules for the sake of rules, wouldn't know whether to be severe with him or not. According to Muriel Parkinson, she would usually laugh it off.

In his Oxford years, his outrageousness did not diminish. When he saw Muriel during those years, he was a tremendous embarrassment to be with; she didn't mind, but her mother, who was strong on manners and propriety, used to find him a great trial. He was very loud in public places, and quite unconcerned about the niceties of dress or table manners. If he was absorbed in developing an idea, reciting a poem, or whatever manner of witty discourse (just as in the incidents of the car that went in the ditch or the teacup smashed on the floor), everything else would be forgotten. When I asked Muriel how his mother's discipline on manners compared with hers, she said, "Oh — his mother would mildly say (as he was waving his bread in the air while he was buttering it), 'Kenneth, put that down'; and he would say, 'Oh, yes,' and put it down, and go on with whatever he was doing." I suspect that his mother, though she kept a semblance of the form of trying to correct him, had enough independence in her to secretly enjoy his flouting of convention, and, perhaps, to appreciate that the idea he was developing just might be more important than putting his bread down. As for his father, he had the same trouble keeping clothes neat as Kenneth did (Bessie remarked of Will, "I fear I shall never be able to make him tidy!") and, by this time in Kenneth's life, I expect his awe of his son would have superseded any fatherly correctional role.

Thumbing his nose at respectability is a repeated theme in his letters; 1928: "Socialism is getting fearfully respectable. I think I shall turn Communist. There are far too many Socialists in Oxford." In 1929, he describes a Methodist conference in London: "the very cream of respectable, Christian Middle-Class Nonconformity lunching off exotic things in the vulgar establishments of the Idle Rich." From his Western tour in 1933: "I take a peculiar delight in walking into respectable hotels in a disreputable condition." And he was overjoyed recently to have a distant cousin unearth a family tree that went back to a widow in Charles II's time who launched his branch of the Boulding clan without benefit of husband — "a delightfully disreputable ancestor!"

Incidentally, the claim to disreputability that he keeps making about himself has certain payoffs: it legitimizes deviance. While giving a nod to the established order, it carves out for him a measure of freedom, a space in which he can be different, whether in clothes, in ideas, or in the influx of the Holy Spirit. It helps to create the expectancy, the image, in other people's minds, as in his own, of a person who, while not quite standard, recognizes

277

the standard and thus can be allowed some deviation from it.

Intellectually, too, rebellion continued, directed in the service of truth. A friend of Oxford years describes it, "Kenneth hadn't the slightest respect for authority. Even if he wanted to believe you he would still want to be convinced with a sound argument." An Edinburgh friend recalls he was always contending for the scope for wickedness and nonuniformity. A Michigan friend says, "He gets a childish delight out of being naughty." Room for the outlaw in the world, wickedness, deviant behavior, and disregard for conventions all go hand in hand, and they are closely allied with the status mobility which was so important in Kenneth Boulding's life, with the breaking of rigidity, the openness to new patterns, and the openness to new knowledge which is essential for society's development. As Norbert Wiener has said, "It is the part of the scientist . . . to entertain heretical and forbidden opinions experimentally, even if he is finally to reject them." [6]

Boulding was in many ways a "marginal man." He was not of the working class; he had to reject his father's occupation and his mother's unsophistication to operate in the world he was fitted for by nature and interest, the world of the mind. Yet he was not of the intellectual class, or not so regarded by society, as he discovered most clearly in his first year in Oxford. Social change comes about, in part, by the resistance of marginal men to the roles that society casts them into — people who are not willing to accept the definitions of status and behavior that are given them. His unconventionality can thus be seen as a continuing protest against unequal status, a questioning of the very terms and definitions of status. His Aunt Flossie was content to slip from one box into another; she made a life out of the attainment of lower-middle-class status, the neat house, the proper clothes, the middle-class amusements. She has never left England, though her two sisters went to Australia and America. But Kenneth was not content with moving into another box; he wanted to break the boxes altogether.

It may be asked, and I have asked myself, why all the young men who were making the same kind of status shift that Kenneth was — in particular, the friends who grew up with him and shared much the same cultural milieu — did not turn out as unconventional as he did. Ron Shaw, it is true, is inventive, and has an entrepreneurial quality in his business, but he has a very mild and unassuming personality; Ernest Dundas is a quiet high school teacher; Robert Shone has been knighted in the service of the government as an economic adviser in the steel industry; Fred Watts has also gone into government service and is very supportive of the established order. Only Bernard Ash seems to have a share of the rebellious attitude so evident in Kenneth. He, like Kenneth, is something of a divided man, writing novels and also conducting an advertising business; also like Kenneth, he made a switch in religious affiliation as well as a considerable advance in economic status in the course of his lifetime. He was not an only child but closer to it than any of the others; he had a sister rather older than he was. We have suggested that the nonconformity of Methodism produced considerable power for social change; Bernard was not a Methodist but the "outsider" status of the minority Jew may have served a similar function in branding him from the beginning as one who did not belong to the main stream. Kenneth's other Methodist friends whom I have met — all more conventional than he — had either a higher or a more stable income than the Boulding family's.

Other factors may have to be combined with low income, a sense of misplaced status, and upward mobility — these were common to all these friends — before a consistent rebel is produced. My guess is that economic uncertainty combined with low level income may be a factor; that belonging to a nonconformist or oppressed religious group may be a factor; that the fact that people are already shocked by one's performance in an area not under one's control (both Bernard and Kenneth were stutterers) may possibly contribute to the adaptation of becoming shocking on purpose in order to gain some control over this segment of life; and that perhaps having conflicting talents, leading one in different directions at once, may keep one aware of the need for flexibility and outraged at the societal crime of putting people arbitrarily in boxes.

I I I

Boulding's impulsiveness and decisiveness are other qualities many of his friends have remarked on. "He works quickly, has good judgment, knows what he wants and goes after it." "He is impulsive; it arouses opposition sometimes but makes him a delightful personality." "He gives presents suddenly, for irrational reasons, never out of a sense of duty." One of his narrative journal-poems begins, "I like a sudden, drastic change of plan." In another (1946), he examines this process rather thoughtfully:

> . . . revelling in the sense of free-will, of the spur of
> the moment,
> Of conventions left far behind, of a world bent close
> to our wish.

> A sudden change of plan
> Reveals a God in man,
> The God whose name is will.
> His voice is never still
> In us he makes much revel
> But is he God or Devil?

This question, of course, he has had to ask himself many times at points of witness for conscience, or when he seemed to be led toward some major decision. Sometimes when faced with a decision, he and Elise have tried to be economic and calculating, to chalk up all the factors pro and con; "and then," she says, "we sort of mentally toss a coin: and we always seem to come out with the same side up!" Sometimes he gives himself time to try something out, as the year at Colgate before he brought his mother over, the year at McGill, after which they decided to go back to Ames, and the year at Boulder before he made the final decision to stay there. And he once made a decision and later changed his mind: after the year at the Center for Advanced Studies in Behavioral Sciences in Palo Alto he accepted a job in California, but, during a few days in the western desert, he rethought the decision, felt it was not the right one, and retracted his acceptance of the new job and his resignation of the old one. But mostly, on everyday matters, he finds decision-making quick and easy, almost automatic. It may be his conviction that in most things it really doesn't matter, that many alternatives are equally good, which contributes to this ease. (On being asked what he wanted for breakfast one day, he replied, "Anything is fine — I'm omnivorous!") And it also may be that his musing about God and Devil has some relationship to the operation of his inner processes, that the gates to various psychic levels are not closed as tightly for him as for most people. We will examine this idea more closely in connection with the creative process, in the next chapter.

But speaking of gates, it would be useful to evaluate his general level of expression of feelings, what comes through and what does not. His own description of his emotional life is given in the introduction to *The Image:*

> I am located in the midst of a world of subtle intima-
> tions and emotions. I am sometimes elated, sometimes a
> little depressed, sometimes happy, sometimes sad, some-
> times inspired, sometimes pedantic. I am open to subtle
> intimations of a presence beyond the world of space and
> time and sense. (p. 5)

He does not mention anger here, though he admits to it in other places ("I am hopping mad" about the denial of a passport to China). Fred Watts's memory of him at Oxford is "I can't remember him ever being angry, ever. . . . He was certainly equable; I can't remember him being in low spirits; he may have been by himself, but not in company." "I never saw Ken punctured," and, "There was great humanity and controlled emotion in him," are other high school and college-years observations. His high school friend Ernest Dundas reported, "When you met him in the morning he'd always come jolly and bursting with joie de vivre; but if things were wrong or he thought them unjust — someone maneuvering people or dictating to them — he would be very indignant." A description by Carlene Blanchard, a friend of his Michigan years, sounds as if time has not changed this very much:

> He has the gusto of carrying through no matter what, an infectious ability to not become enmeshed in despair, to see the larger perspective and keep a real faith that the universe is hopeful and positive. He comes in booming and singing and carried away in realms of ecstasy; it's a relatively continuous quality. He has it there to be tapped all the time and he is down infrequently and not for long.

And Elise, who has lived with him a long time, confirms this picture. Somewhere within him is a continuing source of childlike gaiety.

He has a great store of physical energy, which contributes to a sense of well-being. An impression of total energy comes in a description by Will Baxter from Edinburgh days, of Kenneth bursting in with his (then) black hair, ruddy complexion, and flashing eyes and teeth: "It was a little as if a good Satan had come into the room!" Today, a travel and lecture schedule which would exhaust many a younger man seems instead to inspirit and rejuvenate him.

I would suggest another reason for his inexhaustibility: he has been able to move most of his life activities into the area of play. In a sense, everything he does is play for him, even though it would be hard work for others. He teaches because he enjoys it, writes because there are ideas inside him pushing to come out, lectures because he likes to entertain and it excites and pleases him to instruct, inspire, and amuse an audience. Erikson has said, "To the working adult, play is re-creation. It permits a periodical stepping out from those forms of defined limitation which are his social reality," such as time, or fate and causality, or status.[7] But Boulding has already stepped out of defined limitations. He does not let things touch him that push other people around: the pressure of time, the requirements of other people. He may have to take off to catch a plane; he would stop (a few years ago) to show his new camera to his bedridden mother. He may have publishers dunning him about deadlines; he will write them a calm letter saying he isn't finished yet. He may return from a long business trip to a pile of urgent business; he will say, "First things first," and sit down to show his secretary the sketches he made while he was gone. He carves pieces out of the day for his own renewal, playing the recorder or painting a watercolor while all about him may be desperately responding to the call of duty. If his surroundings are boring, he turns to the entertainment within, and produces a doodle or a limerick that catches the ridiculous essence of the situation.

Professionally, he makes the bargains he chooses to make, then does what he has agreed to because he enjoys it. The things that are not play for him are the things he refuses to do. If he gets into them by accident, he breaks down: administrative details, responsibility for small children, certain money matters; these things he carefully and firmly guards himself against. He does, almost all the time, exactly what he wants to do. People around him learn to adjust to this, and most of the time he is so much fun that it's worth it. And it is because he has moved so much of his life into the sphere of play — and yet found it so fortunately profitable because what he wants to do also serves the needs of others — that he can go on so equably and find the springs of so much energy.

Another dimension of enjoyment and play is his entertainer role. "I don't like Solos unless sung by Me," he put it in 1931. There is some likelihood that it was not just natural wit and talent (though he has that) and the liking for being the center of attention (though he has that) which drew him into this function, which he fills in the classroom, with the family, on the lecture stage, at social gatherings — and, presumably, for himself when he is alone. Guy Swanson has formulated a theory about the determinants of defenses in which he suggests that personal defenses are aspects of an individual's role in a social relationship.[8] In connection with the development of defenses in a child, he pointed out that the parents' deficiencies in interpersonal skills may be compensated for by the children, thus leading them to specialize in some particular problem-solving skill, leading to the overlearning of a particular related defense. The child who adopts the "harmonizer" role, for instance, may adopt with it the defense of reaction-formation, the denial of negative desires and replacement of them with their opposite.

From the record of diaries and letters, it is clear that Kenneth's mother's standards for nonexpression of negative feelings were very high, and that she found it difficult to meet them herself. Any loss of temper was regarded as a disaster. After one such incident in the family (by whom she does not say), her diary records,

> This has been a worrying week and everybody in the house upset through one member of the family loosing their temper! . . . alas! that there should be so many wrecks left on the shore of life when the storm of passion has spent itself. Often broken hearts and shattered nerves are the direct result of bad temper.

Another entry shows her own efforts and failures: "I was feeling very depressed this morning. . . . Mother told me she 'loved the very ground I walked on.' it was lovely to hear it. dear Mother! she tries so hard to keep cheerful under difficulties, I wish I was more like her."

From what we know of the relationship between Bessie and Will, it seems to have been a fairly comfortable one without a great deal of friction; but when Grandpa and Grandma Rowe moved into the top floor at 4 Seymour Street, even Grandma's patience could not contain the explosive mixture of George Rowe and Will Boulding. This was in 1920; Kenneth was ten. The top floor, which used to be his playroom, he was forced to give up now; Grandpa, with his deafness, his black moods, and the pounding of his hammer in the basement blacksmith shop, was now a constant presence; and his mother, given herself to flights of desire and seasons of irritation, had to try to be a buffer between Grandpa's demands and Will's exasperated righteousness. It would not be surprising if such a situation required a harmonizer.

There were a number of alternative models among the adults about him. There was Aunt Flossie, shrewd and tart and a little critical; Aunt Rosie, ineffectual and frequently retreating into illness; saintly and patient Grandma; Grandpa, who said outrageous things and got a lot of attention; Father, who spent a lot of time away from home at work during the week and in good works on the weekends; Mother, who tried to keep herself composed and everybody happy, sometimes wrote poetry for elevation or amusement and sometimes simply escaped the house; and Aunt Ada, who loved to dress up and play-act and liked nothing better than the days when her nephew was dropped off at her house. It looks as if the cleverness of his mother, the dramatic playfulness of his aunt, and the outrageousness of his grandfather, with perhaps the covering aspect of something of the composure of his grandmother, were tried on by this small boy until they made a mix that could set the family laughing and relieve its tensions, and, in the laughter, perhaps soothe some of his own. When he found he could write funny poems, there were good uses for this skill; he could sharpen his wit on a ready audience; but if he should feel angry or aggressive, there was no room for that, unless it was turned into righteous anger, aggression against convention, or a barb that could be laughed at. His father's kindness remained his ideal, but was not easy to put on.

Although the only punishment he can remember getting was for "putting on a show" when they had some elegant company, Kenneth must have been encouraged in his entertaining within the family. That they came to depend on him for the entertainer and harmonizer role may be deduced from comments in letters. After Aunt Ada went to Australia, Kenneth wrote to her every week, and apparently the whole family read his letters for their amusing touches before he sent them, for several times he finished the first page with a false closing for Grandpa to read, and then continued with another page about Grandpa's doings. In one of Aunt Ada's letters to Kenneth, she says, "Why I should feel the end of the world had come nearly, if your letters stopped." And after Kenneth went to Oxford and was also writing to his mother and father regularly, his mother often mentions waiting eagerly for a letter; but the letters were expected to be gay, and almost always were. By the fall of 1930, he reflected in a letter to Aunt Ada:

> You know, really, quite seriously, I'm beginning to think that my stock of jokes is getting used up. One cannot, of course, write a letter brimful of sparkling wit nearly every week for three years without repeating oneself a little . . .

When he was sending home an operetta in sections, his mother's response to one sad song was, "I hope next week's song will be more cheerful." Even when his grandfather died, the letter he wrote telling Aunt Ada about it transformed the event into a symbolic myth in a strongly hopeful vein. Except for one or two letters mentioning being homesick (in a light and humorous way, and only after his mother asked), a reader could not begin to guess the torment of his first year at Oxford. Perhaps he did not even acknowledge it to himself until later.

I V

The child is formed in many ways in interaction with the people around him. Kenneth respected his father for his work in the church, but not for his work as a heating engineer, and while they shared affection, there does not seem to have been a very tight bond between them. From him, however, he may have gotten some stability of temperament, common sense, and humility. He even sometimes seems to be looking at himself in a surprised kind of way, just as his father used to look at him, wondering how this creature had hatched out. With his mother, however, he always had an extremely close relationship. Her intelligence, her sparkle and wit and joy in living, her forthright friendliness, are all reflected in him. And he was the center of her life — not all of it, but its center. She had other activities; she was active in the Chapel; she took care of her husband, and parents, and many guests; she made good friendships wherever she went. But her pride, and her hopes, and, increasingly, her sense of self, circled about her son. In the spring when he was thirteen, she wrote in her diary,

> Will and Kenneth left me this morning to go to Colwyn Bay, the first time Kenneth has ever left me, I dread to think of the day when he may leave me to go out into the wide world, he has been all my world for so long, and he is so good and we love each other so much, but always the thought is there, "he will leave me one day", I hope I shall not be selfish when the time comes, and make it hard for him.

287

Fig. 20. Kenneth and his mother, 1925
(*photo from Michigan Historical Collections*)

When he was seventeen, he wrote a love sonnet for her birthday, and she wrote him long poems for his eighteenth and twenty-first birthdays, and for his fortieth. There were sheaves of letters exchanged, and, all through her life, he sent her postcards from wherever he went on his travels. She sent him a warm and lovely letter on the day she read the news that he had not won the Newdigate Prize, full of her disappointment, her love, her assurance that he could do better next time, good advice (praising her husband and asking Kenneth to try to be like him and to depend on God's guidance), and anticipation of their coming weekend together. On the several times she visited Oxford, Kenneth treated her royally, took her punting on the Cherwell, fixed her a picnic tea basket, took her around to be introduced to his friends. One of these friends, Harold Loukes, contrasted Kenneth's enthusiasm for his parents with the feelings of the rest of the students: "We were all very self-conscious of our social origins, and most of us would keep our parents out of the conversation, but he brought his mother round, though it was obvious she was of simple background. It was a very secure relationship, pure loving; he would make her feel Queen of the May." Kenneth was perfectly conscious that she did not fit in the setting, yet he carried it off. He never would let her know the gap he felt widening between his intellectual and social condition, and hers. And from the time his father died, he had no question that it was his responsibility to be her full support. From then on, until he was married, they made a home together. Even eight years after his marriage, when he took out a new passport, he listed her as the person to be notified in case of accident. Although she was really too old to enjoy her grandchildren (she was sixty-seven when the first one was born), she wrote in her diary in 1952 on receiving a picture of Kenneth, Elise, and their three children, "My heart cracked the day Kenneth was married but a picture like this is excellent surgery!"

It is perhaps a tribute to his very real autonomy and independence, that, surrounded with such devotion, even as a boy Kenneth was not in leading strings of any kind. He started finding his own way and making his own decisions very early, and it is almost as if his parents followed him from then on. His mother, indeed, came to America, and became a Quaker, dropping her own strong Methodist connections as early as Kenneth's Chicago days, because of his choices. The wife he chose was almost a total opposite of his mother, beautiful rather than pretty, tall and statuesque rather than short and elfin, strong and assured rather than anxious, gently deflating rather than effusively praising. "Elise," he wrote in a letter shortly after his marriage, "makes an excellent Elder, and pulls my coat tails when I have said enough!"

It is probably true that the constriction of Bessie's life led her to concentrate far more on her son than if she could have found an independent identity for herself. She was intelligent, literate, with a sensitivity to human emotion and a capacity for humor; she could perhaps, with more education and a broader experience, have been a writer with wider scope and found outlets for her poems, other than the limited printing of hymns and memorials for Brunswick Chapel, the newspaper in Hamilton, and an occasional publication in one of the Friends journals. There was very little range of alternatives for Will, in the setting of his time and class, and even less for her. Dressmaking, housework, or factory work, possibly elementary school teaching, might have been open; before World War I, women did not work in offices or in professions. In any case, when a woman married, it was expected that she stay at home and care for her house and family, pick up all the broken pieces of the lives about her, care for invalid relatives, and the like: and this Bessie did, but not without strain. In 1921 there is a diary entry: "Mrs. G. likes my verses. I am writing some now but never have time to think these days! When I get a thought worth while I am too busy to write it down and when I'm not busy I'm too tired." In 1923, "All my M.S.S. sent back this morning with thanks and regrets etc.! I wonder where they fail, am beginning to think my verses are no use, nobody wants them. I shall have to concentrate on housekeeping after all!" There is an early poem which quite specifically connects her frustrated wishes for fame or heroism with her hope for fulfillment through her son, and a passage from an essay of 1920 carries the same theme:

> I have a little son of ten, he is devoted to me and thinks Mother is perfection, but just think! when he is twenty I shall be fifty, I should hate him to think me old and a back number, I feel I want to do something big. Something that will make him proud of me, something different to keeping house, cooking and shopping, If I could only write a book and make a name for myself! . . . [But] I shall never make myself famous that way. When the Boy grows up he may do some of the things I have always longed to do.

Her impatience with limitations, and her struggle to be brave and noble, run through all these records. Her poems are often about nature or about faith, usually ending with a reassurance of peace or trust in God. Some are light verse and many celebrate special events, birthdays of friends, a new house, anniversaries, the achievement of a term of service in the church. She needed to be needed, and she needed to be busy. The Bookroom was an effort to fill this gap, but it was in the wrong place and time: the neighborhood was not a book-reading neighborhood, nobody had money to spare, and the lack of business acumen hampered both her and Will, so that, like her poems, the bookstore filled time and rendered some service but was not a real success. In some ways, Kenneth's strong tendency to break free of constriction and limitation may be seen as a struggle against being enveloped by her, and in others, as a struggle *for* her, to continue her own drive to break free.

v

To this element in his life, his bond with his mother, Boulding has applied the same sophistication, perceptiveness, and creative handling that he brings to other difficult areas: a measure of acceptance, a measure of walling off (the refusal to get involved in things that are outside his competence), and a measure of conversion (transforming the tension into a creative production) — with, overall, a generous measure of goodwill. Freudian implications have not escaped, but neither have they tormented him. In the schools he went to, psychology was not considered a segment of knowledge at all, and he still has a lingering feeling that delving into the subconscious is rather indecent. He has carried on, for most of his life, a muted feud with Freud, beginning perhaps in response to a talk he heard at Oxford in 1930, "Psychoanalysis and Religious Belief." Around that time, at any rate, he concluded a talk of his own with this "veiled note of warning: The Church might have been well advised had it burnt Sigmund Freud." Another production of the same period was an operetta the butt of whose jokes was a scatter-brained female professor of psychology. Of course, he has matured to a recognition of some usefulness in Freud's insights, but still keeps his tongue in his cheek, as in his verse "Night Thoughts from my Own Couch," written in the middle 1950s, of which I quote about two-thirds:

> I am not greatly overjoyed
> In contemplating Sigmund Freud.
> Nor do I count myself among
> The ardent followers of Jung
> And yet like every normal lad
> I hate my Mother and my Dad.

(A natural feeling which extends
To sisters, cousins, aunts and friends.)
I do not know exactly how Ma
Gave me all my little trauma,
Or in what manner Papa's sex is
Linked to all my guilt complexes.
But Ma (and I) would have done better
If no Papa had ever met her.
For parents are the only source
Of most neuroses now in force.
And parents, being dull or lazy
Tend to drive their children crazy.
And so my deep subconscious wish
Is this: to have been born a fish.
For fish do not have either sex
Of parent breathing down their necks
And live their unrestricted lives
Devoid of husbands or of wives.
Their mental difficulties browse
On thots of food instead of fraus
Their price for straying off the beaten
Path is simply — being eaten!
An end as quick and neat and useful
As man's is slipshod and excuseful.
The evolutionary plan
May not in fact be aimed at man
Who may be climbing on a slim
And quickly tapering branch or limb
While the main trunk prepares a race
Of super-fish to take his place . . .

This quality of being able to back off from emotion-loaded, threat, or problem areas, to be perfectly clear about them but to de-emotionalize them or defuse them somehow, and then to incorporate them in a spoken or written verbalization which is light enough for author and audience to handle, or, alternatively, deep enough to give a sense of communion with greatness that lifts one out of the ordinary (as in his Nayler Sonnets or messages of ministry in meeting for worship), may be called distancing. It is a quality Ernst Kris discusses in his analysis of the creative artist. Kris, in this classic description of "regression in the service of the ego," postulates the ego's allowing hidden levels temporarily to come to the fore, then the detachment of power from the original conflict, the neutralization and fusion of libidinal and aggressive drives, with the result that a wide range of subjects can be presented without too much threat.[9] This description feeds into the dreaming or fantasy that is so important to Boulding, and into his humor. Distancing is perhaps one of the most striking abilities he possesses, and is probably the key to the translation of the conflicts and tensions we have traced as so much a part of his life but so little apparent in his outward mien, into his prolific flow of books, lectures, and articles. Intellectually, in Boulding's thought, this distancing is related to the systems point of view. But even in personal upsets he is often able to step outside the particular and into the larger framework. When he was awarded a ticket for a driving mishap on his 1933 Western tour, he regarded the event not as a disaster but as an interesting introduction to one facet of an unfamiliar culture.

This process of distancing is also very evident in Boulding's TAT record. There is, first, an overpowering sense of uncertainty; hardly a statement is made without some qualification. There is a clinging to the stimulus, returning for more clues, which signifies a reluctance to enter into the situation with empathy and feeling, or to identify with the characters represented. In many ways, he kept himself outside the experience, willing to tell a brief story about the picture but separating it from himself.

In some ways, in life too, this distancing ability can enter between the man and the experience, rather than aiding a transformation of the experience into an expressible form. This seems to happen particularly in relationships with other people in close interaction, where he frequently does not sense the other's need. Combined with his tendency to entertain and be a star, it keeps him from being helpful in a discussion when it is important to sense the movement and feeling of a group, and sometimes prevents him from entering into a feeling someone else is trying to share with him. The natural adoption of the leadership role, the continual sharing of his rich inner processes with those about him to the exclusion of theirs, is a source of enrichment; but it is also a source of trial when it stifles the communication and talents of others. His insight and tenderness for humanity as a whole sometimes seems to leave little room for insight and tenderness for those he is with at the moment. Robert White has thus described the use of humor, which is part of this distancing talent, as defense and adaptation:

> A person with a gift for humor can use it as a technique for preventing serious contact with others. . . . Yet on the whole it is highly adaptive: we owe a great deal to the people who can make us laugh. . . . They sometimes achieve real dignity as social critics, puncturing pretensions and directing the deadly shaft of ridicule against vicious self-seeking and ill will.[10]

V I

Before we conclude this chapter, which has largely relied on the observations of others, it would be well to have a look at the way Boulding sees himself operating in the world. In addition to the TAT, I used what is called a "Q-sort" technique. Paragraphs taken from Murray's definitions of the twenty major personality variables [11] were typed on separate cards, and Boulding was asked to sort them into piles representing those most descriptive and least descriptive of himself. Those he rated as most descriptive of himself were the needs for achievement, understanding, play (particularly emphasizing fantasy), exhibition (that is, "to make an impression, to be seen and heard, to excite, amaze, fascinate, entertain, shock, intrigue, amuse or entice others": this one he was *quite* sure about), sentience (the enjoyment of sense impressions), affiliation (affection and friendship), and nurturance (caring for the weak and helpless). He was ambivalent on four others: counteraction (making up for failure by restriving; searching for difficulties to overcome), succorance (being taken care of), dominance (controlling one's human environment), and autonomy (resisting coercion and restriction, defying convention, shaking off restraint). We can see reflected here the values of the intellect, aesthetics, and religion (if we equate religion with care and friendship). The entertainer role and the fantasy-distancing process are also to be found here, but it is striking that the need for autonomy which I have seen as so central he views as questionable.

The needs represented by the characters in his TAT stories closely parallel these, with achievement and autonomy most positively weighted and sentience next most frequent. Entering in minor roles are the needs for affiliation, avoidance of harm, nurturance, counteraction, exhibition, order, and succorance.

His images of himself through the years may also be seen in his excursions into fancy dress and fantasy. In 1919, he dressed as Robin Hood for the Peace Parade in Chard; in 1934, he was the Knave of Hearts for a costume party. Both these characters are bad but not wicked: Robin Hood robbed the rich to give to the poor, and the Knave stole the tarts because he was hungry and mischievous. Boulding's self-image now is more like Pooh bear, tolerant, big, and bluff, enjoying things and letting them go their way.

He produced, in 1968, a visual autobiography, reproduced here (fig. 21) in response to a question at a party, "Tell something about yourself without using any words." It includes Liverpool and a ferry on the Mersey, Oxford and a mortarboard, John Wesley and George Fox (the

Fig. 21. Self-Portrait by Boulding

founders of Methodism and Quakerism), the skyscrapers of Chicago, the mountains of Boulder, love, economics, children, books, and a frantic lecture schedule. And he tried hard, but he could not quite refrain from using any words!

If we could picture the major goals he has demonstrated in his life as the two channels they seem to flow in, we could call them being productive with his mind and being of service to God and man. The latter includes something of a sense of mission, in which his mother's prayer before he was born may have played a part after all. He has been known to say, "I rather fancy myself in a John-the-Baptist role," and "I really am a soldier in the Lamb's war" (counted on to fight Christ's battles). But the two streams flow together. As we know, the roles of scientist and saint have battled all his life for preëminence within him; he endows both with the quality of mission in the passage, "The scientist and the saint have strictly complementary tasks: the scientist to show where we are, the saint to show where we ought to be," and in his dis-

297

cussion of the "diseases of the value system," for which, he
suggests, the social sciences and religion together may develop a therapy. The use of the mind in the service of
man, and particularly a literary gift, comes to the fore in
his references to the important part that images play in
shaping our lives, and writers in shaping images. "It is not
reality by which we are moved, but our image of it, and
our image of it is largely created by rhetoric. . . . Rhetoric is the fulcrum of social power." [12]

A conscious goal is part of what moves man, and as
Boulding looks over the satisfactions of his life, he notes
the achievement of professional status, wealth, a happy
family, and a recognized place in his chosen religious
group; but all these, one gets the feeling, came rather
after the fact of his doing just what he wanted, with some
attention to what God's will for him might be. As in the
Nayler sonnet about goodness (No. 2), he gives the impression of operating more from inner springs than a distant call:

> Ask the sweet spring upon the mountain top
> What makes his sinless water flow so free:
> Is it the call of some far-distant sea,
> Or the deep pressure that no crust can stop?

VII

Some of this inner pressure relates to what may be called
his compulsion to write. He sometimes replies to a friend
who asks him what he is working on now, "my bibliography!" His bibliography is already practically a book, with
the single-spaced typewritten list of each year's publications now reaching the length of one and a half to two
pages, exceeding even the degree of fever mentioned by
Robert Merton in his diagnosis of the itch to publish, *in-
sanabile scribendi cacoëthes*. In this disease, age is an important predisposing factor; attacks are recurrent, never
conferring immunity. "Onset is as a rule sudden, pre-

ceded by a slight, scarcely noticeable publication. The fever to publish is intense; rising rapidly, it may within a few years reach the degree of 15 or 20 publications annually . . ." [13]

The compulsion to write is fed partly by the tremendous store within — a magnificent mind operating at full speed most of the time — partly by the entertainer, partly by the missionary, very greatly by the audience demand (most of his recent articles are solicited); and it is held in check occasionally by the saint. The battle between cleverness and wonder, pride and humility, is fought on the field of shaping what comes out. An unpolished, uncopied poem without a date may introduce us to a feel for the struggle:

> Because I have a constipated mass
> Of stuff within my mind, I have to write,
> Although I know the brilliant crusty blight
> Of cleverness will make me out an ass
> And this stale age, bloated with verbal gas,
> (Ha, Muse, think you to trap me in a sonnet —
> I'm done with corsets — and refuse to bonnet
> My straying ends of thought) — this age, I say
> (This age, being what I have seen through my own
>   Knothole,
> And not including the opinion of the last hottentot)
> This age, having lost simplicity,
> Humility, Tranquility,
> Or at least, not having them — whether lost or not,
> Now worships cleverness, admires obscurity,
> Allusiveness, and likes to have in hand
> Poetry that it cannot understand.
> Then I, being clever, not averse to praise,
> Not liberated yet from this world's ways
> Sophisticated in my love of God,
> Yet hankering after steps some ancients trod,
> My eye united with the scene it sees,
> And half infected with the same disease,
> I shall be tempted into saying things

That are not true, because the words have wings
And I shall find
In the vast, ripe, confusion of my mind
Bright threads of clarity, drawn on the string
Not of the true, but of the interesting.

There are probably other roots to the need to write
and speak. Perhaps counter-reaction to his stuttering is a
factor. It is likely that since writing and speaking are the
tools of the intellect, and the intellect became Kenneth's
major mode of finding success in the years of latency when
he was probably doubting that success would come, they
have a great appeal for him. It is also possible that we can
find factors further back, in the years when he was learning to walk and talk. Innate traits are important, as Robert White points out in *Lives in Progress,* because of the
encouragement they give to certain kinds of learning, and
the limits they set on other kinds. We can only read back-
wards and make guesses from meager clues, for we have no
real evidence on when Kenneth started to walk, though
there is a record of his saying words by his second spring,
as he was being pushed in a carriage. However, a mother
pushes a baby in a carriage long after he can walk, for his
speed and endurance take years to develop to the limits of
her tolerance. But we know that Kenneth was big for his
age, which might have made his walking later than normal, and that he was described in his childhood as awkward and badly coordinated, as "slouching and ambling."
If we postulate a high innate verbal ability and a fairly
low muscular ability, we can see how this contrast could
have become even more pronounced (leaning still on
White). If a child learns to talk early but walk late and is
praised for verbal prowess, "he presses forward along the
line of his excellence, maximizing his competence and
building it into his main interests, meanwhile neglecting
his physical activities, with the result that a difference in-
nately small becomes a difference actually enormous." [14]
What Erikson calls the "locomotor-genital" period, then,

the years from three to five, would have been doubly difficult for him as he tried to penetrate his environment
with less-than-perfect coordination and work through the
classical conflict of infantile sexuality. The middle of this
critical period brought the sudden constriction of his environment, in the fall of 1914, with the move back to Liverpool, compounding both his maturational problems
(coming to terms with his sex as well as penetrating his
surroundings competently) at the same time. The verbal,
locomotive, and intellectual connections in this period
overlap, as is made clear by Erikson's description:

> The *intrusive mode* dominating much of the behavior of
> this stage characterizes a variety of configurationally "sim-
> ilar" activities and fantasies. These include the intrusion
> into other bodies by physical attack: the intrusion into
> other people's ears and minds by aggressive talking; the
> intrusion into space by vigorous locomotion; the
> intrusion into the unknown by consuming curiosity.[15]

That Kenneth's locomotion was not just awkward but
remained an uncrossed emotional hurdle may be guessed
from several later evidences. He remembers a game from
childhood, making the little boys "do Charlie." Now the
main characteristic of Charlie Chaplin that could be imi-
tated would be his walk, the shuffling, slouching gait.
That Kenneth got enjoyment from seeing smaller boys
walk in a scarcely competent way would indicate he had
just conquered, or barely conquered, the skill himself.
Phyllis Greenacre has observed that a child shows pleasure in making fun of another's failure when his mastery
of a skill is still uncertain: he repeats his victory to overcome half-assimilated fear that he can't do it.[16] Kenneth's
lifelong aversion to competitive athletics also has the emotional tinge of feeling "no good at it." And there was his
continued yearning for, and leadership of, rambles into
the countryside — intrusions into the environment, literally so when he displayed his penchant for trespassing. It

is almost as if he was redoing the incomplete locomotor-genital stage. And finally, we have the record of his minor accidents with cars and bicycles and the rare times when his emotional balance is completely lost, which seem to occur most frequently in connection with travels — locomotion — in the midst of complicated traffic or confusing directions.

The continuing pleasure in the verbal mode and the continuing blocks in the locomotor mode may be the opposite sides of the same developmental coin. He climbed Long's Peak in 1969, one of the highest peaks in the range of the Rockies just behind Boulder, where he lives. He trained for the feat (he had done no climbing and little hiking for years) by swimming, which was the one sport in which he deigned to indulge in secondary school. Swimming, like hiking, is noncompetitive, not bound by arbitrary rules. When I asked him why he suddenly hauled off and climbed a mountain, he said, "It was an aberration." An intrusion into the sky, it was a fitting aberration.

A final major facet of Boulding's personality is his share of pride and humility, measured by his image of what a man can do and what the world looks like. His sense of his own competence, gained in experience with people, is tremendous. It is self-esteem, built out of efficacy in action and others' response to what one has done, rather than the narcissistic interest of self-love. But pride is a shadow always dogging his footsteps, a trap to trip the extremely capable man, and humility is his salvation. He does not see the world wholly as his oyster, or even as man's, but as God's also. It is the "precious little planet, this blue-green cradle of life with its rosy mantle," which carries an "immense wealth and variety of evolutionary freight and evolutionary potential." [17] His view of the environment as presented in all his TAT stories put together may be summed up in two words: exploitable and ambiguous. It may be dangerous or hostile, friendly or protective, or useful. I would judge (and he concurs) that

Boulding's world-view contains a good deal of darkness; that he sees himself endowed with enough resources to overcome the "things that go bump in the night" but, at the same time, he recognizes that they are there and that for most people (and for the world as a spaceship unit) the struggle is touch and go. If the light triumphs, it is because of its quality, not its quantity.

Humility, he claims, plays an adaptive function in the evolutionary process. It has been so for him; Will Baxter, who was in Edinburgh at the time of Kenneth's major battle against stuttering, told me that the secret of curing his stammer was meekness, relaxation, letting go. Boulding often trades on humility for humor: "Every time I read a transcript of my own remarks, it always sounds like complete nonsense, and it all sounds like me." But quite soberly, his humility is genuine. He has expressed his surprise that he was made a prefect at Liverpool Collegiate ("It gave me delusions of grandeur"), and that he got the best "first" in his field at Oxford, feeling himself quite ordinary and run-of-the-mill. When he recounted to me the major decisions that had shaped his life, the general feeling he gave was that a lot of things were decided for him, were accidental, or not his doing — when actually, as I have pointed out, he was, for the most part, very active in making things happen. His view of man, and himself, is only occasionally inflated, and here, as in many other conflict and tension areas, he walks a careful middle course. "Economic man is a clod, heroic man is a fool, but somewhere between the clod and the fool, human man, if the expression may be pardoned, steers his tottering way." [18] Recently I asked him brashly, "When did you begin to feel eminent?" His first, heroic answer with a laugh, was "About 1918." (He would have been eight at the time.) And then, the sober economic answer: "I don't really feel eminent." And finally, the human answer: "I'm still that little boy back in Seymour Street; the whole thing is a bit of a fraud."

14

Career and Creativity

It is much easier to think something up than to look it up.

— KEB, "Ecology and Environment" in *TransAction*

I

It is our task now to pick up Boulding's career where we left it in chapter 12, at the point where he had published his "monumental book" and could turn his attention from work to marriage.

During his last year at Edinburgh he had taken on an extra job on the side, a piece of research into the milk and meat problems in British agriculture, funded by the Rowntree Trust. It was probably through people who had known of his work there that he was invited in 1941 to a post with the League of Nations, whose economic and financial section had recently moved its headquarters to Princeton. The salary was attractive, and he had already decided to make this move before he met Elise; but it simplified his newly married status to make a physical change to a different place as well. He enjoyed his work there, particularly the anomalies he discovered (for example, that most of Europe's food was grown in *industrial* regions), but had to resign, as described in chapter 6, over his supervisors' objections to the statement on disarmament that he and Elise prepared. He then took the offer of a job at Fisk.

304

Tom Jones, a Quaker friend, was president of Fisk University at the time Boulding went there, in 1942. It was a productive year; both Kenneth and Elise enjoyed living on campus and interacting closely with faculty and students. It was no doubt here that Kenneth first identified his own sense of deprivation with the problems of black students in America. He recalls almost "passing" for black on a faculty of all shades among whom categories of blackness and whiteness were never spelled out.

But, in the next summer, though reluctant to leave Fisk, he was enticed by an offer from a department which, though obscure, he regarded as one of the best in the country. It also promised him a good deal of freedom. Albert Hart, his friend from Chicago days, was his major contact there. Theodore Schultz, the chairman of the Economics Department at Iowa State College, wanted to give a general economist a year to study labor and move toward becoming a labor economist, without any teaching duties until after that first year. Boulding, an abstract theorist whose only move toward specialization or empirical research had been his work in agriculture, was an interesting choice. Schultz appreciated the creative potential of a fresh approach to a field. "He had the idea," Boulding recalls, "you ought to have a labor economist among the cows; this had to be somebody impartial, and the only way you'd get somebody impartial in this field was to find somebody who knew nothing about it at all."

Boulding jumped at the opportunity to broaden his knowledge. He spent the year doing a good deal of reading and going about the country visiting offices of labor unions, attending conventions, and interviewing labor people. He credits this year of mastering a new field with being the impetus which led him into tackling the broader reaches of social dynamics. "I had been taught at Oxford that sociology didn't exist, so I didn't have to study it, and psychology was negligible . . . the only thing which existed was economics and maybe philosophy. . . .

305

Getting into the labor field made me realize that if you were going to tackle anything of an applied nature in social systems, you had to have all the social sciences to do it."

It was also helpful in this broadening process that economics and sociology at Ames were very closely related departments; faculty people and their wives from both groups shared in frequent conversations, both academic and social. Kenneth began to pick up sociological concepts and modes of thinking from his colleagues, and the rest he got through "domestic osmosis" after Elise decided to pursue the field of sociology.

For the academic year of 1946–47, Boulding was invited to be chairman of the Economics Department at McGill University in Montreal. (In the course of that year Elise went to Syracuse for the birth of John Russell, their first baby, because "we want to have a President!") Housing was very tight in Montreal; they had to live with another family while they were there; and although they enjoyed the picturesqueness of the city and the department at McGill, the constrictions of the British social system seemed to weigh on them even in French Quebec. Boulding also discovered that administration was not his meat, and forever after refused all offers to become chairman of a department. In the end, the fact that they still had a house in Ames and none in Montreal may have tipped the coin. They went back to Ames at the end of the year, and stayed there until they made the move to the University of Michigan in 1949.

The years at Michigan with the beautiful interlude in California have been described in earlier chapters. Though Boulding made many weekend speaking trips, and, in the summer of 1953, spent two months in Brazil, his enlarging family made it difficult to consider seriously any possibilities of a year's leave in some exotic place. But children grow, and soon after the crisis point when the parents were just emerging from ten years of diapers only to look forward to fifteen years of teenagers, they decided to accept a visiting year in Kingston, Jamaica. Boulding found paradise in the tropics, as their Christmas letter of 1960, after their return to Michigan, indicates:

> . . . On summer's horizon, Jamaica
> Sails like a great green galleon of an isle
> Glowing in sun on the sapphire garment of sea.
> Bleak northern December makes father a little homesick
> Like Adam for Eden, for home that is time, not place,
> But our Viking children are glad for the north again . . .

Along with his work that year on *Conflict and Defense,* he had spent three weeks in the summer in a seminar in Leningrad, with Russian and American students and some from other countries, trying to throw a thin guy wire across the communication chasm. Following that, he attended the Christian Peace Conference in Prague. "Father is working mainly/ In disarmament theory," the letter resumes. "The children still play with guns . . ."

The next three years of increasingly frenetic teaching, speaking, and writing were Ann Arbor-based, and marked by the death of Kenneth's mother, who had been ill and very feeble for several years, and of his Aunt Ada, who had spent a last happy summer visiting with the family. Boulding was spending more and more time "speaking to the conscience, the intellect and the spirit of many communities, often in the academic world, sometimes in the business world, and occasionally in the schizophrenic world of 'government circles,'" as the 1962 Christmas letter, written by Elise, recounts. His improbable schedule, she goes on, "is managed by the knit-one, purl-one, drop-one technique. Elise handles family life, peace research and peace action by somewhat the same technique, on a smaller scale." We are reminded of George Fox's admonition to the early Quakers in 1656: "Walk cheerfully over the world, answering that of God in every one." Except for the substitution of airplane wings for legs and horse-back, it could not have been fulfilled more literally.

In 1963–64 the Bouldings went to the International Christian University in Tokyo for another year of visiting professorship. This proved to be a year almost as momentous in Boulding's thinking as the year at the Center for Advanced Studies in Behavioral Science in Palo Alto. The exposure to Japanese society, with its intricacies of organization, tradition, and aesthetic expression, to Japanese history, almost completely outside the Judaic-Christian and Greco-Roman stream which constitutes history for the Western world, and at the same time to Japan's fantastic development in terms of modern production and use of resources, had a powerful impact on him. It was after this that he began thinking in terms of the Christian "phylum" as one branch of a tree of sacred histories. The re-exposure to Marxism through Japanese students reactivated his own early appreciation of its idealistic and heroic qualities; and the tension between this and his mature analysis of history in terms of the evolutionary process produced a creative interaction. He tends to think of Marxism now rather as a fourth great Judaic religion than as a valid system of social analysis. It is, he feels, the kind of twisted image which as a guide for economic decision-making can lead a whole society down the path to ruin.

He was able to prove, through a research study carried out with his guidance by a fellow International Christian University faculty member, what he had always believed: that a country destroys more of its resources at home during wartime than the destruction it inflicts on its enemies; and that defeat can be tremendously profitable.[1] The richness of Japan's culture, its extraordinary rate of growth of per capita income (8 percent per annum since 1945, the highest in the world),[2] and its smooth adjustment from defeat and loss of empire to economic leadership, even though it faced, at the same time, tightly constricted resources and far too many people for its land, led him to the conclusion that Japan may well be the first country to step into the twenty-first century. By that he means the solution of the "re-entry" problem, the requirements of the spaceship earth for recycling its closed resources. All in all, Japan left him with a "new sense of the infinite and marvelous variety in the ways of being man."

Three more years were spent at the University of Michigan, and then, in 1967, came a major decision. It was, as he views so many of the turning points of his life, about as much surprise as plan:

> . . . Almost by accident, at Boulder
> Where the Rockies thrust through the plains, Kenneth,
> Lecturing in November, set in motion a notion
> a commotion an emotion — ah, so schön! is Boulder
> With an Upshot an Uproot. . .[3]

In short, the family would move for a trial year to Boulder, where, at the University of Colorado, both Kenneth and Elise were offered teaching positions, in economics and sociology respectively, with each holding a part-time research appointment at the Institute of Behavioral Science.

Unfortunately, it was a year too soon for Elise, since she had to write her dissertation and begin full-time teaching at the same time — on top of resettling the not completely overjoyed family. But I suspect it was not wholly accidental for Kenneth that the move came then. Though he had always been fond of the University of Michigan and respected it as a great institution, it seemed to him that the state was not supporting it with the funds necessary to keep it that way. It had always been difficult to raise the amounts he envisioned for the effective functioning of the Center for Research on Conflict Resolution, both within and outside the university, and while he was grateful that the university allowed this vital venture, it had to be done "under the rug," as it were.

There was something, too, in having been in one

place for a long time. He probably knew, by either an inner or an outer sense, what Pelz and Andrews discovered in a study of creativity in scientists,[4] that creative performance is sustained best over time with a periodic change in project, field, or situation. "There comes a time," as Elise said (Kenneth credits the phrase to Henry Cadbury), "when people, like plants, need re-potting."

The freedom of half time for letting thought and research lead where they would, in an environment of a general behavioral science approach, was certainly very appealing and something Boulding had been looking for. In some ways, it was the challenge of beginning again, of repeating the good years at Ann Arbor: a growing university that could become a center of learning for the whole Rocky Mountain area, a small, friendly community, and a small Friends meeting, all with great potential. And the physical surroundings were a strong attraction. The mountains thrusting through the plains, breaking the crust of rigidity and convention, could also serve as a protecting wall or an encircling arm for the dream house that snuggled under them.

But their roots were strong in Ann Arbor; friends and colleagues and Friends Meeting were hard to leave. The decision needed to grow by trial. On the other end, too, the decision was given some trial. Boulding was appointed as a visiting professor, and, in the middle of the year, was recommended for a full-time professorship with tenure. Two conservative regents opposed the appointment, presumably on the basis of the salary, but other regents charged the opposition was really because of Boulding's political views. It was a painful matter of mutual recriminations and newspaper publicity, with his tenure upheld by a split vote of four to two. It is a pity the regents did not realize what a moderate radical they were getting!

The sudden blow of not being wanted must have been, all unexpected, a revival of Edinburgh. His soreness

was again translated into poetry, in a letter sent out for
Ash Wednesday, 1968:

> The University is split by political strife
> And Kenneth, not by design, became a small symbol
> Of conflict between the old ways and the new,
> And only now have the Regents confirmed his appoint-
> ment,
> And still by a split vote. In this lean season
> There is no elation in victory, and cutting the ties
> of the past
> Is not easy to do, but we do look forward now
> To new tasks of the Boulder years; our little troubles
> A tiny eddy in the maelstrom of Manunkind —
> Compared to Vietnam, to Biafra, to Jordan, to Harlem,
> A trifle; but our cockleshell twists in it,
> And we sense in the ripple the agony of the flood.

In the fall of that same year, 1968, Boulding was the
center of another storm. That was the year of the unholy
Democratic Convention in Chicago, and it was the year
that he was president of the American Economic Association, which was scheduled to hold its annual meeting in
Chicago in December. Many professional groups — the sociologists, the psychologists, and the historians — moved
their meetings out of Chicago after the convention deba-
cle as a protest against the city's administration. There
was a lot of agitation for the AEA to do the same; the executive committee split down the middle on the issue, so
Boulding had to cast the deciding vote.

At first, as we might guess, and as most people expected, he favored the move. Protest was no stranger to
him, and he too was appalled at the trampling of civil
rights and the distortion of the political process that had
occurred under the billy-clubs of the Chicago police. If
the executive committee had shown a majority for the
move, he would have voted with them. Yet he was split
as the membership was split, on the sharp ridge of the
heroic–economic rock. In the end, he wrote a letter to the

membership, spelling out his decision to hold the meeting in Chicago after all. He did not approve of indirect sanctions, or hurting the people (the hotelkeepers) who were not the ones to blame; and he feared in the breaking of an agreement the destruction of trust, "a subtle but fragile structure on which much of our social organization depends." He was anxious, too, about the widening gap between academics and the rest of society; he hoped, indeed, the meeting could serve as a reconciling force for social change.

The meeting in Chicago was boycotted by many AEA members, and even a number of his friends could not understand his decision and did not feel it had the effect he intended. Among those who came, as the minutes of the business meeting reflect, feelings were still high on both sides; and the executive committee held a special meeting to reaffirm the base of AEA as a nonpolitical society. But afterwards Boulding still felt the decision was the right one, and that perhaps he, as a known liberal, was one of the few people who could have made it.

> It seemed to me a mistake to view the professional associations as part of the threat system, on the ground that if you use something as a club that wasn't designed for this you'll bend it. . . . An individual has every right to be heroic, but you don't have a right to demand that an organization be heroic; in fact it causes trouble when organizations try to be heroic — that's the trouble with the national state.[5]

The conflict in the AEA was the conflict in Boulding writ large, the heroic vs. the economic: the purity of protest and witness vs. the muddledness of trying to calculate effects and results. And the decision to be economic rather than heroic, conservative rather than radical, is one he has leaned to more and more in recent years. (Paradoxically, it took more courage in this case to make the economic decision than the heroic.) His presidential address at that

December meeting, "Economics as a Moral Science," [6] was a defense of the humdrum. In it he presented an analysis of the moral overlap into the economic sphere, showing where the moral becomes nonheroic and how the nonheroic is also moral.

For one who feels the pull of the Spirit as strongly as Boulding, the de-radicalizing, the reservation of some areas of life to operate in a humdrum way, is perhaps essential. One needs to move into a quiet room sometimes, out of the blinding light and away from the sharp insistent call.

I I

The story of Boulding's career should certainly include some description of him as a teacher. In this area, perhaps more than any other, observers will be likely to have radically differing opinions, depending on their point of view. After an hour in a University of Colorado class, in which Boulding took off like a rocket from a simple birth-rate graph he had found in a journal article, to range over the unpredictability of social trends ("If anyone finds a reason for this I'll give him a prize"), World War II as a "trivial entertainment" compared to the number of people killed by cars, the comparison of birth to getting a Ph.D. ("a rite of passage into a more complex organization"), the terrifying prospect of immortality, sex vs. race discrimination, the principles of growth and form for buildings, people, and organizations, to the Roman and British empires, the United States Constitution, and the spaceship society — after all this, at a rate about as breathless as this sentence, a student remarked as he walked out, "I've got to get out of this class; I've done all right in the physical sciences, but I don't dig this social science at all!" But other students are stimulated to make their own rocket takeoffs. Once Boulding accepted as a term paper in an economics class an illustrated economic fairy tale, and encouraged its author to make a series of animated cartoons out of it for a possible teaching device.

A batch of student evaluations from the early 1950s at Michigan rates him consistently above the middle on a scale of five possible ranks. On four out of eight items the average ratings of his teaching by all his students was between "good" and "very good"; on the other four it was between "very good" and "superior." The item on which he received the highest average rank was "ability to arouse interest and stimulate thinking." But the range is represented in these two comments:

(1) I know no other teacher on the campus that can take a class at 4 P.M. and keep them on their toes until 5:30 P.M. the way Prof. Boulding can. Rate him tops.

(2) He may well be the great economist he is reputed to be, but in conducting the class he has shown himself to be very nearly incompetent *as a teacher*.

It is very much like the difference between Boulding's and Robert Shone's reactions to Frank Knight's teaching in Chicago days. Shone found it worthless; Boulding found it delightful, particularly when Knight went off the subject, as he usually did.

William B. Palmer, a Michigan colleague who knew him well, describes Boulding's courses as "about as unstructured and chaotic as one could imagine," as he started off with something predictable, then suddenly had an inspiration and followed it off on a tangent for several days. "It might be fruitful or a blind alley, one never knew." But, added Professor Palmer, he kept recommending to his students that they "take a course in Boulding; the sensitive, bright students realized they were experiencing something pretty unique, watching something closely akin to genius." Another colleague, Daniel Fusfeld, felt one of Boulding's major contributions had been in showing students that you could be heterodox and still have status in the world; that the recent rise of radical economics through the department at Michigan had been closely related to Boulding's impact in this direction.

Boulding himself would rather start someone else off on his own track than have anyone follow in his footsteps. He detests the idea of disciples or of having someone closely dependent on him, and feels that learning has to come from within:

> As every good teacher knows, the business of teaching is not that of penetrating the student's defenses with the violence or loudness of the teacher's messages. It is, rather, that of cooperating with the student's own inward teacher whereby the student's image may grow in conformity with that of his outward teacher.[7]

"The main business of the teacher is to guide the student in his reading and to cheer him up!" he commented to me. "I never thought I taught anybody anything he didn't know already, in a way." He has chosen undergraduates over graduate students because, he feels, they are more open-minded and can take a more general, interdisciplinary outlook on things.

He told me also that he had done very little thesis work, had very seldom been chairman of a doctoral committee, partly because he didn't like to do this, partly because he is a theorist and theses in theory were very rare. The same impression was expressed to me by several other faculty members who had served with him at Michigan, that during his years there he had had relatively few doctoral students under him. It is interesting to note, however, that a tabulation of the membership of all the doctoral committees in economics in the period when Boulding was on the faculty at Michigan shows that of twenty-five faculty members serving as chairmen of doctoral committees, Boulding ranked tenth in the number of times he was chosen as chairman. (These ranks are adjusted to reflect the number of years each member served in the department during the period of tabulation.) Of all the doctoral committee *members* (a total of 161 individuals), Boulding ranked fourth in the number of committees on which he served: in nineteen years he was on forty-five doctoral committees. In actuality, then, though not remembered, he was very frequently chosen as a doctoral committee member. Perhaps this was because ideas came so easily to him and were so readily shared. He was chosen somewhat less frequently — but not at all negligibly — as chairman (perhaps not oftener because the duties of meeting deadlines and calling committee meetings came less easily to him).

His function as a team member on a teaching staff, except as a stimulator of ideas, was almost nil. He "bought his free-thinking and wide-ranging impact somewhat at the price of friendship," as one colleague put it. Perhaps it was not so much a matter of friendship as of solid dependability: if he took on a job, such as chairman of a committee, he might be diverted to something else and go off on another track. His mind would constantly take him on flights of fancy, whether in faculty meeting, classroom, or lecture platform; and anyone who appreciated only careful, methodical, well-worked out points of view found this very disturbing. He is not a team thinker, he is a lone thinker: he can think alone in a crowd, but collaboration, bringing out a joint product, is almost impossible for him.

Looking back over his life as a learner, one can see that he treats others in the way he found most fruitful for himself. After his elementary school years and his Methodist summer-camp experiences, there was no teacher to whom he felt particularly close, no one at all at Oxford who did more, as he remembers, than set him on to reading. He was stimulated by Frank Knight at Chicago, and credits Jacob Viner with useful insights; and, recently, he has come to recognize that Schumpeter in the two or three months he worked under him at Harvard probably influenced him more than he thought at the time. (The idea that it is not the economic man, who works with equilibrium, but the innovators, the destroyers of equilibrium, who are the movers and shakers of the world, is Schumpeter's thesis.) But for most of his early life he learned more from books than any other way.

On the other hand, as his life went on, his learning came more and more from interaction with contemporaries, and he is very free in acknowledging this. Again and again he has said, "I got all my best ideas from Albert Hart"—who was a fellow graduate student with him at Chicago, now teaching at Columbia. In fact, he had a lingering feeling that Albert Hart should have been president of the AEA instead of himself. (It is interesting to note that two other major names among current American economists, Paul Samuelson and Milton Friedman, were also at Chicago at the same time Boulding was, Samuelson as an undergraduate, Friedman as a graduate student; but I have found no record of impact or communication between either of them and Boulding at that time.) From the interdisciplinary seminars he conducted at Michigan, and from his work at the Conflict Resolution Center, he is quick to name a number of people in various fields from whom he learned a great deal; and we have mentioned already the continuous mutual learning between him and Elise.

He is now part of the "Invisible College," the people on the fringes of new knowledge in general systems and conflict resolution (he has never felt part of an Invisible College in economics), who meet at conferences, exchange mimeographed papers as they work out ideas, and create a thin but penetrating worldwide layer of the noösphere — the web of shared knowledge that parallels the biosphere and stratosphere. One could observe that the strong resistance to dependence we have seen in Boulding is operating here both ways: for him, learning can occur only among equals. He could not learn from anyone in an authoritarian position over him, nor does he want to take such a position over anyone else.

But though he himself feels a general debt to many thinkers (as he wrote of his new science of eiconics, "So multisexual is the reproduction of images . . . that it comes not with the pedigree of two parents alone, but with many"),[8] people who have worked with him and observed him conclude for the most part that he gets most of his ideas and stimulation from within. Even in his early days, as a 1930 letter spells out, writing something out of his own thought was easy, while getting it from books was work: "A Philosophy essay you can do with a bit of cheek all out of your own head but a History essay has to be read for. Hence the quantity of work, as I am doing entirely History (Political and Economic) essays this term."

As time goes on he has moved increasingly, I believe, to the use of levels of the mind that are not tied on the strings of reason and consciousness. Early in his student days he was very methodical, taking copious notes on what he read, writing comments in the margins, classifying and indexing notes for future reference. In 1939 and 1940, when he was writing *Economic Analysis,* he had a schedule of writing ten pages a day over the summer, and plotted his progress on a graph, driving himself a fair amount to keep to his plan. More recently, when he reads a book (mostly those sent him for reviewing) he makes brief notes on the flyleaf, jotting down only those ideas he considers new. He still may collect sheaves of notes for a projected book, but when he begins to compose, he scarcely looks at notes at all though he usually has some kind of an outline in mind. He writes by extended dictation, and unless the publisher has strict space requirements that require cutting or expanding, he rarely revises more than a few words from the first dictation. There is a good deal of what one might call "casual empiricism," picking up data and statistics from various sources and using them later in perhaps startling combinations as dramatic illustrations of something else. He seems to soak up information, and he lets it sink to some level where it brews for a while and mixes with other ingredients, and then when it is ready — perhaps years later, in a process quite different from driving himself to compose something — it comes out in a new shape. Surroundings are important to him: quiet, and warmth, and, if possible, beauty. He retreats when he can to a cabin on a lake or by the sea or in the mountains; but of necessity much of his writing is done in office or study or hotel room.

An important factor in this "sinking and return" process is a memory which all observers agree is extremely exceptional. In any casual conversation he is likely to come out with a phrase or a poem quoted whole to illustrate something he is saying. In 1949, he attended a seminar held in a castle in Austria and wrote a poem growing out of the experience; ten years later, when he returned to another seminar in the same castle, he recalled the poem and rewrote it from memory, with only minor changes of a few words. The same kind of recall of poem and place occurred in revisiting Rio de Janeiro. The bits and pieces of knowledge about geography, or architecture, or history, that most people take in and promptly forget, he keeps in a fabulous memory bank ready to be withdrawn on call. His cousin Eddy, who has had occasion to be enriched from this bank on many holiday trips with Boulding, feels it is partly a matter of his not allowing himself to be diverted by unimportant things; Boulding observes very closely when he chooses to observe, but many times would be concentrating on inner processes while Eddy was distracted by the goings-on about him.

Memory is one segment of intelligence, which is a topic we have not discussed directly. It is clear from any layman's observation that an extremely high order of intelligence operates in Boulding. IQ tests were never a part of any school program he was enrolled in, and I doubt if there is any such test that could take such a mind at a mature level and tell us anything useful. There is, however, a kind of educated guess that we are fortunate enough to have access to, and I present it for whatever it may be worth. Harold Loukes, a well-known British Quaker writer, was a friend of Kenneth's in Oxford, and is now teaching at Oxford in the Department of Education. In the course of his work, he has made professional IQ evaluations of many students, and relating this experience back to his knowledge of Kenneth's style of thinking in Oxford days, he came up with an estimate of an IQ of around 175 to 180, as compared with a normal range at Oxford of 130 to 150. He ranked him "among the half-dozen best minds I have ever met."

III

But we need to go beyond intelligence to the talent for creativity, which has been distinguished by many investigators from the concept measured by the usual intelligence test.[9] That Boulding is an unusually creative thinker has been shown both in testimony and example. (One example I can't resist comes from his "American Journal," written in his first year and a half as a transplanted Britisher: "A waffle, I might explain, is a thing like a gridiron made out of batter cooked in an apparatus that looks like a large oyster caught in the act of doing a crossword puzzle.")

Creativity, in a composite of many definitions, involves some measure of the original and unfamiliar (an intuition or discovery process) plus some measure of pattern, form, or usefulness, bringing what is new into relationship with what is already known. "Creative production is at once action and revelation; new movement of the subjective energies and emergence of new meaning amid the universe of meanings."[10] These two elements, the looseness and the tightness, can be found in Boulding's own statement, "Creativity in the sciences as well as in the arts comes from a combination of excitement, hard work, and discipline." But he adds something else: In

320

many of his references to creativity he describes it as an action out of necessity in a difficult situation. I have noted his defense of continuing conflict in terms of its creative potential, and his description of his own poetically most creative periods as a response to internal stress. He equates creativeness likewise with the use of scarce resources: "All creativity is making the best of a bad job." [11] Turning to something new, in his perception, is a way out of a tight spot: the looseness is a response to the tightness. On the other hand, it is clear that the creation of a poem involves the return from the freedom of inspiration to a stringency of form, so it is an alternating process.

It is probable that Boulding is right about constriction being at least one triggering motivation for creativity, for among the characteristics of the original productive scientist, combined from a number of studies, are "a high degree of autonomy, self-sufficiency, self-direction," "marked independence of judgment, rejection of group pressures toward conformity in thinking," and "a special interest in the kind of 'wagering' which involves pitting oneself against uncertain circumstances in which one's own effort can be the deciding factor." [12] All of these would predispose an individual to react against constriction or move into a field because of a challenge. They are certainly all descriptive of Boulding.

From one point of view, we could read much of his personality, his reactions against the class system, principles of ideal social organization, and even his religious views, as aspects of a general drive to make room for creativity at both the individual and societal level. The creative person needs a measure of security and love to be able to tolerate ambiguity; he needs freedom of expression and movement to explore the unknown; he needs contact with contradictory views and different perspectives to bring the unlike into juxtaposition; he needs sufficient material wealth to leave a margin of time and energy beyond the requirements of subsistence; he needs acceptance rather than punishment for deviant thoughts and acts to bring the range of potentialities into play; he needs to be open to the nonrational elements in himself and man, and temporarily at their mercy, for this is at the core of the creative process. Here we can see, caught in one net, a conglomerate set of Boulding's preferences and values: love, autonomy, pluralism of all sorts (cultural and interdisciplinary), wealth (for society as well as for the individual), the reward for the prophet and tolerance for the crank, and indeterminism, mysticism, and humility.

Drawing on his studies of creativity, Frank Barron has summarized the characteristics one would expect in creative people. They are more observant, and pick out particularly what goes generally unrecognized, with a special interest in truth and accuracy; their more complex universe leads them "to prefer much tension in the interest of the pleasure they obtain upon its discharge"; they have exceptionally strong egos and are both more destructive and more constructive than the average person; and finally,

> When the distinction between subject (self) and object is most secure, this distinction can with most security be allowed to disappear for a time (mysticism, love). This is based on true sympathy with the not-self, or with the opposite of the things which comprise defensive self-definition. The strong ego realizes that it can afford to allow regression, because it is secure in the knowledge that it can correct itself.[13]

The creative process itself has been the focus of much thinking and investigation. Among various theories it seems well agreed that there is some kind of alternation, in psychoanalytic terms, between id and ego, or between unconscious, preconscious, and conscious levels; in common parlance, we might call this the intrusion of the nonrational on the rational, and, in turn, the shaping of the nonrational by the rational. But the distinction between creative and neurotic persons, who both share this intrusive quality of the nonrational, is that the creative person is able to *consciously* change levels, to withdraw control in order to allow the unconscious to operate, to unfasten his attention, as it were, and let it blow loose in the wind — then button it again when he chooses.

Ernst Kris's formulation of this theory, "regression in the service of the ego," was given in the preceding chapter. In his words,

> The process involves a continual interplay between creation and criticism, manifested in the painter's alternation of working on the canvas and stepping back to observe the effect. We may speak here of a *shift in psychic level,* consisting in the fluctuation of functional regression and control. When regression goes too far, the symbols become private, perhaps unintelligible even to the reflective self; when, at the other extreme, control is preponderant, the result is described as cold, mechanical, and uninspired.[14]

It is recognized that this ability to shift psychic levels is related on one hand to security, ego-strength and self-confidence, and on the other hand, to unsolved problems and tensions, which shape the content which emerges from the unconscious. Just why some people have better access to this content than others remains something of a mystery; but Phyllis Greenacre has given a very reasonable hypothesis to help understand the unusually creative individual. Such a child is born with a potential capacity for deep sensitivity and responsiveness to the world. This may include a special awareness of form and rhythm and an unusual ability to perceive patterned relationships, readying him for a multiplicity of experience, making symbolization both easier and more necessary for him than for the less perceptive. He senses a greater "richness in the texture and pile of the fabric of sensation." [15] This, from the beginning, gives him more resources and more extensive symbols, and as he faces the successive crises of infancy and childhood, he may be able to retreat more easily from his personal trials to such collective substitutes as fantasy. This would both keep more open the path between primary- and secondary-process imagery and thinking and leave some of his maturational problems less firmly solved.

The continued access to the states of early childhood is characteristic of the creative thinker. "A certain quality of naïveté may be indispensable to great discoveries," wrote Pelz and Andrews,[16] and this is also T. S. Kuhn's major finding in his historical study of scientists.[17] Greenacre suggests the same of graphic and literary artists. In addition to specific recollections of early childhood typical of artists, the whole diffuse feeling of inspiration, "characterized by a general sense of power and awareness reaching beyond the limits of the individual self — a haunting and compelling sense of boundlessness," is related to the memory traces of the infant's unity with the mother. This may be felt as a masculine position, the penetration into the mysteries of the cosmic mother, or the receptive feminine one of the acceptance of the great gift of creation from the god-father; there is likely to be, through the unusual empathy generated by increased sensitivity, a predisposition to bisexual self-awareness. But in the state of inspiration, there is always an element of surrender to a power felt as though outside the self.[18]

I V

We can put together, in the light of this general analysis of the creative person, a number of bits and pieces of what we know about Boulding. Both behaviorally and in his writings we find evidences of his slipping the bonds of the secondary process almost at will. There is Leslie Stone's reference to his early being "gormless" at school — but able to answer a question with a shake of his head. We have seen instances of heedlessness of various kinds, symbolized perhaps by the many times he forgot his hat (I have notes of this happening at widely distant times and places from three separate observers). People who are close to him are well aware of times when he seems to be doing nothing, but much is going on within. The importance of "dreaming" in his TAT stories is another such evidence.

The intensity of his observation has been recorded, too, from very early in his life. From his baby carriage he noticed the leaves coming out on the trees. (When he was three days old, his father played the organ in the next room and asked Bessie to watch him carefully to see if he had a "musical ear," but she did not, unfortunately, record what she observed.) His letters home from Oxford include a careful description of the marsh gas he and his friends stirred up from the muddy bottom of the Cherwell, which could be ignited with a match and would go off with a pop; of the awesome spectacle of Mayflies coming out of their cases; and, again and again, of flowering trees, shrubs, gardens, and fields. We have mentioned the magnifying glass he keeps in his pocket, to look at a bud on a tree branch, dissolve a magazine picture into dots and lines, or analyze a stone picked up on a walk. Observation leads to relationships. He is reminded of something else by what he sees wherever he goes.

The action of the primary process can be recognized from within by its inaccessibility to reasonable explanation, or might be attributed to some outer agency. We find frequent references in Boulding's writings to how much we do not know, particularly about the learning process (though this is an area where, in fact, there is a good deal of empirical evidence) and there are specific passages such as "poems *are* made by fools like us by processes which are largely hidden from us," [19] as an example of our utilizing systems we do not really understand. In the composition of poems, he has always attributed the agency to something outside himself. In his youth, while his mother or Aunt Ada would blame themselves for failures in their writing skills, he would brazen it out by blaming the typewriter for mistakes, or, more frequently, the Muse, if his poems did not come up to his hopes in quantity or quality — or he would talk about getting carried away by aesthetic passion, or "exuding" poems. Of one of the sonnets to Elise in 1941 he wrote, "It had evidently been living at the corner of Olden Lane and Ober Road, and I walked right through it and carried it off." More soberly, in a letter in 1944, he likened the composing of sonnets to the formation of a crystal, something that happened almost without volition in his mind.

In larger things, too, as we know, he has felt moved by forces outside himself. It is my guess that his continual effort to be open to the Inward Light, to the guidance of what he apprehends as divine, is related to his hesitancy to ascribe autonomy to himself, observed both in the Q–sort evaluation and in his feeling about his major life decisions. It is possible that the impulsivity of the primary process also enters into his sense of the randomness of much of life, as it certainly does into the comments of many observers about his actions. There was one instance of his forgetting to apply before the deadline for a scholarship which he would almost certainly have gotten, which would have kept him in England for one or two more years of graduate study instead of coming to America on the Commonwealth Fellowship. The deeper reason for his "forgetting" was, no doubt, hidden somewhere in that unconscious psychic level, but the perception of it looks like the hand of fate. "Chance," writes Ernst Kris, "is always tinged by the conception of fate. It stands for what in religious terms may be called the will of God, in the last analysis for God himself." [20] I am not willing to stand on the bald promontory where Kris takes his position, that inspiration is nothing but the mechanisms of projection and introjection, though this is certainly true sometimes and possibly true all the time; but openness to the creative process and openness to the "subtle intimations of a presence beyond the world of space and time and sense" are certainly related, in whatever terms we wish to cast our theory of what is "really" happening.

Boulding's childlike qualities are also related to his creativity. "He does enjoy listening to himself," remarked his friend and colleague, Herbert Kelman; ". . . Nobody can be creative unless he gets pleasure, like a child, out of putting things together in a novel way." Kelman went on to say the child in Boulding is intermittent, co-existent, with the man who lives and understands at a very deep level.

It may be the child in him, still living through the unclosed conflicts of infancy, that is the key to a number of seemingly unrelated items. If we postulate, for instance, some struggle involving oral deprivation in the earliest years, the emotional remnant of this unmet *need to be taken care of* could explain his own inability to take responsibility for his children when they were small and needed much physical care, his throwing up his hands and calling for an aunt to come and help when his mother was sick in Edinburgh, his overreaction to conditions of physical discomfort, his agonized irritation when the administration under which he is working does not provide the support he expects of it, his interpretation of salary level not so much in terms of need as in terms of somebody's caring for him and for what he is working to achieve.

If we move on to the oedipal period of three to five years, when, as we have already suggested (in chapter 10), there was considerable outward reason for difficulty in crossing the maturational hurdle, a leftover feeling of needing to be taken care of or of being shut away from resources would have intensified his problems. Five-year-old Kenneth was shut in, away from the sun and the stars and the trees, and, at the same time, shut out from the usual care of his mother. Shutting in and shutting out could well become emotion-laden, conflicted symbols for him. This would go far toward explaining the tremendous impact on him of being shut out of the circles of the learned and mighty, both at Oxford and at Edinburgh. And might we not also include his repeated use of the figure of the expulsion from Paradise, with the angel of the flaming sword guarding the gate?

The wall, of course, is the means of shutting in and shutting out, and walls indeed appear as a powerful recurring symbol, particularly in his sonnets. (The form of the sonnet is itself a wall, as has been pointed out.) There are at least three early poems (1927–28), a sonnet from 1941, four of the Nayler sonnets (about 1942) and one of the sonnets for Elise (1949) which revolve around the theme of walls.[21] One of the early ones is quoted in chapter 10, in which the speaker is standing outside the castle of understanding and trying to get in. There is one other with the outsider image, carrying more terror and aloneness, but again with a beckoning tower which promises a haven. In the other seven, the figure is that of being shut in by a wall. The verse from Oxford days about being shut in is full of violent images of breaking, bursting, and smashing walls and chains; but in the later ones, three of the walls are protective, with the sun or friendly fire inside and unknown terrors without (though twice there is also a suggestion that they prison as well as protect). In three, he stands inside, with God walled out by pride or outward righteousness. Strangely enough, in all these later "wall" images, he is not trying to break out but rather, when he is out, to get inside, and when he is in, to let God in. God breaks down, or is asked to break down, the wall with his "sudden tide" or "seas of brightness."

Let me digress for a moment, to return to the walls after a detour. If I am right in my theory about the significance of locomotion, spelled out in the preceding chapter, then there is more meaning in Boulding's lifelong fondness for maps than I have yet developed. A map represents order, plan, an organized representation of our surroundings: it gives them meaning. A map is also a tool of autonomy, used to facilitate locomotion — to get around without depending on anyone else. Boulding has always had a greater confidence in his sense of direction than the facts warranted, but he hates to ask the way, and for such a person a map is an extremely adaptive device. Particularly if it is a contour map, it is also aesthetically pleasing, with a form and pattern that is intriguing for its own sake. It was, in fact, one of Boulding's devices for relaxation when work lay too heavy in Edinburgh, Hamilton, and Ames, to draw contour maps of imaginary countries. They spilled over from one sheet of paper to another, a whole set done in colored pencil with a key in smaller scale, one a mountainous territory, another an island. And maps, as any Boulding reader will soon discover, are a favorite figure in his writing for the plan of a field of knowledge, which is usually viewed as a piece of land complete with cliffs, plateaus, and mountains. Some of his economics diagrams, too, actually turned into contour maps with top view and side elevation.

A third symbol has been particularly persistent in Boulding's life: the castle. We know from his diary and his mother's accounts that building sand castles was one of his favorite pastimes when he was very young (and not all small boys build sand castles: cousin Eddy built a sand motorboat when he was visiting). We know from Robert Shone's note in the journal of the great Western trip that Kenneth built sand castles when they stopped at a beach in 1933. We know from his own journal of the trip to California in 1954 that "Elise and Russell canoed into the yellow sunset and Daddy and the others stayed on the beach and built sand castles." We know from a friend of Ames and Ann Arbor days that Kenneth liked to build castles of tooth picks and damp sugar when sand was not handy. And, like the baby bear when he saw Goldilocks, we know from the castle still existing — though in somewhat battered condition — that he really *did* like to build castles. (See fig. 22.) This one, about a foot square and two feet high, is a plasticene model of a castle on the Rhine built during his days in Ames, on a mountain of cardboard and cement. In addition to it, his architectural talents have been displayed on a cathedral, built during Oxford days (which his father wired with electric lights), a kind of palladium or state capitol built in Edinburgh, and an intri-

Fig. 22. The Castle (*photo from Michigan Historical Collections*)

cate monastery he designed and constructed in Hamilton (shown in Figure 1, chapter 1), all in plasticene, with details inside as complete as those outside.

It has occurred to me that a castle is a combination of walls and maps. It is tall and formidable, well defended by cliffs and moats in addition to thick walls — but inside, it is a three-dimensional map or plan, with a maze of passages and rooms and stairways. And by great good fortune, we have a guide to the maze in an essay Kenneth wrote at sixteen called "My Dream Castle." The castle's outward appearance is a combination of grimness and the cheerful wink of hundreds of tiny windows.

> But inside this lordly palace: there would lie the glory of the whole construction. What an endless maze of passages and rooms, of queer little winding staircases which will insist on coming out at most unexpected places, of wide galleries and vast banqueting halls, of myriads of little one-roomed turrets, gables, roofs and chimney pots, all culminating in the masterpiece, the Tower. Here lies the essence of my dream, a lofty place, above the common level of the plains, a place where I can rest my eyes on infinite distances, a place to receive the freshest, the purest, the sweetest of the four winds of heaven, a place to retire to in the solitude of eventide.

The castle would be peopled with fairytale and fictional characters, "not the dull people who appear in history books," who would fill all the rooms with life and laughter for his enjoyment.

> But crowd and castle melt away, and I am left alone in the same old world. Who shall say, though — Is not this life a dream, or a nightmare, through which, when half asleep we dimly see the shadow of another world — Why, even the castle of my dreams, might come true, the vision of my waking thoughts be verified.

First he is outside, then enjoying the delights within; then the castle melts away, but he wonders whether it may not

331

be more real than the "real world." Masculine symbol, feminine symbol, religious symbol, and a bow to the near-supremacy of the primary-process fantasy are all wrapped up in this castle.

Erik Erikson has developed in some detail, through play therapy with children, the finding that there seems to be a difference between the kinds of constructions most boys make, given a free choice of building materials and toy figures, and the constructions that most girls make. The boys mostly choose "outer space," tall buildings and streets, while the girls build "inner space," enclosed rooms with figures peacefully inside.[22] Kenneth built plenty of towers and bridges and crossing gates with his Meccano set as he was growing up, and his castle has its massive walls, its frowning keep, and its masterpiece, the tower. And yet it has also its inside, with its jolly company of fairy characters. The poems on "walls" seem to be even more a depiction of "inner space," with the two in which God breaks down the wall including the intrusion of something desired from the outside — another frequent characteristic of the girls' constructions, and, of course, symbolic of the female's physical acceptance of the intrusion of the penis.

I think we must return, especially considering the content and setting of the Nayler sonnets, to Phyllis Greenacre's description of the religious imagery used by many creative people and to the bisexual awareness and sense of receptiveness accompanying the feeling of inspiration, which may be based on memory-traces of the mother–child relationship of earliest infancy. Erikson, too, has pinpointed the earliest, oral stage of development as the necessary foundation for the institution of religion and the basic trust on which society must be built. "Trust born of care is, in fact, the touchstone of the *actuality* of a given religion." [23]

To top off the "castle" discussion I would add the last castle-poem, which Boulding wrote in 1952, and which I think would be his answer to all the psychoanalysts:

> Build up these palaces of prayer, nor think
> Them insubstantial, vacant, though you can
> Not live there, see them, walk therein, nor plan
> Their elevation — they stand on the brink
> Of man-space, mind-time, in an odd skew chink
> Of not-this-earthly light, playing on man
> From utterly elsewhere, built on a span,
> Between somewhere and nowhere, a bright link.
>
> And think it not dream-castle, though the walls
> Shimmer and fade — it's you who are the ghost,
> Out of the corner of your ear listen — the host
> Is welcoming; how noiselessly he calls,
> Invites us — where? to His home — O strange guilt,
> To think that our hands His great house have built.

v

The breadth of Boulding's creativity should, perhaps, be mentioned, though piece by piece we have touched on most of it. Most obvious, of course, is the tremendous flow of his writing, in which metaphor, the very mode of creativity, plays such a large part.

> Metaphor serves as a stimulus to functional regression because the primary process is itself metaphoric and imagistic. The dream life, for instance, is predominantly visual, and shows a marked tendency to note similarities (especially by way of similar emotional responses) that escape the practical orientation of waking life. Metaphor serves, not to bring poetry close to the dream, but rather close to the psychic processes underlying both art and fantasy.[24]

Boulding's serious poetry is a facet of his creativity which has not received the public recognition accorded his prose. He sent the Nayler sonnets to eight publishers without success before A. J. Muste at Fellowship Press asked him if they could publish them. (They have sold consistently from 1945 to the present, with several reprintings.) There is a growing collection of unpublished manuscripts of mixed quality and polish, but including some fresh and exciting pieces of expression.

Beyond this, the area of private creativity extends to the setting of an occasional poem to music; funmaking poetry and dramatic productions; watercolor sketching and oil painting; the plasticene architectural masterpieces; three-dimensional geometric figures made out of index cards; the cake village every Christmas, and many cake decorations for birthdays and weddings and general jollities; and the topographical maps. The list would not be complete (I am not sure it is anyhow) without his doodles. The doodles are almost legion (they are produced at every boring meeting) and would fill a small whimsical book. I will include three (fig. 23), with the quatrains that accompany them. The implications I will leave the reader to develop for himself.

Being creatively productive, sensing the world in all its complexity and transforming it into meaning, is more at the heart of him than nonconformity, Keynes, Quakerism, or any other facet we have described; it is this that underlies and gives power to all the manifold aspects of the man. A passage in a letter to Elise of June, 1941, describes his working out a new formula for price determination, and being so excited by it that he jumped up and knocked over his table lamp, scattering white shards all over the floor. "There is something about lighting on a new truth," he exclaimed, "that is more exciting than anything else in the world — even than writing poetry: its the same kind of excitement as poetry, only unfortunately one cant share it with people so easily."

Creativity has been the guiding element all through his life. It was symbolized by his response to the surprise card in the TAT set: a blank card, with nothing on it at all. For this card, with the possibility of saying absolutely

The Homo Genius is so bright
He keeps himself awake at night
And finds before his life is
*   done*
Two heads are not as good as
*   one*

The one, neglecting State &
*   Church*
Devotes itself to Pure Research,
The other plunges towards the
*   sky*
In clouds of vague Morality.

The Noble Gesture
Is mostly vesture
What's really him
Is very slim

The Unbelievable Success
Can not withstand the World's Caress
And Usually comes to grief
In trying to confirm Belief

Fig. 23. Doodles by Boulding

anything, he chose to fantasize himself painting a picture
of his beloved mountain in Boulder: a picture which
would never do justice to the beauty and intricacy of what
was given out there in reality.

> It's almost like being a Japanese painter where you have
> to look at it for twenty years before you dare put the
> brush to the paper, I mean it's such an exquisite land-
> scape that I've really been afraid to try to paint it. . . .
> Anything you put on the paper couldn't possibly catch
> the complexity and the depth and the structure of the
> mountain.

Toward this, nevertheless, he had to strive.

We see in Boulding a predominant and persistent
awareness of the conflicts Erikson describes us all as un-
dergoing: the trust vs. rage of the oral-sensory stage; the
pride vs. humility of the muscular-anal stage; the freedom
vs. security (infantile exuberance of growth potential vs.
internalized parental guidance and regulation) of the locomotor-genital stage; the fear of ego loss in situations of
self-abandon (intimacy vs. isolation, the adolescent stage);
the battle for meaning against despair of the stage of full
maturity.[25]

His inward knowledge of the importance of conflict
for creativity accords with psychologists' observations; but
psychologists have also seen the fruitful managing of such
conflicts, as have we.

> We can . . . learn much from self-actualizing, highly
> healthy people. They teach us that there is no real oppo-
> sition between caution and courage, between action and
> contemplation, between vigor and speculation, between
> tough-mindedness and tender-mindedness, between seri-
> ousness and (Olympian) humor. . . . In these people
> there is no need to deny reality to experiences of tran-
> scendence or to regard such experiences as "unscientific"
> or anti-intellectual. That is, such people feel no need to
> deny their deeper feelings. Indeed, it is my impression

that, if anything, they tend rather to enjoy such experiences.[26]

The creative individual is one who not only attempts complex solutions of problems external to himself through special attention to and preference for apparent disorder, but also attempts to *create himself* through commitment to a complex personal synthesis.[27]

It is thus the creative process itself which both builds on and binds together the polarities which are so much a part of Boulding.

15

A View from the Watershed

The social system you save may be your own.

— KEB, *The Impact of the Social Sciences*

The artist and the poet have always been valued for their special quality of vision, or for seeing what others could not see so clearly. Sensitivity to inner and outer reality, and the translation of such observations into terms that most men can understand — basically, the arrangement of perceptual chaos into some sort of order which makes sense once it is pointed out — is a function for which society relies on its gifted and creative people. They serve as the lens which brings into focus what to the normal eye would be indistinct or invisible.

Beyond the lens which focuses what *is,* the growth of human knowledge demands something like a slide projector which adds a new picture to the scene, or one frame after another, which can be judged in terms of its applicability and relevance. The "slide projector" is the thinker or creative scientist. In discussing the progress of science, the importance of making unusual connections, of conceptualizing a new image or a new relationship between parts, is frequently emphasized. Philosopher Morris Cohen, for instance, analyzing discovery and invention, considers it directly dependent on the application of existing images to new fields: "The number of available analogies is a determining factor in the growth and progress of science." [1] Boulding has stayed in the midst of new connections. He entered economics when it was in a flurry of revolution, and when it became a field of greater consensus he moved toward fields of less consensus — the other social sciences, ethics, and peace research. He seems to find his natural place as the spanner of the gap, the builder of the paradigm, the launcher, like Whitman's soul, of filament after filament "till the ductile anchor hold."

Thus it is the "imaging" of the creative thinker, artist, poet, or scientist, which gives society its mental pictures, and builds the next step up the staircase of knowledge. Images and imaging, metaphor and analogy, as we have learned, are exactly what Kenneth Boulding is most at home with. Seeing in familiar objects what no one else has seen before is one of the functions his mind excels in. One of the most concise descriptions of him in this role is in a 1953 book review:

> Now and again a book comes along that racks up the mental tenpins in your private bowling alley. An idea here — perhaps only a phrase — puts the things you know into a form you can recognize and understand. Such a book is Kenneth E. Boulding's *The Organizational Revolution.* . .[2]

Society, in other manifestations, has extended Boulding a hand of thanks. We already know about the John Bates Clark Medal for Economics in 1949. In 1952, Boulding received a grant of $5,500 from the Ford Foundation, one given to "creative scholars" to use as they please. The American Council of Learned Societies selected him as one of ten American university professors in 1962 to receive prizes of $10,000 each "in recognition of their distinguished contributions to humanistic learning." Still, in 1964, when he was notified that he was among the five professors at the University of Michigan to receive the

Distinguished Faculty Achievement Award of $1,000, he responded to William Palmer, who had gathered the material for his nomination, "I don't know when I've been more pleased and felt more humble because I really don't deserve it." His citation for this award pointed out his "remarkable creative imagination and an eagerness to undertake new and difficult problems." The thirteen colleges and universities which have bestowed honorary degrees on him in a steady stream since 1962 have praised him as a "respected economist," "creative scholar in social systems," "pioneer in conflict resolution," teacher, philosopher, "inspiring poet," and "citizen of conscience and concern" (the latter two were especially emphasized by the three Quaker colleges on the list).[3]

One could not seriously suggest that Boulding has been the central lens through which our society has formed its images; yet he has caught certain aspects of its pattern and reproduced them with his own distinctive stamp. Society's fabric has many strands at any one moment, and it takes a number of lenses and projectors to envision the pattern and cast the glow of the next bright colors to be woven in. Certainly one of the major themes of the pattern of the present age is the reaction against the fragmentation of man, and it is this pattern or trend which Boulding most clearly formulates and brings into focus.

Floyd Matson in *The Broken Image* has extensively documented the double movement of the splitting of the scientific from the humane culture over the last three centuries and the beginning of their rapprochement in the middle years of the twentieth century. The mechanistic universe of Galileo and Newton and the social-Darwinist movement of Spencer which placed man at the mercy of impersonal mechanical forces brought forth their fruit in the image of man as a machine, which has been developed by Watson, Skinner, and others. Complete order and control, "objectivity," detachment, and prediction, were the great hope for the study of man as well as of physics.

The historical reliance of the social sciences upon root metaphors and routine methods appropriated from classical mechanics has eclipsed the ancient liberal vision of "the whole man, man in person" (to use Lewis Mumford's phrase) — and has given us instead a radically broken self-image. The tragic history of the breaking of the human image parallels the disintegration of the inner sense of identity, the flight from autonomous conduct to automaton behavior, in the modern world.[4]

As we know, the sense of brokenness, of man's alienation from himself, has become more and more conscious, from the time Durkheim pointed out one of its sources in the division of labor growing out of industrialization, through Camus and Sartre and the Theater of the Absurd, to the "outsiders" and the reactive movements of the "counter-culture" and the "greening of America" which form so large a part of the unrest in the world today.

The movement toward rapprochement of the two halves of the culture, the gluing together of the broken image, has come not only from the literary and humane culture but from the scientific culture itself. As Matson points out, there has been recently an

affirmative countermovement in post-modern science — from its sources in the new physics of uncertainty and complementarity, through its consensual endorsement in the biology of freedom, to its several distinctive formulations in those adventurous outposts of psychology which seek to dissolve the barriers of detachment and disinterest between observing man and man observed.[5]

The widespread adoption of ecology, a generalist kind of science, the study of whole organisms and global ecosystems, is symptomatic of the growing trend in higher education to move toward a problem-centered, whole-centered, rather than a discipline- or part-oriented approach to learning. Boulding, in chapter 10 of *The Image,* traces parallel movements in the various disciplines that are aimed at bringing the pieces of man together, at viewing in terms of the pattern of the whole as the notion of the Image does, rather than assuming that the whole can be described if we know its parts. Peter Drucker, himself an economist who has taught philosophy, politics, and management science, described this shift from emphasis on parts to emphasis on whole or pattern as the new world-view which we have come to almost unawares, out of the mechanistic, Cartesian philosophy of the universe. This new world-view is one of purpose, of process, is organic rather than mechanistic, dynamic rather than static, "and one of its latest and most persuasive expressions is provided by the distinguished economist, Kenneth Boulding, in a small book called *The Image*." Drucker's final charge in his article is that we need a discipline which will take down the fences between the universe of matter and the universe of mind, a discipline which

> explains events and phenomena in terms of their direction and future state rather than in terms of cause — a "calculus of potential," you might say, rather than one of "probability." We need a philosophy of purpose; a logic of quality, and ways of measuring qualitative change; and a methodology of potential and opportunity, of "turning points" and "critical factors," of risk and uncertainty, of constants and variations, "jump" and continuity. We need a dialectic of polarity, one in which unity and diversity are defined as simultaneous and necessary poles of the same essence.[6]

This balancing of diversities, the containing of polarities, the reaching toward wholeness which has been shown to be one of the definitive movements in modern culture, is exactly what Boulding has exhibited, in his life and in his writing. Here, in the larger science, is the outward reflection of inward integration: scientific method plus intuition, hard intellect plus sensitive feeling. Here is the emphasis on purpose, will, choice, uncertainty: the fear plus the hope of the future. Here, too, in Boulding, is the combination of the two main choices of identities that

Erik Erikson sees facing today's youth, the technological and the humanist.[7] Drawn to the technologies which have grown inevitably out of man's increasing knowledge and which promise to bridge the chasm between us and the mountain of Zion, Boulding is still a universalist, a humanist, full of compassion, his face set against regimentation. Erikson describes these two orientations as totally opposing yet requiring each other; Boulding has the battleground within. A nineteenth-century Christian individualism and inner-directedness is brought in him into combination with the twentieth-century technocracy of organization, invention, and development.

Today, Boulding has an even more intense sense of the "appalling fragility of human society" than in 1964 when he called attention to the unprecedented system-changes of our days and to the potential for good and evil that lay in the moment of transition. "Civilization is passing away, and . . . this is the meaning of the twentieth century."[8] But, he contended, if we were intelligent and lucky enough, and applied ourselves to the conscious development of the integrative system, civilization would be replaced by postcivilization, which would be better. Alvin Toffler, the sociologist who recently published the book *Future Shock,* wrote of Boulding,

> Only a tiny handful comprehend that the changes they observe in their own sphere of interest are part of a tremendous shock wave of social development sweeping over mankind, gathering force, smashing traditional institutions and relationships, creating a totally new society. And only a still smaller number understand — in their viscera as well as in their brain pans — that now is a nodal moment.
>
> Kenneth Boulding is . . . a member in good standing of this select circle.[9]

The polarities that are emerging in American society today, the stretching of differences almost to the breaking point, lay a very heavy strain on creative management of tension. It is a time of being shaken. Management of conflict has been Boulding's message, and balance of tension has been his life. All of his images of discontinuities — the hurdle, the watershed, the system break — may be coming to a focus in the immediate now in the question of whether the opposites in our society, the feeling and the thought, the freedom and the control, the scientific and the religious, the body and the spirit, the black and the white, the poor and the rich, the powerless and the powerful, the technocrat and the humanist, the dove and the hawk, the hardhat and the longhair, the male and the female, the young and the old — can be held together in some kind of balance that leaves room for growth, and variety, and joy.

Appendix A

Thematic Apperception Test

The TAT is a series of pictures, each capable of a number of interpretations, for each of which the subject is asked to make up a story about the characters represented — what has happened to them, what they are doing, and what will happen in the future. An analysis of various elements in the responses often gives insight into what problems are uppermost in a person's life, how these are likely to be handled, and some of his feelings about relationships between people and environment.

The TAT, with a selection of thirteen pictures,[1] was administered to Boulding by a clinical psychologist in January of 1969. The responses were tape-recorded and later transcribed. My analysis of the TAT protocol has been based for the most part on the methods developed by Silvan S. Tomkins and Leopold Bellak, supplemented by the approaches of Morris Stein and David Rapaport.[2]

Tomkins, using the concepts of need and press worked out by Henry A. Murray (the originator of the TAT test),[3] breaks down each TAT story into words or phrases and then classifies these in a number of different ways — by "vectors" dealing with the direction or emotional content of the action (for instance, *toward* another person or thing, depending *on*, receiving *from*, etc.); by "levels" of psychological functioning (behavior, thinking, feeling, etc.); by "conditions," states of lack or abundance of various kinds of physical or mental resources; and by "qualifiers," having to do with time sequence, certainty or uncertainty, causal relationships, etc. This method makes possible some interesting quantitative analysis without losing the sense of what is being said. The pattern of behav-

345

ioral sequences, the psychological levels used most often, the types of vectors most frequently entering the stories, and the kinds of conditions most often described, are among the useful distillations from this brew. In addition, Tomkins includes a look at the relative emphasis and treatment of the major areas of life in all the stories put together. I have noted his caution that one instance does not make a pattern, but that repeated sequences do have significance as pointing to the general outlook and perceptions of the subject about the way things happen between people and how the world treats them.

Leopold Bellak also worked with Murray on methods of TAT analysis. Bellak's analysis, leaning a little more toward psychoanalytic practice and theory, consists of a series of questions applied to each story, looking mainly for needs, conflicts, and defenses, and drawing inferences from these. This method has provided me with supplemental clues and cross-sectional summaries at a different level.

Among the major findings in Boulding's TAT protocol are the generally optimistic outcome of all the stories, the sense of distance and, in the main, lack of involvement with the story characters, and the romantic stereotyping of the male–female relationship, together with its representation as a negative experience. The series shows a backing off from strong emotion; romantic or extreme behavior either brings suffering or is brought up short with an anticlimactic quip: both sex and aggression seem to be strongly repressed.

The protocol has some qualities described by Rapaport and others as indications of obsessive-compulsiveness, a characteristic often connected in the literature with stutterers' personalities. These include continual return to the picture-clues, dwelling on description more than the making up of a story, and the conflicts, doubts, and alternative versions so frequently present.[4] (Ten out of the thirteen stories had multiple versions.) These qualities may also be a manifestation of underlying ambivalences requiring him to keep several alternatives open.

In the stories, interpersonal relationships are very important, and personal aggression is almost entirely ruled out, but the highest positive value-rating is given to autonomous action even if this means risking valued personal relationships. Achievement (though not monetary or vocational achievement) ranks next in value, and dreaming or fantasy is an essential ingredient in the stories for the accomplishment of any goal. Punishment for antisocial behavior is kept in the realm of inner suffering. The environment is seen as more negative than positive, but definitely exploitable for an individual's purposes. Repeated conflict patterns represent variations on a broad freedom–restriction range, including order–ambiguity, affiliation–autonomy, and the system vs. the self-directed man.

The picture of Boulding that emerges is of a man under considerable inner constraint who sees the world as dominantly negative, often fuzzy, but ripe with opportunities for positive autonomous action; for whom such action is as often in the realm of dreaming, thought, or feeling as it is in the realm of the physical; who finds occasion for strong feelings both against and for people, but who does not allow antipersonal acts to enter the sphere of real events — and for whom the polarity and tension between freedom and bonds of many forms are of continuing and central interest.

Appendix B

Boulding Chronology

1902 May 21	William C. Boulding and Elizabeth Ann Rowe married in Chard, Somerset
1903	Will's stepfather died, and Will took over his heating business in Liverpool
1904	Will and Bessie moved to 4 Seymour Street, Liverpool
1910 Jan. 18	Kenneth Boulding born
1912	Bouldings moved to Wallasey, across the Mersey River
1914 Nov.	Bouldings moved back to Seymour Street
1915(?)	Kenneth started school at St. Simons
1919 spring	Entered Hope Street School
1920	George and Mary Rowe, Bessie's parents, came to live with Boulding family
1922 June	Kenneth won Earl of Sefton Scholarship
summer	Entered Liverpool Collegiate School
1926 Dec. 19	Joined Brunswick Methodist Church
1927 Feb. 18	Mary Austen Rowe died
Mar. 15	Aunt Ada left for Australia
March	Bessie and Will opened Methodist Bookroom
spring	Kenneth won scholarship to Liverpool University, but decided to stay at Liverpool Collegiate and try for Oxford or Cambridge

349

1928 spring   Won Open Major Scholarship in Natural Sciences at New College, Oxford

Aug. 6   George Rowe died

fall   KEB entered Oxford (student there 1928–32)

1929 June 12   Decided to change fields from chemistry to humanities

1930   Won Webb-Medley Junior Scholarship in Economics, Oxford

1931   B.A. with 1st Class Honours from School of Philosophy, Politics, and Economics, Oxford

Nov. 25   Joined Liverpool Friends Meeting

1932   Won Commonwealth Fellowship; left for study at University of Chicago, 1932–34

1933 summer   Western trip with Robert Hall and Robert Shone

July 27   William C. Boulding died; KEB returned briefly to England

fall   KEB studying at Harvard; hospitalized with collapsed lung

Dec.   KEB's mother joined him, and went back with him to Chicago

1934 fall   Began job as Assistant in Economics, University of Edinburgh (1934–37)

1935 Sept.   To Oxford and London for Magdalen Fellowship exam and other job interviews

1936 April   "Cosmops" conference at Melrose, Scotland

Submitted book manuscript to Harvard Press

On Northern Friends Peace Board (1936–37)

1937   *Paths of Glory* published

summer   Delegate to Friends World Conference in Philadelphia

Sept. 15   Accepted job as Instructor at Colgate University (1937–41)

1938		KEB's mother joined him in Hamilton, N.Y.
1939	April	M.A. from Oxford
		Writing *Economic Analysis*
1940	May 15	"Out of Blackness": experience of love overcoming hate
		Writing Nayler sonnets
1941	April 25	*Economic Analysis* published
	May 4	KEB met Elise Biorn-Hansen
	Aug. 31	Elise and Kenneth married
	summer	KEB began working as economist for League of Nations Economic and Financial Section, Princeton (1941–42)
1942		*New Nations for Old* published
		The Practice of the Love of God (William Penn Lecture) published
	July	Kenneth and Elise sent out epistle, "A Call to Disarm"
	Aug.	Month of "traveling in the ministry"
	Sept.	KEB appointed as Professor of Economics, Fisk University (1942–43)
1943	fall	Associate Professor, Iowa State College, Ames (1943–46)
1945		*Economics of Peace* published
		There Is a Spirit: The Nayler Sonnets published
	Aug. 31	Kenneth and Elise inaugurated Friends Student Colony
1946	Jan.–Feb.	KEB incapacitated with pneumonia
	fall	To Montreal as Professor and Chairman of Department of Economics, McGill University (1946–47)
1947	June	John Russell born
	Aug.	Back to Ames as Professor, Iowa State College (1947–49)
1948		Writing *Reconstruction of Economics*
	Dec.	U.S. citizenship granted

1949		Elise earned M.S. in Sociology, Iowa State College
	spring– summer	Kenneth, Elise, and Russell to England and Europe; Salzburg Seminar in American Studies
	Sept.	To Ann Arbor as Professor, University of Michigan (1949–68)
	Nov.	Mark born
	Dec. 29	KEB awarded John Bates Clark Medal, American Economic Association
1950	spring	Began interdisciplinary faculty seminars, University of Michigan
		Reconstruction of Economics published
1951		Writing *The Organizational Revolution*
	Oct.	Christine born
1952		Award from Ford Foundation for "creative scholarship"
1953	spring	"Growth" seminar
	July	Philip born
	July–Sept.	KEB to Brazil, lecture series
		The Organizational Revolution published
1954	summer	Family to Stanford, Calif., for KEB's year as Fellow at Center for Advanced Study in Behavioral Sciences (1954–55)
	Dec.	Society for General Systems Research formed
1955	Aug.	Wrote *The Image*
	summer	Back to Ann Arbor
	Dec.	William born
1956	spring	"Conflict" seminar
		The Image published
	Dec.	First of a growing number of conferences on arms control and disarmament
1957	March	*Journal of Conflict Resolution,* first issue
		Sonnets for Elise privately published
		KEB President, Society for General Systems Research (1957–59)

1958	April 4	Vigil at the flagpole on U. of M. campus, protesting continued nuclear tests
		Principles of Economic Policy published
		Skills of the Economist published
		Vice President, American Economic Association
1959	July	Center for Research on Conflict Resolution began operation
	fall	To Jamaica as Visiting Professor, University College of the West Indies (1959–60)
1960	Aug.	Leningrad Seminar of Russian and American youth
	Sept.	Christian Peace Conference, Prague
1961	Mar. 30	Elizabeth Ann Boulding (KEB's mother) died, Ann Arbor
	Nov.	Elise to conference of Soviet and U.S. women
1962		*Conflict and Defense* published
		Honorary degree, Pace College
		Aunt Ada visited in the summer, died in England in September
		KEB to Pugwash Conference, London
		Received American Council of Learned Societies Prize for Distinguished Scholarship in the Humanities
	Nov.	Elise to international conference, Brussels
1963		Honorary degree, Colgate University
		Family to Japan: KEB Danforth Visiting Professor, International Christian University, 1963–64
		Disarmament and the Economy published
		Elise started editing *International Peace Research Newsletter*
1964	Jan.	KEB to Pugwash Conference, Udaipur
	Mar. 24	Teach-In, University of Michigan
		The Meaning of the Twentieth Century published

The Evolutionary Potential of Quakerism
(James Backhouse Lecture, Australia)
published

Honorary degree, Earlham College

1965   Conferences and lectures increasing exponentially

1966   *Impact of the Social Sciences* published

Honorary degrees becoming too numerous to be interesting

KEB Vice President and Chairman of Section K, American Association for the Advancement of Science (1966–67)

Delegate to Church World Conference, Geneva

Elise ran as write-in peace candidate for Congress

1967   *Mayer/Boulding Dialogue on Peace Research* published

fall   Family to Boulder; Kenneth and Elise to teach at University of Colorado (1967 to present)

1968   *Beyond Economics* published

KEB President, American Economic Association

1969 April   Elise awarded Ph.D. in Sociology, University of Michigan

1970   *Economics as a Science* published

A Primer on Social Dynamics published

The Prospering of Truth (Swarthmore Lecture, England) published

1971 June   Mark married

Aug. 31   Termination of Center for Research on Conflict Resolution

Collected Papers, vols. 1 and 2 (of projected 5) published

1973   *Collected Papers,* vol. 3 published

Oct.   Russell married

Notes

CHAPTER 1

1. *American Economic Review: Papers and Proceedings*, XL, Supplements (May, 1950), 582–83.

2. KEB, *The Skills of the Economist* (Cleveland, Ohio: Howard Allen, 1958), p. 131.

3. KEB, "A Liquidity Preference Theory of Market Prices," *Economica*, n.s. 11, XLII (May, 1944), 55–63. Reprinted in *Readings in Price Theory*, ed. W. C. Stigler and K. E. Boulding (Homewood, Ill.: R. D. Irwin, 1952), pp. 311–28.

4. KEB, *Sonnets for Elise* (Ann Arbor: Kenneth E. Boulding, 1957), No. 38.

5. KEB, *Beyond Economics* (Ann Arbor: University of Michigan Press, 1968), p. v. (Subsequent page references to this work in the text and in the notes are cited *B.E.*)

6. Norbert Wiener, *The Human Use of Human Beings* (Boston: Houghton Mifflin, 1950 and 1954; New York: Avon Books, 1967), chap. 2.

7. In *The Fiscal Revolution in America, 1932–1964* (Chicago: University of Chicago Press, 1969), p. 162.

8. "Heretic Among Economists," *Business Week*, January 4, 1969, pp. 80–82.

9. The last three quotations are from: (1) "World Wide Labor Newsletter" of the UAW, (2) *The Moderator*, October, 1968, (3) Spencer Pollard, "Budgets for Food and Virtue," *Saturday Review*, November 16, 1968, p. 49.

10. Herbert Kelman, "Internationalizing Military Force," *Preventing World War III — Some Proposals*, ed. Quincy Wright, William Evan, and Morton Deutsch (New York: Simon and Schuster, 1962), pp. 106–22.

11. Thomas S. Kuhn, *The Structure of Scientific Revolutions* (Chicago: University of Chicago Press, 1962, 2d ed. 1970).

CHAPTER 2

1. Letter from Registry Clerk, Oxford University, January 12, 1971.
2. Letter to KEB from D. H. McGregor at Oxford, March 20, 1939.
3. Henry C. Simons, reviewing *Economics of Peace, Journal of Business,* XIX, no. 1 (January, 1946), 46–47.
4. Gerhard Colm, in review of *Principles of Economic Policy, Science,* April 25, 1958, p. 1.
5. Ben B. Seligman, *Main Currents in Modern Economics* (New York: The Free Press of Glencoe, 1962), chap. 8, section *viii*, p. 687.
6. KEB, "A Liquidity Preference Theory of Market Prices," *Economica,* n.s. 11, XLII (May, 1944), 55–63.
7. By the "grants economy" Boulding means the segment of the economy which consists of one-way transfers without tangible return — that is, gifts to charities, support of nonproductive children or aged parents, foundation grants for research or study, welfare payments, etc.
8. KEB, "The Consumption Concept in Economic Theory," *American Economic Review,* XXXV, no. 2 (May, 1945), 1–14; and "Income or Welfare?", *Review of Economic Studies,* XVII (1949–50), 77–86.
9. KEB, *B.E.,* p. 282.

CHAPTER 3

1. KEB, *B.E.,* p. 84. Originally published in *Management Science,* II, no. 3 (April, 1956), 197–208.
2. KEB, "An Application of Population Analysis to the Automobile Population of the United States," *Kyklos,* II (1955), 109–24.
3. KEB, "Professor Knight's Capital Theory: a Note in Reply," *Quarterly Journal of Economics,* L (May, 1936), 524–31.
4. Anatol Rapoport, "Modern Systems Theory: an Outlook

for Coping with Change," *Yearbook of General Systems,* XV (1970), 15–25.

5. See Ludwig von Bertalanffy, "General System Theory," *Main Currents in Modern Thought,* XI, 4 (March, 1955), 75–83.

6. This was an idea arising from D'Arcy Thompson (*On Growth and Form* [Cambridge: Cambridge University Press, 2d ed., 1952; abridged ed., Cambridge, 1961]). It came into prominence in Boulding's thinking about this time and has proved startlingly fruitful in his analysis of the development of such varied items as architecture and social institutions. It begins with a simple geometrical observation: The volume of an organism increases as the *cube* of the linear dimensions, but the area of its skin or any section increases only as the *square* of the linear dimensions. While weight, and the number of cells to be fed, depend on the volume, strength depends on cross section of bone and muscle, and the absorption of nutrients depends on the areas of the tissues in contact with the supporting nourishment. Therefore an animal such as an insect, which breathes through its skin, cannot develop beyond a very small size. Absorption of air and food and communication among its parts are major limits to the increase in size of animals, unless adaptations such as the convolutions of the lungs and digestive system can expand the absorbing area, or intricacies of the brain and nervous system improve the communications.

7. Richard Dyer McCann, reporting in the *Christian Science Monitor,* August 11, 1955.

8. James G. Miller, "Toward a General Theory for the Behavioral Sciences," *American Psychologist* X, no. 9 (September, 1955), 513–31.

9. They have since been published: Lewis Richardson, *Arms and Insecurity* (Pittsburgh: Boxwood Press, 1960), and *Statistics of Deadly Quarrels* (Chicago: Quadrangle Books, 1960).

10. One of Boulding's often-repeated mottoes is, "Knowledge is gained by the orderly loss of information." See his article, "Ecology and Environment," *TransAction* VII, no. 5

(March, 1970), for a summary of the minimum knowledge of the social sciences we need to transmit to all children. The need for minimizing knowledge by finding new organizing concepts runs, too, all through Alfred Kuhn's *The Study of Society: A Unified Approach* (Homewood, Ill.: Richard D. Irwin, 1963).

11. George A. Miller, Eugene Galanter, and Karl H. Pribram, *Plans and the Structure of Behavior* (New York: Holt, Rinehart, and Winston, 1960).

12. Marshall McLuhan, *Understanding Media: The Extensions of Man* (New York: McGraw-Hill, 1964, paperback 1965), p. 10.

13. Leon Festinger, *A Theory of Cognitive Dissonance* (Evanston, Ill.: Row, Peterson, 1957).

14. Miller, Galanter, and Pribram, p. 2.

15. There is an interesting discussion of this problem by men actively engaged in innovations and predictions, in "The Nature and Limits of Forecasting," *Daedalus: Toward the Year 2000: Work in Progress,* LXXXXVI, no. 3 of the Proceedings of the American Academy of Arts and Sciences (summer 1967), 936–47. See especially 941–44.

16. Fred Polak, *The Image of the Future* (New York: Oceana Press, 1960).

17. Robert A. Smith III, review of Bertalanffy, *General System Theory,* in *Yearbook of General Systems,* XV (1970), p. 239.

18. Science historian Derek de Solla Price traces the origin of this term in the early name of what became the Royal Society in London, around 1650. It was he, as Mr. Boulding pointed out to me, who resurrected it to describe the "new Invisible Colleges, rapidly growing up in all the most hardpressed sections of the scholarly research front" (Price, *Science Since Babylon;* New Haven: Yale University Press, 1961, pp. 54, 99).

CHAPTER 4

1. KEB and Emile Benoit, eds., *Disarmament and the Economy* (New York: Harper and Row, 1963).

2. KEB and Milton Mayer, *The Mayer/Boulding Dialogue on Peace Research,* edited by Cynthia Kerman and Carol Murphy (Wallingford, Pa.: Pendle Hill, 1967).

3. KEB, *B.E.,* pp. 299–300.

4. Quincy Wright, "Project for a World Intelligence Center," *Journal of Conflict Resolution* I, no. 1 (March, 1957), 93–97.

5. KEB, *Perspectives on the Economics of Peace,* pt. I of *Economic Factors Bearing Upon the Maintenance of Peace* (New York: Institute for International Order, 1961), p. 23.

6. KEB, "Social Sciences," *The Great Ideas Today,* edited by R. M. Hutchins and M. J. Adler (Chicago: Encyclopedia Britannica, 1965), p. 278.

7. *Journal of Conflict Resolution,* XV, no. 3 (September, 1971), 279–80.

CHAPTER 5

1. Erik Erikson, *Identity: Youth and Crisis* (New York: W. W. Norton and Co., 1968), pp. 133, 189.

2. Silvan Tomkins, "Left and Right, a Basic Dimension of Ideology and Personality," *A Study of Lives,* edited by Robert W. White (New York: Atherton Press, 1964), p. 389.

3. George Bernard Shaw, *Everybody's Political What's What,* p. 49, quoted in Eric Bentley, *Bernard Shaw* (London: Robert Hale, 1950), p. 95.

4. KEB, *B.E.,* p. 14.

5. George Bernard Shaw, "Immaturity," an autobiographical essay, quoted in Bentley, p. 218.

6. KEB, unpublished sonnet, 1961.

7. Bentley, p. 112.

8. KEB, *The Organizational Revolution* (New York: Harper and Brothers, 1953; Chicago: Quadrangle Books, 1968), p. xiv.

9. Martin Meisel, *Shaw and the Nineteenth Century Theater* (Princeton, N.J.: Princeton University Press, 1963), p. 446.

10. H. G. Wells, *Experiment in Autobiography* (New York: Macmillan, 1934), p. 197.

11. Edmund Wilson, *Axel's Castle* (New York: Charles Scribner's Sons, 1931), p. 268.

12. Quoted by Robert Sklar, in *F. Scott Fitzgerald, The Last Laocoön* (New York: Oxford University Press, 1967), pp. 18, 19.

13. William Leuchtenburg, "Introduction," Walter Lippmann, *Drift and Mastery* (Englewood Cliffs, N.J.: Prentice-Hall, 1961), p. 2.

14. This is, in fact, the persistent misquotation in which he was caught in print, referred to on p. 20. He knows (now, at least), that the first word should be "Bliss" ("The Prelude," XI, line 108).

15. KEB, *The Meaning of the Twentieth Century* (New York: Harper and Row, 1964), pp. 176–77.

16. KEB, *Economic Analysis*, 1st ed. (New York: Harper and Brothers, 1941), pp. 408, 347.

CHAPTER 6

1. This quotation, together with supporting incidents, is taken from an unpublished 124-page autobiographical account written by Kenneth's mother, Elizabeth Ann Boulding (partly based on her diaries), over several years in the early 1940s. Subsequent references to this source will be cited EAB. In all the quotations from this source and from diaries, letters, and early school essays, as well as unpublished poetry, I have kept the original spelling and punctuation, which varies in some cases from the standard form.

2. This poem, describing his experience, was published under the title, "Out of Blackness" in *The American Friend,* June 6, 1940.

3. KEB, *There Is a Spirit: The Nayler Sonnets* (Nyack, N.Y.: Fellowship Publications, 1945), p. 3.

4. Boulding's impulse to be shocking here outran exactness of meaning. "What I should have said" (he noted on reading the manuscript): "'I became a citizen by experiencing the help of God, rather than by invoking it.'"

5. KEB, "Violence and Revolution: Some Reflections on Cuba," *Liberation,* V, no. 2 (April, 1960), 7.

6. M. Brewster Smith, Jerome Bruner, and Robert W. White, *Opinions and Personality* (New York: John Wiley and Sons, 1956). See also Daniel Katz, "A Functional Approach to the Study of Attitudes," *Public Opinion Quarterly,* XXIV (1940), 163–204.

7. *Bulletin of the Atomic Scientists,* XXI, no. 8 (October, 1965), 18–20.

8. There are variant recollections of the event. Boulding's memory of it, related in a letter of July 9, 1971, is this: "The real mediator was Theodore Newcomb, who did meet with the original group, but who also was involved in meeting with the dean and the Center for Conflict Resolution. As I recall it, the actual idea for a teach-in was suggested to me over the telephone by a professor of education . . . [named by others as Claude Eggertson]. I passed on the idea to the group meeting in the dean's office, and Newcomb was excited by it and undertook to take it to the original group, who finally accepted it after a very long discussion."

William Gamson, a leader of the protest group, credits (in a conversation January 19, 1972) the original proposal of the night meetings to Herbert Kelman (another nonsigning sympathizer) and its real facilitation to a six-man subgroup within the "striking" forty-six, led by Eric Wolf.

But the meeting of the group with the dean, Boulding's proposal at that meeting, and the interchange of messages between the groups are supported by several other observers.

Chapter 7

1. T. S. Gregory, *According to Your Faith* (London: Epworth Press, 1966), p. 85.

2. W. B. Yeats, *Essays and Introductions* (New York: Macmillan, 1961), p. 128.

3. KEB, *B.E.,* p. 190.

4. KEB, *The Image* (Ann Arbor: University of Michigan Press, 1956; paperback, 1961), p. 146.

5. David S. Tillson, in *American Anthropologist,* vol. LXVIII, no. 1 (February, 1966), p. 290.

6. KEB, *B.E.,* p. 191.

7. Ibid., p. 206 (article written in 1952).

8. KEB, *Economics as a Science* (New York: McGraw-Hill, 1970), p. 135. This chapter was originally given as the AEA Presidential Address in December, 1968.

CHAPTER 8

1. The fullest genealogical information on Jane Austen is given in William and R. A. Austen-Leigh, *Jane Austen, Life and Letters* (London: Smith, Elder, and Co., 1913).

2. Herbert Hyman, "Value Systems of Different Classes," *Class, Status, and Power,* ed. Reinhard Bendix and Seymour Lipset (Glencoe: The Free Press, 1961), pp. 426–42; Joseph Kahl, *The American Class Structure* (New York: Holt, Rinehart, and Winston, 1961), chap. 6; Edward O. Laumann, *Prestige and Association in an Urban Community* (Indianapolis: Bobbs-Merrill, 1966), chap. 3; Gerhard Lenski, *Power and Privilege, a Theory of Social Stratification* (New York: McGraw-Hill, 1966), pt. III.

3. Josephine Kamm, *Hope Deferred: Girls' Education in English History* (London: Methuen, 1965), p. 160.

4. *The Children's Encyclopedia* (10 vols.) was edited by Arthur Mee, who also edited a children's magazine published during Kenneth's school years. In 1928, Will Boulding sent a testimonial to the editor, crediting him with having a large part in Kenneth's winning scholarships to secondary school and Oxford. This testimonial was used in advertising the encyclopedia, and Will carried the advertisement in his wallet until he died.

5. Wilfred Smith, ed., *A Scientific Survey of Merseyside* (Liverpool: University Press of Liverpool, 1953), p. 132.

6. David Caradog Jones, ed., *The Social Survey of Merseyside,* vol. III (Liverpool: University Press of Liverpool, 1934).

7. Jones, p. 135.

CHAPTER 9

1. Edward Lucie-Smith, ed., *The Liverpool Scene* (New York: Doubleday, 1968).

2. David Caradog Jones, ed., *The Social Survey of Merseyside*, vol. III (Liverpool: University Press of Liverpool, 1934), p. 285.

3. Jones, p. 298.

4. Jones, pp. 305–14.

5. My information on the development of Liverpool from 1891 to 1908 draws on a series of letters sent to my father during that period from a school chum of his in Liverpool, Will Rowlands, of roughly the same social class and exactly the same age as William Boulding.

6. Jones, p. 295.

CHAPTER 10

1. Charles Van Riper, *The Nature of Stuttering* (Englewood Cliffs, N.J.: Prentice-Hall, 1971), p. 361.

2. Van Riper, pp. 395–96.

3. D. A. Barbara, *New Directions in Stuttering: Theory and Practice* (Springfield, Ill.: Charles Thomas, 1965), p. 47; and Wendell Johnson, *Stuttering and What You Can Do About It* (Minneapolis: University of Minnesota Press, 1961).

4. Joseph Sheehan, "Conflict Theory of Stuttering," *Stuttering: A Symposium*, ed. J. Eisenson (New York: Harper and Bros., 1958), pp. 121–66.

5. I. Peter Glauber, "The Psychoanalysis of Stuttering," Eisenson, pp. 71–119.

6. Van Riper, pp. 142, 211, 213.

7. Gertrud L. Wyatt, *Language Learning and Communication Disorders in Children* (New York: Free Press, 1969).

8. Havelock Ellis, *A Study of British Genius*, 2d ed. (Boston: Riverside Press, 1926), p. 178. A recent survey of many studies states that they point to an incidence of a little over 1 percent in Europe and a little less than 1 percent in the United States (Oliver Bloodstein, *A Handbook on*

Stuttering; Chicago; National Easter Seal Society, 1969, pp. 71–72). Ellis's "geniuses" came out 2 percent.

9. Israel Shenker, "The Affected Stammer as a Mark of the English Gentleman," *New York Times,* November 8, 1970, p. 90.

10. Liverpool school statistics in this chapter are taken from D. C. Jones, ed., *The Social Survey of Merseyside,* vol. III (Liverpool: University Press of Liverpool, 1934), pp. 167, 168, 173.

11. David Butler and Jennie Freeman, *British Political Facts, 1900–1967,* 2d ed. (London: Macmillan, 1968), p. 191.

12. Butler and Freeman, p. 198.

13. Josephine Kamm, *Hope Deferred: Girls' Education in English History* (London: Methuen, 1965), p. 238.

14. T. S. Gregory, *According to Your Faith* (London: Epworth Press, 1966), pp. 57–61.

CHAPTER 11

1. Letter from Registry Clerk, Oxford University, January 12, 1971.

2. "Scots University Education 'Sitting on its Haunches for Past Fifty Years,'" *The Scotsman,* Edinburgh, April 6, 1936, p. 9.

3. *The Student,* XXXIII, no. 9 (March 9, 1937), 232–33.

CHAPTER 12

1. David Butler and Jennie Freeman, *British Political Facts, 1900–1967,* 2d ed. (London: Macmillan, 1968), p. 191.

2. KEB, *A Reconstruction of Economics* (New York: John Wiley and Sons, 1950), p. 7.

3. Some clinicians might draw an inference of latent homosexual tendencies from this apparent anxiety about heterosexual relations and negative attitude toward marriage. See, for example, Gardner Lindzey, "The Thematic Apperception Test: The Strategy of Research," *Journal of Projective Techniques,* XXII (1958), 173–80.

4. KEB, "Violence and Revolution: Some Reflections on Cuba," *Liberation,* V, no. 2 (April, 1960), 8.

5. KEB, *The Impact of the Social Sciences* (New Brunswick, N.J.: Rutgers University Press, 1966), p. 76.

CHAPTER 13

1. Robert W. White, *Lives in Progress,* 1st ed. (New York: Dryden Press, 1952), p. 133.

2. KEB, *The Organizational Revolution* (Chicago: Quadrangle Books, 1968), pp. 64–65.

3. Kurt Eissler, *Leonardo da Vinci* (New York: International Universities Press, 1961), pp. 235–36.

4. KEB, *The Skills of the Economist* (Cleveland, Ohio: Howard Allen, 1958), p. 107.

5. Erik H. Erikson, *Childhood and Society,* 2d ed. (New York: W. W. Norton and Co., 1963), pp. 258–61.

6. Norbert Wiener, *God and Golem, Inc.* (Cambridge, Mass.: M.I.T. Press, 1964), p. 5.

7. Erikson, p. 213.

8. Guy Swanson, "Determinants of the Individual's Defenses Against Inner Conflict — Review and Reformulation," *Parental Attitudes and Child Behavior,* ed. John Glidewell (Springfield, Ill.: Charles C. Thomas, 1961), pp. 5–41. See especially p. 39.

9. Ernst Kris, *Psychoanalytic Explorations in Art* (New York: International Universities Press, 1952). For a discussion of regression in the service of the ego, see pp. 24–30, 60–63, 177, 197–98, 312–18.

10. Robert W. White, *Lives in Progress,* 2d ed. (New York: Holt, Rinehart, and Winston, 1966), p. 354.

11. Henry A. Murray, *Explorations in Personality* (New York: Science Editions, 1965), pp. 142–242.

12. References in this paragraph, in order of citation, are (1) *The Organizational Revolution,* p. 69, (2) *The Impact of the Social Sciences,* p. 99, and (3) "After Rage, What Kind of Power?" (Boulding office file, 1969), p. 15. (Mimeographed.)

13. This is from sociologist Robert Merton's spoof of the academic world, *On the Shoulders of Giants; a Shandean Postscript* (New York: Free Press, 1965), pp. 83–84.

14. White (1st ed.), p. 238.
15. Erikson, p. 87.
16. Phyllis Greenacre, *Swift and Carroll* (New York: International Universities Press, 1955), pp. 269–70.
17. KEB, *The Meaning of the Twentieth Century*, pp. 192, 193.
18. KEB, *Economics as a Science*, p. 135.

CHAPTER 14

1. KEB and Alan Gleason, "War as an Investment: The Strange Case of Japan," *Peace Research Society (International), Papers,* vol. III, edited by Walter Isard and J. Wolpert (Philadelphia: 1965), pp. 1–17.
2. KEB, *A Primer on Social Dynamics* (New York: The Free Press, 1970), p. 141.
3. KEB, "Letter for Candlemas, Groundhog Day, February 2, 1967."
4. Donald Pelz and Frank Andrews, *Scientists in Organizations* (New York: John Wiley and Sons, 1966), pp. 200–13.
5. KEB, conversation in April, 1969.
6. Included as chapter 6 of *Economics as a Science* (New York: McGraw-Hill, 1970), pp. 117–38.
7. KEB, *The Image* (Ann Arbor: University of Michigan Press, 1956), p. 18.
8. KEB, *The Image,* p. 149.
9. *See* J. W. Getzels and P. W. Jackson, *Creativity and Intelligence* (New York: John Wiley and Sons, 1962), and Michael Wallach and Nathan Kogan, "Creativity and Intelligence in Children's Thinking," *TransAction,* IV, no. 3 (1967), 38–43.
10. Brewster Ghiselin, "Ultimate Criteria for Two Levels of Creativity," *Scientific Creativity: Its Recognition and Development,* edited by Calvin W. Taylor and Frank Barron (New York: John Wiley and Sons, 1963), pp. 41–42.
11. KEB, "General Systems as a Point of View," *Views on General Systems Theory (Proceedings of the 2nd Systems*

Symposium at Case Institute of Technology), edited by Mihajlo D. Mesarovic (New York: John Wiley and Sons, 1964), p. 37; and KEB, *B.E.*, p. 226.

12. Calvin W. Taylor and Frank Barron, eds., *Scientific Creativity: Its Recognition and Development* (New York: John Wiley and Sons, 1963), pp. 385–86.

13. Frank Barron, "The Needs for Order and Disorder as Motives in Creative Activity," *Scientific Creativity . . .* , edited by Taylor and Barron, p. 159.

14. Ernst Kris, *Psychoanalytic Explorations in Art* (New York: International Universities Press, 1952), pp. 253–54.

15. Phyllis Greenacre, *The Quest for the Father* (New York: International Universities Press, 1963), p. 15.

16. Pelz and Andrews, p. 197.

17. T. S. Kuhn, *The Structure of Scientific Revolutions* (Chicago: University of Chicago Press, 1962; 2d ed., 1970).

18. Greenacre, *Quest for the Father*, p. 18.

19. KEB, *B.E.*, p. 95.

20. Kris, p. 297. The interested reader is referred to the chapter, "On Inspiration," pp. 291–302.

21. Nayler Sonnets 11, 17, 19, and 24; and No. 52 of *Sonnets for Elise*. The others are unpublished except for the one I have quoted.

22. Erik Erikson, *Childhood and Society*, 2d ed. (New York: W. W. Norton and Co., 1963), pp. 97–108.

23. Erikson, p. 250.

24. Kris, p. 258.

25. Erikson, pp. 247–74.

26. Abraham Maslow, *The Psychology of Science* (New York: Harper and Row, 1966), p. 144.

27. Frank Barron, "Needs for Order and Disorder . . . ," p. 158.

CHAPTER 15

1. Morris R. Cohen, *The Meaning of Human History*, 2d ed. (La Salle, Ill.: Open Court, 1961), p. 249.

2. Burton Crane, in *New York Times,* February 23, 1953, p. 31.

3. Earlham (1964), Swarthmore (1967), and Haverford (1968). The other degrees were awarded by: Pace College (1962), Colgate University (1963), Western Michigan University (1966), Case Institute of Technology (1966), Marquette University (1966), Carthage College (1968), Michigan State University (1969), University of the South (1969), Loyola University (1970), and Colorado College (1970).

4. Floyd W. Matson, *The Broken Image: Man, Science and Society* (New York: George Braziller, 1964), pp. *vii–viii.*

5. Matson, p. *viii.*

6. "The New Philosophy Comes to Life," *Harper's,* CCXV (August, 1957), 39 and 40.

7. Erik Erikson, "Memorandum on Youth," *Daedalus,* LXXXXVI, no. 3 of the Proceedings of the American Academy of Arts and Sciences (Summer 1967), 860–70. Also discussed in Erikson, *Identity: Youth and Crisis* (New York: W. W. Norton and Co., 1968), pp. 31–39.

8. KEB, *The Meaning of the Twentieth Century* (New York: Harper and Row, 1964), p. 84.

9. KEB, "Passage to Post-Civilization," *New Republic,* December 12, 1964, pp. 17–18. *Future Shock* was published in New York by Random House, 1970.

APPENDIX A

1. Pictures used, from Set No. 2, were: 1, 2, 3BM, 6BM, 7BM, 8BM, 11, 13MF, 14, 16, 17BM, 20, and 15, in that order.

2. Silvan S. Tomkins, *The Thematic Apperception Test* (New York: Grune and Stratton, 1947); Leopold Bellak, *The TAT and the CAT in Clinical Use* (New York: Grune and Stratton, 1954); David Rapaport, *Diagnostic Psychological Testing,* vol. 2 (Chicago: The Year Book Publishers, 1946); Morris I. Stein, *The Thematic Apperception Test; An Introductory Manual* (Cambridge, Mass.: Addison-Wesley Publishing Co., 1955).

3. Henry A. Murray, *Explorations in Personality* (New York: Oxford University Press, 1938; Science Editions, 1962).
4. See Rapaport, pp. 443–45; also Eva R. Balken and Jules H. Masserman, "The Language of Phantasy: III," *Journal of Psychology* IX–X (1940), 81–82.

Bibliography

Works by Kenneth Boulding

BOOKS

Beyond Economics: Essays on Society, Religion and Ethics. Ann Arbor: University of Michigan Press, 1968; Ann Arbor Paperbacks, 1970.

Conflict and Defense, a General Theory. New York: Harper and Row, 1962; Harper Torchbooks, 1963.

Collected Papers. 5 vols. Boulder: Colorado Associated University Press, 1971–.

Disarmament and the Economy (Edited with Emile Benoit). New York: Harper and Row, 1963.

Economic Analysis. 1st ed., New York: Harper and Brothers, 1941; 2d ed., New York: Harper and Brothers, 1948; 3d ed., New York: Harper and Brothers, 1955; 4th ed. (2 vols.), New York: Harper and Row, 1966.

Economics as a Science. New York: McGraw-Hill, 1970.

Economics of Peace. New York: Prentice-Hall, 1945. Reprinted for Essay Index Reprint Series; Freeport, N.Y.: Books for Libraries, 1972.

The Image: Knowledge in Life and Society. Ann Arbor: University of Michigan Press, 1956; Ann Arbor Paperbacks, 1961.

The Impact of the Social Sciences. New Brunswick, N.J.: Rutgers University Press, 1966.

The Meaning of the Twentieth Century: The Great Transition. New York: Harper and Row, 1964; Harper Colophon Books, 1965.

Bibliography

The Organizational Revolution. New York: Harper and Brothers, 1953; Chicago: Quadrangle Books, 1968.

A Primer on Social Dynamics: History as Dialectics and Development. New York: The Free Press, 1970.

Principles of Economic Policy. New York: Prentice-Hall, 1958.

A Reconstruction of Economics. New York: John Wiley and Sons, 1958; New York: Science Editions, 1962.

The Skills of the Economist. Cleveland, Ohio: Howard Allen, 1958.

There Is a Spirit: The Nayler Sonnets. Nyack, N.Y.: Fellowship Publications, 1945.

PAMPHLETS

The Evolutionary Potential of Quakerism. Wallingford, Pa.: Pendle Hill, 1964.

The Mayer/Boulding Dialogue on Peace Research (with Milton Mayer; edited by Cynthia Kerman and Carol Murphy). Wallingford, Pa.: Pendle Hill, 1967.

New Nations for Old. Wallingford, Pa.: Pendle Hill [1942].

Paths of Glory. London: Friends' Book Centre, 1937; John Hornman Trust, 1938.

Perspectives on the Economics of Peace, Part I of *Economic Factors Bearing Upon the Maintenance of Peace.* New York: Institute for International Order, 1961.

The Political Consequences of the Social Sciences. Kalamazoo, Mich.: Michigan Center for Education in Politics, 1966.

The Practice of the Love of God. Philadelphia: Friends Book Committee, 1942.

The Prospering of Truth. London: Friends Home Service Committee, 1970.

Religious Perspectives of College Teaching in Economics. New Haven, Conn.: Hazen Foundation, 1950. Reprinted in *Religious Perspectives of College Teaching,* edited by Hoxie N. Fairchild, pp. 360–83, New York: Ronald Press, 1952; and in *Beyond Economics,* pp. 179–97.

Sonnets for Elise. Ann Arbor: Kenneth E. Boulding, 1957.

Bibliography

WORKS DEALING WITH BOULDING'S ECONOMIC THEORY

Kerber, Walter. *Die Verteilungstheorie von Kenneth E. Boulding*. Berlin: Duncker und Humblot, 1966.

Seligman, Ben B. *Main Currents in Modern Economics;* Chapter 8, Section *viii,* "Kenneth E. Boulding: The Economics of Organization." New York: The Free Press of Glencoe, 1962.

Index

Index

Index

Index